AF600706

NORTHROP FRYE AND AMERICAN FICTION

CLAUDE LE FUSTEC

Northrop Frye and American Fiction

UNIVERSITY OF TORONTO PRESS
Toronto Buffalo London

Toronto Buffalo London
www.utppublishing.com

ISBN 978-1-4426-4769-5

Frye Studies

Library and Archives Canada Cataloguing in Publication

Le Fustec, Claude, author
Northrop Frye and American fiction / Claude Le Fustec.

(Frye studies)
Includes bibliographical references and index.
ISBN 978-1-4426-4769-5 (bound)

1. American fiction – 20th century – History and criticism. 2. American fiction – 19th century – History and criticism. 3. Frye, Northrop, 1912–1991 – Criticism and interpretation. 4. Transcendence (Philosophy) in literature. 5. Postsecularism. I. Title. II. Series: Frye studies

PS379.L37 2015 813'.5409 C2014-907542-1

University of Toronto Press acknowledges the financial assistance to its publishing program of the Canada Council for the Arts and the Ontario Arts Council, an agency of the Government of Ontario.

Canada Council for the Arts Conseil des Arts du Canada

University of Toronto Press acknowledges the financial support of the Government of Canada through the Canada Book Fund for its publishing activities.

Contents

Acknowledgments

As for all labours of love, this book owes its existence to a long chain of solidarity. First of all, I am most indebted to my institution, Rennes 2 University, for granting me a sabbatical that made this book possible. My sincere thanks also to the staff of Rennes 2 University library, notably its interlibrary loan service and in particular Mrs Emmanuelle Le Pouliquen, for their efficiency in providing me with the necessary research material. I also wish to acknowledge Sará Tóth's most generous sharing of a great deal of critical material on Northrop Frye. Besides, I do not know what I would have done without my colleague Guénola Pondemer-Dewulf's professional assistance in the final formatting of my manuscript.

Pertaining to the psychological and emotional support that is essential to the progress of such a book, special mention should also be made of my first editor, Ron Schoeffel, who assisted me through the various stages of the writing and died suddenly just before he was to receive the final manuscript. I am most grateful to his successor, Siobhan McMenemy, for taking up the project with such supportive competence and to Professor Alvin Lee for recommending my manuscript to the University of Toronto Press in the first place.

I also feel deep gratitude to the colleagues and friends who were my first readers: Adrian Morfee, Ellen Lévy, Milagros Ducassé-Turner, Ann Runnalls, with a very special thank you to my old friend, Jim Lenette. Finally, for their crucial material help and encouragements, I keep a very special place in my heart for my dearest friends Robert and Véronique Mari, Isabelle and Alain Auffray, and Hania and Philippe Marlière. This list, of course, could not be complete without due reference to my children, Maël and Laurent, for their patience, and last but certainly not least, my mother, Michèle Le Fustec, for her unfailing love, support, and sympathy.

Abbreviations

AC *The Anatomy of Criticism* (Frye)
B *Beloved* (Morrison)
DV *The Double Vision: Language and Meaning in Religion* (Frye)
GC *The Great Code: The Bible and Literature* (Frye)
GG *The Great Gatsby* (Fitzgerald)
GW *The Grapes of Wrath* (Steinbeck)
LN *Northrop Frye's Late Notebooks, 1982–1990* (Denham, ed.)
MM *Myth and Metaphor. Selected Essays, 1974-1988* (Denham, ed.)
OR *On the Road* (Kerouac)
RT *Northrop Frye's Notebooks and Lectures on the Bible and Other Religious Texts* (Denham, ed.)
RV *Northrop Frye: Religious Visionary and Architect of the Spiritual World* (Denham)
SL *The Scarlet Letter* (Hawthorne)
TE *The Europeans* (James)
WP *Words with Power: Being a Second Study of the Bible and Literature* (Frye)

NORTHROP FRYE AND AMERICAN FICTION

Introduction: Re-enchantment, Postsecularity, and the Return of Transcendence in Western Culture

Two of the most frequently encountered quotations in the last hundred and fifty years are probably Nietzsche's assertion that "God is dead" and Malraux's alleged prediction that "the twenty-first century shall be religious or shall not be."[1] Reputedly made some seventy-odd years apart, these two pronouncements bespeak an immense shift in Western religious attitudes since the nineteenth century.

To situate such a shift in the wider perspective of the secularizing process in the modern West, Charles Taylor's *A Secular Age* provides an illuminating context. As he states:"We have moved from a world in which the place of fullness was understood as unproblematically outside of or 'beyond' human life, to a conflicted age in which this construal is challenged by others which place it (in a wide range of different ways) 'within' human life."[2] This "immanent frame," according to Taylor, characterizes "the spiritual shape of the present age"[3] and "puts an end to the naïve acknowledgement of the transcendent, or of goals or claims which go beyond human flourishing."[4] As he demonstrates, this current secularity came to be "along with the possibility of exclusive humanism, which thus for the first time widened the range of possible options, ending the era of 'naïve' religious faith."[5]

Clearly, as the philosopher points out, both religious naïveté and the pretence of universality have been ruled out in our global age. Somewhat surprisingly, however, this "new plural, non-naïve predicament" does not spell the ultimate death of transcendence.[6] While some do experience secularity as a "closed immanent order,"[7] for others, it remains "inherently open to transcendence."[8] Besides, even when the former attitude is espoused, as in the case of exclusive humanists, the utter rejection of transcendence remains problematic when one faces issues related to final sense-making.

Charles Taylor's analysis regarding the persistence of transcendence in Western culture could seem, in a way, to echo Peter L. Berger's global desecularization thesis. As Berger cogently argued, the secularization theory according to which modernity necessarily leads to a decline in religion has been proved wrong, for global developments suggest "*counter*-secularization is at least as important a phenomenon in the contemporary world as secularization."[9] As Berger also remarks, however, there are two major exceptions to this global trend: Western Europe, where "if nowhere else, the old secularization theory would seem to hold" and "an international subculture composed of people with Western-type higher education, especially in the humanities and social sciences."[10] It is particularly this "globalized *elite* culture"[11] that this book wishes to address.

Berger also allowed, however, that a number of recent works in the sociology of religion have questioned the relevance of the secularization theory even as applied to Europe, on the basis of "a body of data indicat[ing] strong survivals of religion, most of it generally Christian in nature, despite the widespread alienation from the organized churches. A shift in the institutional location of religion, then, rather than secularization, would be a more accurate description of the European situation."[12]

Directly supporting this claim regarding the relocation of religion in the West, Christopher Partridge's central argument in *The Re-Enchantment of the West* is that, "the theories posited by [Berger's] globalized elite are being challenged by emergent, detraditionalized forms of popular spirituality."[13] Claiming "there seems to be a gradual, yet ubiquitous growth of 'spirituality' in the West,"[14] Partridge turns to popular culture to examine the "variety of ways increasing numbers of Westerners are discovering and articulating spiritual meaning in their lives."[15] Coining the term "occulture" to refer to this "new spiritual environment in the West," Partridge analyses a vast array of beliefs and practices "sourced by Eastern spirituality, Paganism, Spiritualism, Theosophy, alternative science and medicine, popular psychology, and a range of beliefs emanating out of a general interest in the paranormal."[16]

There is, arguably, a disquieting aspect to this new "cultic milieu,"[17] which is sometimes interpreted as a fundamentalist type of response to the spiritual vacuity famously associated with the development of Western scientific rationality in Max Weber's disenchantment theory. Such is George Levine's stance in *Darwin Loves You* (2006). Alarmed by the new religiosity manifesting as "the cultism of the late twentieth century and emerg[ing] with political and financial power in the frightening fundamentalisms of the new century,"[18] Levine argues for a new reading of Darwin as "a model of an engaged secularism, a demonstration that secularism and naturalism need not entail disenchanting aridity."[19] "An argument for the possibility of an enchantment within a secular world in which science keeps its major explanatory voice," Levine's "alternative Darwinian narrative" is a convincing if undeniable retreat to the safe harbour of secularism,[20] which he presents as "opposed to the inadequate alternatives – a religious view of the world that explains it in transcendental terms and makes the experience of this world secondary to that of the transcendent, or a naturalistic view that reduces biology to mere mechanism."[21] I would suggest yet another possibility: a religious (non-cultic) attitude that would not make the experience of this world secondary to that of the transcendent but rather claim it as the very locus of a possible experience of transcendence.

Nearly at the same time as Peter Berger, Mark C. Taylor also noted the remarkable global resurgence of religious beliefs and practices, a fact questioning historians' and social theorists' secularization theory, still very much in vogue in the 1960s. In a cogent analysis of the effects of modernization, Taylor suggested that modernization was rather to be understood as marked by the "interiorization of religion": "To identify modernization merely with the eclipse of religion is to fail to discern the religious dimensions of modernity itself. Religious devotion and belief do not simply disappear but initially are turned inward in a way that renders them as invisible as the transcendent God who is present as an abiding absence."[22]

The central aim of this project is to make this invisible turn inward visible, illustrating Mark Taylor's claim that "even when appearing resolutely secular, twentieth-century culture is haunted by religion."[23] In this perspective, the current project intersects with a body of theory addressing the postsecular character of Western contemporary culture. While William E. Connolly claims "secularism is coming apart at the seams" and demands refashioning because it "ignores or devalues some dimensions of being that need to be engaged more actively,"[24] Graham Ward also describes the "implosion of the secular [as having] facilitated a new return to the theological and a new emphasis upon re-enchantment."[25] John A. McClure, for his part, defines postsecularism as a "disenchantment with secular values and modes of being and a determination to invent alternatives,"[26] which, Ward argues, is both the child and condition of postmodernity. As Ward states, "the emergence of the postmodern has fostered post-secular thinking," while on the other hand, "we have not yet attained to the postmodern until we recover for our time the world before and beyond the secular."[27] Placing transcendence at the forefront of postmodern concerns, Ward's remark, interestingly, heralds Regina Schwartz's in her introduction to a later collection of essays entitled *Transcendence: Philosophy, Literature, and Theology Approach the Beyond*: "In each [response to heal the split between immanence and transcendence], the urgency of interest in transcendence is an outcome of postmodern thinking. No longer confident in reason's capacities to know and to master, [...] no longer positing a self-present idealist subject, and no longer preoccupied with definitions of God, [our contributors] turn to what? Transcendence, but without proposing 'a return or recovery of previous figures of transcendence.'"[28] Such a paradoxically new recovery of transcendence thus appears as the major challenge of our "postmodern condition," which, Kevin J. Vanhoozer insists, "is at once intellectual/theoretical and cultural/practical, a condition that affects modes of thought as well as modes of embodiment."[29]

With this remark, we come to the issue of the importance of the challenge. For if Vanhoozer is right to see the postmodern as a "revolution in consciousness" affecting the whole of human experience,[30] renewing our bond with transcendence ceases to be the sole province of theology and religion. In fact, as Graham Ward argues, the return of the transcendent is "not signalled by theologians but by filmmakers, novelists, poets, philosophers, political theorists and cultural analysts."[31] A global cultural phenomenon that precedes theorizing and resists doctrinal definitions, this unprecedented, multifacetted return of the transcendent both meets with unavoidable resistance and poses challenging intellectual problems in terms of its conceptual delineation.

The main resistance comes from within the postmodern itself. As Brian D. Ingraffia argues in "Is the Postmodern Post-Secular?" postmodernism's free play of interpretation and discarding of belief in any final, authoritative meaning would seem to preclude religious interpretations of postmodern culture.[32] Vanhoozer himself admits that there are "nihilist versions of postmodernity," which he sees as "the logical culmination of basically modern tendencies" to deny God's transcendence: "The 'God' thus known, however, is only a conceptual idol manufactured by human reason; and the 'God' proclaimed dead or unbelievable by Nietzsche is, likewise, only the construction of modern 'ontotheology.'"[33]

Vanhoozer and Ingraffia thus concur in considering that the metaphysical God rejected by both modernity and postmodernity is not the God of Christian revelation.[34] While posing as a reaction to modernity, postmodernity, paradoxically, runs the risk of falling into the same nihilistic trap, made even more dangerous by postmodernity's emphasis on the necessary deconstruction of modernity's "prideful constructions – buildings, conceptual systems, political regimes, theologies":[35] "The besetting temptation of the postmodern condition is [...] *sloth*. According to Dorothy Sayers, sloth is the sin 'that believes in nothing, enjoys nothing, hates nothing, finds purpose in nothing, lives for nothing, and remains alive because there is nothing for which it will die.' *The question is whether certain forms of postmodernity act as corrosives to the conditions for the possibility of commitment, poisoning the will by depriving it of anything in which to believe ultimately.*"[36]

Graham Ward, for his part, maintains that, "at the end of modernity we come [...] to a forking of the ways": "The primrose path is the aesthetics of nihilism in its various contemporary forms: a culture of seduction and flagrant, self-consuming sexuality; a culture of increasingly sophisticated drugs and drug-use; a culture of virtual, video-taped realities. The thorny way is the practice of faith. The latter is a difficult path, fraught still with all the dragons, giants and demons of *The Pilgrim's Progress*."[37]

These are serious warnings, outlining as they do a postmodern condition at the crossroads between ultimate destruction and exacting fulfilment. The old heaven-and-hell battle resurfaces, but its potential resolution through renewed bonding with transcendence will have to find new cultural forms to fit the postmodern condition and its insistence on the embodied nature of knowledge. These new cultural forms will have to be concrete. In Christian terms, they will have to "embody in new situations the wisdom and love of God embodied in the cross."[38]

Postsecular Postmodernity and the Spiritual Role of Fiction in an Age of Experience

This necessarily "embodied" character of the postmodern quest for transcendence brings another concept to the forefront – spirituality: "The shape of life – the habitual patterns of thinking, of speech and of action – constitute the 'spirit' of an individual or a culture. [...] The condition of postmodernity is neither simply philosophical nor simply socio-political, but *spiritual*, a condition in which belief and behaviour come together in the shape of an embodied spirit."[39] In our postsecular times, the "spiritual" is usually credited with being quite an inclusive concept, as, for instance, in Paul Fiddes's definition: "With the aim of overcoming dualism [between body and spirit], and in order to affirm the wholeness of embodied existence, [the word 'spirituality'] has often been used to express the 'reaching out' of the whole person towards realities which transcend the world of the senses."[40]

In turn, the comprehensive and embodied character of the search for transcendence expressed in such a definition of the "spiritual" may account for its contemporary currency as a term much preferred to that of "religious," involving a more abstract and doctrinal approach. As Philip Sheldrake notes: "Spirituality has become a word that defines our era. Certainly a growing interest in spirituality is one of the most striking aspects of contemporary Western culture, paradoxically set alongside a decline in traditional religious membership."[41] In an era of non-creedal belief,[42] the paradox is not difficult to sustain, and spirituality probably remains the best word to designate the concrete character of the contemporary quest for transcendence. Such is its relevance to our times that, as both Philip Sheldrake and Arthur Holder note in their respective introductions to their *Brief History of Spirituality* and extensive *Blackwell Companion to Christian Spirituality*, "the subject of spirituality is now an important academic field,"[43] focusing on "the lived experience of Christian faith and discipleship."[44]

If experience is undoubtedly a key word regarding the type of knowledge postmodern seekers are after,[45] language also features prominently in postmodern concerns. Kevin Vanhoozeer even speaks of a "linguistic condition of postmodernity" to designate the centrality of this concern.[46] This, in turn, takes me to a consideration of what appears as the ideal linguistic form, where belief and behaviour, the two poles of the postmodern spiritual condition, coalesce and respond to the postmodern urge for "embodied knowledge": literature.

Significantly, as Vanhoozer again observes, "the most important contributions to postmodern thinking have come from the domain of literary theory. Indeed, according to several French postmodern thinkers, literary theory has come virtually to displace philosophy, or, rather, philosophy has come to be seen as a species of rhetoric and literature."[47] This again supports my argument regarding the centrality of experience to the postmodern as a postsecular spiritual condition. Indeed, as compared with the lofty abstractions of philosophy, literature does convey embodied knowledge, which makes it a medium much better suited to the specificities of the postmodern quest for wisdom.[48]

At this point, there arises the traditional objection regarding the incompatibility between literature as a secular linguistic mode, on the one hand, and religious discourse, on the other, particularly where the novel is concerned. In his systematic examination of the "spiritual potential of the novel" as a secular art form, Paul Fiddes, however, makes much the same observation as Mark Knight and Thomas Woodman in their introduction to their more recent collection of essays on *Biblical Religion and the Novel, 1700–2000*: "There are deep-rooted similarities and analogies between the novel and religious discourse. The most central is the role of story in both."[49] In this same collection of essays, proceeding to show how fiction may mediate the transcendent, Martin Corner's close reading of Updike and Ford, in particular, makes a persuasive point regarding the difference between "religious" and "spiritual" discourse:

> Taken together, Updike's and Ford's writings embody a withdrawal from the position that made spirituality coincident with religion to one that makes it integral to humanity. [...] [They] tend toward a recovery of the ordinary, the everyday texture of human life, from being a weight that crushes (as it was for Modernism) to being recognized as the mediator of mystery. The literal opens on the hiddenness within which its being is grounded. [...]
>
> Whereas religion as organized, exclusive discourse will always tend to the monologic, and threaten the life of the novel, spirituality will always tend to dissolve such language, by redirecting human awareness in openness to what is given in experience, to the true mediation of the mystery.[50]

This typically postsecular distinction between the closure of dogmatic religious discourse and the openness of the spiritual one as constitutive of human experience is crucial. Still, Corner's demonstration runs the risk of suggesting that all religiously inflected discourse is incompatible with fictional creativity. This would run counter to the current convergence of theological and literary concerns, duly noted by Knight and Woodman: "The development of what is commonly known as Narrative theology has especially concentrated attention on the functions of story in religious life. Not only is the Bible primarily a narrative, but Christians are encouraged to assimilate their own personal stories in the great meta-narratives of salvation and conversion."[51] As a matter of fact, Knight and Woodman's remark echoes Vanhoozer's own call for a postmodern theology that should "strive for a shape of life that repeats differently the life of Jesus, [...] a *story* that plumbs the heights and the depths and which inserts us into the dramatic flow of evangelical reality."[52]

As it is, in their own way, contemporary literature and literary theory seem to be in the process of fulfilling this wish: after John McClure's study of the "new, weakened and hybridized, idioms of belief" in post-secular fiction,[53] Andrew Tate points to a direct engagement of contemporary fiction with Christian themes: "[This book] explores the complex religious impulses at play in the fictions of our postmodern moment. Major and emerging Anglophone novelists [...] persistently return, both explicitly and in less overt ways, to theological questions. [...] This introductory chapter examines the implications of 'post-secular' culture for the novel and identifies a number of distinct, if overlapping, thematic approaches to Christianity that are crucial to the spiritual sensibilities of contemporary fiction."[54] What Tate suggests is a weakening of the neat postsecular distinction between the religious and the spiritual. This, however, in no way suggests the return of the primacy of monologic religious discourse. On the contrary, as Tate shows, the openness associated with postsecular spirituality has come to permeate contemporary literary approaches to the Christian tradition. In keeping with the spirit of postsecularism, "a mode of being and seeing that is at once critical of secular constructions of reality and of dogmatic religiosity,"[55] contemporary fiction features "ostensibly secular novels [that] can be profoundly theological" or "disbelieving narratives [that] accentuate a yearning for the language and hopes of theology."[56] Besides, in her discussion of postmodern belief as expressed in the literature of the United States, Amy Hungerford also notes "the remarkable religious valence of the literary in the secular context of twentieth-century America."[57] It is with just such "religious valence" that the present work is concerned.

Frye, American Literature, and Religious Literary Criticism: Introductory Methodological Remarks

For all that has been said about the resurgence of spiritual-cum-religious interests in contemporary Western culture,[58] large parts of the academic world still remain deaf (and dumb) to it. Dennis Taylor's urgent call for a religious literary criticism, already more than a decade old, deserves quoting at length:

> A great critical need of our time is for ways of discussing religious or spiritual dimensions in works of literature. We live in an age of critical discourses that are expert in discussing the dimensions of class, gender, textuality, and historical context. Yet an important part of the literature we read goes untouched by our discourses, or is deconstructed, historicized, sexualized, or made symptomatic of covert power relationships. The negative hermeneutic of such reductive discourse has been thorough and successful. Attempts at a more positive non-reductive hermeneutic tend to be soft discourses, appealing to general unexamined values and a preconverted audience. There is a need in our time for religious interpretations that are substantial enough to enter into a productive and competitive relation with the reigning critical discourses. The answer to the dilemma of skepticism and softness may simply be a sense of the intricacy of the subject.[59]

The result of twenty years' teaching American literature to a French public,[60] this study stems from an acute awareness of the "religious valence" of fiction in the United States, probably made all the more obvious in the context of French academia's entrenched secularism.[61] Particularly striking in such a context is the strong biblical hypotext permeating the fiction of the United States.[62] Though it is the undisputed "great meta-narrative of Western society," as Knight and Woodman note, in the twentieth century, the Bible has come to have a much less secure role in our culture. As they also remark, however, "the decline of faith meant a reworking or transmutation of traditional religious motifs, not their abandonment."[63]

Focusing on this transmutation of biblical content in American secular fiction has led me to turn to the equally undisputed authority of Northrop Frye in the field of Bible and literature studies. As David Bevan states in his own collection of essays on *Literature and the Bible*: "There is little doubt that since the appearance of Northrop Frye's *The Great Code*, the Bible has been definitively recuperated as a, as *the* paradigmatic literary text, at least in Western literature, and is now relentlessly subjected to the entire gamut of recent and emergent critical approaches. [...]. But, of course, in addition to the richness of the Bible *as* literature, there is its at least equal importance *for* literature, as perhaps *the* central document of our Western heritage."[64]

Also, Bevan rightly notes, the contemporary relationship of literature to the Bible has often been one of "recuperation" or "appropriation" as a "treasure-house of myths, characters, ideas, narrative modes and patterns into which novelists and poets dip continuously."[65] However, a major characteristic of Frye's theory regarding the relationship between the Bible and literature – and I would argue, probably one reason for the persistence of its authoritative aura – is that it makes the Bible into much more than a dead cultural "document" for a secular age to plunder. Rather, what Frye's work suggests is not the mere continuing relevance of the biblical text to our present age, but its ongoing influence on the Western psyche, as indicated by his image of the "great code" to designate the Bible as the key to Western literature. Beyond issues of declining faith and obsolete thematic concerns, this "great code" imagery points to a structural correspondence, even an affinity, between the Bible and Western literature:[66] "The *axis mundi* seemed to me significant because [...] being as frequent and central outside the Bible as within it, it illustrates my 'great code' principle that the organizing structures of the Bible and the corresponding structures of 'secular' literature reflect each other" (*WP*, xxi–xxii).

This subtle affinity is what this project seeks to delineate, basing itself on Frye's definition of the Bible's structural specificity: "The Bible is held together by an inner core of mythical and metaphorical structure: mythical in the story it tells of the redemption of man from between the beginning and the end of time; metaphorical in the way that its imagery is juxtaposed to form an 'apocalyptic' picture of a cosmos constructed according to the categories of human creative energy" (*WP*, 102).

The intertextual relationship between the novels chosen, on the one hand, and the Bible's myth of redemption and metaphorical construction of space, on the other, will thus be structuring concerns of this study.

Still, beyond exposing the continuing though often-ignored power of the biblical hypotext in American literature, the present work is interested in an even more shunned topic: the spiritual import of fiction. In his seminal *Northrop Frye: Religious Visionary and Architect of the Spiritual World*,[67] Robert D. Denham documents the traditional academic resistance to such an approach of literature in his introductory reference to a conference devoted to the legacy of Northrop Frye in the 1990s: "It has been almost a dozen years since Margaret Burgess, speaking at a conference devoted to the legacy of Northrop Frye, examined the anxieties surrounding the religious scope of Frye's thought, anxieties that produced in her view a widespread resistance to directly confronting things spiritual. Craig Stewart Walker, speaking at the same conference, observed in a similar vein that in the modern world it has become increasingly difficult to speak about religion because 'the language of religion is widely regarded with suspicion and indifference.'"[68] However, as apparent in a conference on the religious contexts of Frye's work held a decade later, this "resistance to religion" may be diminishing, which Denham takes as a good omen for his own analysis of the centrality of religion in Frye's work as a whole. In the same optimistic vein, and taking up where Denham left off, my aim is to apply the now recognized religious character of Frye's theory to American literary texts.

A first distinction is then to be made between "religious" and "spiritual," two key adjectives that are used with near equivalency in Denham's study, resulting in a conceptual ambiguity that he makes no attempt to hide: "I have not tried to define in any systematic way the nouns lying behind the adjectives 'religious' and 'spiritual' in my subtitle, both of which are what W.C. Gallie calls 'essentially contested concepts' – words about whose meaning and use there is widespread debate."[69] For the sake of clarity, but also, as I hope will become clear in this study, because of the specificity of Northrop Frye's theoretical imagination, I shall try to restrict the word "religious" to an explicitly Christian, theological frame of reference, whereas "spiritual" will refer to those aspects of Frye's theory that, though often drawing from the framework of Christianity, far exceed the usual limits of the Christian theological terrain. This distinction is to be related to Frye's double allegiance, both to traditional Christianity and to "'esoteric spirituality,' an umbrella phrase that [notably] includes mysticism and certain practices and concepts in Eastern religious traditions."[70] In keeping with the core difference at the heart of Eastern and Western religious heritages, respectively, this double allegiance undoubtedly accounts for the tension noted in Frye's work between "a doctrine of the radical immanence of the divine, as opposed to divine transcendence" and "a strong current running throughout Frye's work which moves in a direction opposite from immanence."[71] Besides, this also manifests a temper impatient with doctrinal straitjackets, most evident in Frye's dislike of organized religion and in his own affiliation to the United Church of Canada.[72]

Yet, Frye's central double allegiance is, of course, to religion and literature. Both keep feeding each other in his work, making him the perfect theoretician of the manifestation of transcendence within the immanent realm of words. This, in turn, is his way of responding to an exclusively secular vision, which he sees to have been caused by theologians' narrow dogmatism,[73] while suggesting a whole new vision and practice of literary criticism, should it open up to the non-secular dimension of literature. In Ian Sloan's terms, "Frye the minister brings a positive attitude to literary criticism to bear against a negative attitude to theology and makes of them contraries through which he forges contributions to both literary criticism and theology."[74]

In the field of literary criticism, one of the most illuminating aspects of Frye's spiritual theory is that leading to his delineation of "verbal modes" in the first part of *Words with Power*, the completion of his foray into language as conducive to the sharing of a force or an energy.[75] In their refutation of the "metanarratives" of modernity, prevailing postmodern theories have, indeed, been more concerned with the critique of ideology than with the effect of language on human consciousness.[76] In his examination of verbal modes, however, Frye tackles the difficult issue of the specificity of a verbal mode mediating religious Revelation, all the while tracking its presence in secular literature. While this approach offers a key to understanding the power of "great" literary texts, the examination of the dominant verbal mode in a work of fiction suggests the possibility of evaluating its relationship to transcendence from a non-thematic viewpoint. In each of the novels under study, the congruence between the prevailing type of verbal mode observed and that novel's relationship to transcendence, as expressed through its reconfiguration of the myth of Redemption and of biblical cosmology, has been the matter of some surprise: it is a tribute to the profound coherence and visionary power of Northrop Frye's theory.

Religious vs Spiritual Criticism: Further Methodological Remarks

Besides delineating the admittedly unusual and unfashionable critical path this study purports to follow, the preceding remarks should also make it obvious why it will not rely on Frye's pre-eminent work for the arts and humanities, *The Anatomy of Criticism* (1957). The best formulation to account for such a paradoxical critical choice is, once again, to be found in Robert Denham's *Northrop Frye: Religious Visionary and Architect of the Spiritual World*:

> As I have followed the contours of Frye's career, I have become more and more convinced that what is fundamental to his work is not so much the principles outlined in the *Anatomy*, though that is surely a book that will

> remain with us, but the values that emerge from those works that serve as the bookends of his career, *Fearful Symmetry* at the beginning and fifty years later the two Bible books and *The Double Vision*. During the past two decades I have had a developing intuition that the central feature of the superstructure Frye built is its religious base. This intuition has been strengthened during the ten years I have been pondering Frye's notebooks, especially his late notebooks.[77]

This also means that the present work owes less to the content of Frye's literary-cum-social analyses than to his heuristic assumptions concerning literary criticism, a central one being holism. Frye himself already claims it as a guiding principle in his famous "polemical introduction" to *The Anatomy of Criticism*.[78] Stating his intention to examine "the possibility of a synoptic view of the scope, theory, principles, and techniques of literary criticism" (*AC*, 3), Frye then proceeds to stress his basic postulate regarding criticism: "the assumption of total coherence" (*AC*, 16), a belief in criticism as *theoria* that he repeats thirty three years later in his introduction to *Words with Power*. Besides, still in *The Anatomy*, he observes, in a telltale and surprising image for a work written at the height of the formalist period, that "what critics now have is a mystery-religion without a gospel" (*AC*, 14), suggesting the religious type of direction a truly comprehensive type of criticism should take. Yet again, after over three decades of influential critical writing, Frye's introduction to *Words with Power* bears the mark of the consistency of this critical direction:

> This book continues the study begun in a book published some years ago called *The Great Code*, subtitled "The Bible and Literature." The significance of the "and" was that I was not attempting to isolate the literary features of the Bible, or deal with "The Bible as Literature." [...] I wanted to suggest how the structure of the Bible, as revealed by its narrative and imagery, was related to the conventions and genres of Western literature. [...] The present book puts more emphasis on critical theory, and tries to re-examine the Bible on a level that makes its connection with the literary tradition more comprehensible. It is therefore something of a successor also to the much earlier *Anatomy of Criticism* (1957). In fact, it is to a considerable extent a summing up and restatement of my critical views. (*WP*, xi–xiii)

A "holistic thinker [...] who saw his separate books and essays as informing parts of a larger whole,"[79] Frye's critical coherence is grounded in his fundamental belief that "literature is not only the obvious but the inescapable guide to higher journeys of consciousness" (*WP*, 28). Spiritual, in his definition, being "the highest intensity of consciousness" (*WP*, 128), this amounts to saying that Frye's central heuristic assumption was his belief in the spiritual power of literature. Vested in Christian terms because of his "suspicion" that "Christianity has at least as much to be said for it as any other religion," Frye's central credo is in "the role of art as a potential liberator of whatever gets liberated."[80] To this extent, his is a kind of spiritual criticism intent on showing "how literature contributes to what he called the architecture of the spiritual world."[81]

This brings me back to the distinction between "religious" and "spiritual" as meaningful regarding the specificity of Frye's critical endeavour, which I mean to take as a model. Indeed, "spiritual" for Frye seems to designate a heightened state of consciousness that "does not run away from its physical basis or cut off its physical roots" (*WP*, 128), recalling my earlier remarks on the embodied character of postsecular spirituality. Interestingly, the context of this quote from *Words with Power* is Frye's discussion of kerygma as a verbal mode where language becomes an instrument of spirituality:

> Valéry, in an essay on Mallarmé where he is following Mallarmé's thought very closely, says that in Mallarmé language becomes an instrument of spirituality, which he explains as "the direct transmutations of desires and emotions into presences and powers that become 'realities' in themselves." [...]
>
> It is not hard to understand that spiritual may be used to mean the highest intensity of consciousness. But Valéry and Mallarmé are saying much more than that [...]. They are in fact suggesting that the initiative excluded hitherto from the imaginative and poetic, the principle that opens the way into the kerygmatic, is the principle of the reality of what is created in the production and response to literature. (*WP*, 128)

To try and circumvent this paradoxical notion of a physical-cum-spiritual reality that should be the hallmark of the kerygmatic in the literary experience, one should return to Frye's own definition of works of literature as "powers to be absorbed": "Great literature doesn't simply present beautiful forms or constructs, but releases articulate power. Using literature to tune in to that power and to shape one's own articulateness is the end of a literary education."[82] Spiritual literary criticism, then, would be dedicated to the study of literature as "articulate power," thus encompassing but also transcending religious criticism with its traditional focus on the intertextual relationship between theology as doctrinal content and literature. To put it differently, spiritual criticism would address the study of words as "spiritual realities": "In the Word and Spirit dialogue, proclaimer and listener, signifier and signified are identified: words become spiritual realities" (*LN*, 1: 286).[83]

In a significant remark encapsulating the difference between a religious type of literary criticism focusing on doctrinal content in literary works and spiritual criticism, Frye notes: "Word and Spirit have nothing to do with doctrine and everything to do with experience" (*LN*, 2: 704).[84] This Word and Spirit dialogue, Ian Sloan notes, is "what Frye means by kerygma, which he understands as a mode of language that reverses the usual direction of language. Humans usually direct language to God and to each other. In kerygma, the direction is turned inside out: kerygma is a 'two way street, the interpenetrating of Word and Spirit, not the "proclamation" of God to Man.'"[85] A central concern for Frye, this Word and Spirit dialogue is to be related to Blake's lifelong influence on him. To quote Blake's critic, Nelson Hilton: "At the beginning of *The Four Zoas*, Blake quotes John:14: 'And the Word was made flesh, and *dwelt among us*' [...]. If the Spirit has been incarnated in language, then it should be possible to move through the corporality of the word back to the Spirit, to recognize – to name – the Word in the word. [...] [For Blake] the word has a spirit of its own, more expansive than the individual mind through which it speaks or is read."[86] Similarly, in his essay "Sacred and Secular Scripture(s) in the Thought of Northrop Frye," Alvin Lee turns to Frye's *Fearful Symmetry* (1947), a book-length study of Blake, to bring out a key conception of Blake's, which is his "metaphor identifying God and man, in which the creative impulse in man, the human imagination, is God in Humankind."[87] In the same way, Sára Tóth's analysis of Martin Buber's influence in Northrop Frye's late work focuses on "Frye's views on the divine aspect or 'otherness' of the human imagination."[88]

The Word within the word or the kerygmatic power of literature is thus a central preoccupation in Frye's work and one that also animates this study of the literature of the United States.[89] More is now to be said about the structure of the present work and its relationship with Frye's own theoretical imagination.

The Spiral and the Cross: Northrop Frye's Theoretical Imagination

Bringing ample evidence of Frye's continuous focus on the interrelatedness between the human and the divine through the binding force of language, his last and posthumous publication is entitled *The Double Vision: Language and Meaning in Religion* (1991), an image once again borrowed from Blake. Characterized by its author as "something of a shorter and more accessible version" of his magnum opus on the Bible and literature,[90] this publication of some of Frye's last lectures reads as the concluding chapter in a global work of criticism that appears structured by two significant symbols: the spiral and the cross. Indeed, as Denham notes, "if Frye is an intuitive thinker, he is also a schematic one. [...] While it is true that he thinks 'in cores or aphorisms,' it is no less true that he thinks geometrically, and such thinking is a feature of Frye's mental life that was with him from the beginning."[91] The spiral and the cross are tentative symbolic projections of Frye's spiritual and religious imagination, respectively, which is a distinction without division to take up Denham's formulation regarding Frye's dialectic of Word and Spirit.[92]

The image of the spiral, first, is suggested by the progression of Frye's theory, from a focus on an individual author (Blake in *Fearful Symmetry*, 1947) to a concern with the whole of Western literature (in *Anatomy of Criticism*, 1957), culminating in his comparative study of the Bible and literature. In his 1975 essay "Expanding Eyes," Frye himself described his own work as a "spiral curriculum, circling around the same issues, though trying to keep them open-ended."[93] This ever-widening field of critical interest, with its pattern of repetitive concepts and literary tropes constantly revisited, thus conjures up the image of the spiral, the traditional esoteric symbol,[94] and an apt one to describe Frye's "critical and spiritual vocation."[95] Typically, Frye also regarded the symbol in Christian terms, as imaging resurrection:

> "The way or journey is a series of cycles [...] where we get 'up' in the morning and 'fall' asleep at night. At a certain point the cycle stops for us [...]. We all take that road; the question is whether (or when) an upward spiral moves against it. It does, of course, but there must be a point at which rebirth must give place to resurrection (*LN*, 1:289)."
>
> "Without that point we are 'trapped in a squirrel cage' of endless repetition (*MM*, 213)."[96]

The preceding entry from Frye's *Late Notebooks* demonstrates the centrality of the spiral to his critical and spiritual imagination. It illustrates his key heuristic assumption regarding the liberating power of literature as well as the aim of criticism. In Imre Salusinszky's terms, Frye saw criticism as a "mission [...] liberat[ing] literature, and religion, from the limitations of the society into which they are born. [...] One of the deepest themes in Frye, suggested by his frequent use of forms of the word *liberate*, is the release of energy that accompanies the relegating of something to a new context."[97] While this intersects with a number of key concepts in Frye's work such as his vision of imagination as a new creation or the dialectic process of *Aufhebung*,[98] I am primarily interested in this spiralling design and process as the symbol of Frye's vision of the redemptive character of literature. All the while, as this formulation indicates, I am also aware of the interpenetration between the Christian and more widely esoteric-cum-spiritual valence of such a vision, which will, in turn, model my own.

Another equally important structuring symbol in Frye's critical universe is the cross, as suggested by the intersection of two key concepts in Frye's theory of language: myth and metaphor. A symbol of the specifically Christian dimension of Frye's thought, the cross appears to literally shape Frye's conception of criticism, summed up by Salusinszky in the following terms: "As total *dianoia*, criticism is what allows us to reconfigure the horizontal movement of literature though time into a vertical vision of simultaneous meaning."[99] This echoes Jeffery Donaldson's claim that "any discernment of continuity in Frye's overall thought [...] would have to return to the abiding principles in Frye of metaphor and myth, words in space and words in time,"[100] which I now propose to do.

One aspect of this connection of myth to time and metaphor to space is related to Frye's analysis of the reading or listening experience as "a movement in time, which is the *mythos* properly speaking, up to and followed by an act of understanding where the *mythos* is 'seen,' or apprehended as a unit, [...] [which makes myth] inseparable from another verbal phenomenon, the metaphor": "Metaphor, then, suggests a state of things in which there is no sharp distinction between subject and object. That is, a metaphorical statement is not so much an assertion that A is B as an annihilation of the space separating A and B. [...] Just now we must note that the myth does to time what the metaphor does to space. It does not say so much 'this happened long ago' as 'what you are about to see, or have just seen, *is* what happened long ago.'"[101] A key to Frye's near obsession with myth and metaphor, these remarks shed light on a possible reason for it: as linguistic vehicles of a timeless and spaceless experience, they are potential verbal purveyors of the apex of spiritual experience.

Besides, in the Bible, too, according to Frye, myth and metaphor appear as structuring principles. The former projects a horizontal axis where the sequential *mythos* told is that of the redemption of man. The latter shapes a vertical universe divided into several levels, going all the way from Eden to Hell. The cross thus appears as a major symbol of Frye's theoretical approach to the biblical verbal universe, "the great code" of Western literature. It is also a relevant emblem for his whole critical system with its repeated references to the intersection of a vertical and horizontal axis, whether in his definition of the poet's relation to society or in his analysis of the literary experience:

> I think of a poet, in relation to his society, as being at the center of a cross like a plus sign. The horizontal bar forms the social and ideological conditioning that made him intelligible to his contemporaries, and in fact to himself. The vertical bar is the mythological line of descent from previous poets back to Homer (the usual symbolic starting point) which carries on into our own time. (*WP*, 47)
>
> I am not connecting Jesus' metaphor ["I am the way"] here with a structure of belief, but with the response of a reader to a verbal structure. Following a narrative is a metaphorical journey, and the journey is metaphorically horizontal, going from here to there. Coming to the end, and trying to understand what we have read, introduces a vertical metaphor of looking up and down. That is why the second half of this book deals with the vertical metaphor of the *axis mundi*, the journey of consciousness to higher and lower worlds. (*WP*, 95)

Frye's constant emphasis, then, is on the intersection of a metaphorically "horizontal" dimension of consciousness, connecting us to our daily secular environment, with a "vertical," spiritual one, relating us to the whole of humankind's experience. In his view, this intersection marks the point where a potential experience of revelation, the acme of human consciousness, may take place through language. This spiritual vocation of language is what Frye's study of the Bible and literature purports to theorize, most notably through his delineation of verbal modes.

Defined as the "variants" into which the relation of signifiers to signifieds develop (*WP*, 3), "verbal modes" appear to answer Frye's wish to capture "the positive linguistic force [...] cutting across the variety of *langues* employed" (*GC*, 5).[102] Perusing Western literature from Homeric times to the eighteenth century, Frye's history of language, initially presented chronologically in *The Great Code*, appears in reverse fashion in the first half of *Words with Power*. In this sequel, it is presented as a progression from "the less inclusive to the most inclusive verbal mode" (*WP*, 4) in terms of the relationship of these modes to human consciousness. Culminating in the kerygmatic, Frye's sequence of modes ends on the distinction between those addressing, respectively, the psyche through the senses, reason, and emotion, and that which addresses what he refers to, in Paulinian terms, as "the *soma pneumatikon*, the spiritual body (I Corinthians 15:44)" (*WP*, 124). This is where Frye's religious imagination turns into spiritual vision.

Frye and Kerygma: From Theology to Spiritual Literary Criticism

As Robert Denham notes, the reason for Frye's obsessive concern with critical theory is his own religious quest, which "is not a matter of belief, though it stems from the conviction that life has a point," and it is marked by a number of epiphanies. In the *Late Notebooks*, Frye himself noted: "I've spent nearly eighty years trying to articulate intuitions that occupied about five minutes of my entire life" (*LN*, 2: 636).[103] In the same notebook, Frye even speculates that his main two epiphanic experiences were "essentially the same illumination, perhaps: the movement from the esoteric to kerygma" (*LN*, 2: 621).[104] In this context, Frye's spiritual criticism may be defined as his effort to describe the experience of expanded consciousness in linguistic terms. In Denham's words: "At the center of [Frye's] speculations [about his book on religion in Notebook 21] are scores of entries, which he expanded over a period of some eight years, having to do with the development of human consciousness from its natural to its imaginative or mythical (sometimes mystical) state."[105] Far from being motivated by doctrinal content, Frye's critical quest thus investigates higher levels of consciousness, especially what he initially termed "the fourth awareness," which "does turn out to be revelation, [...] the excluded initiative of the imaginative":[106] "'So what is revelation?' Frye asks. And his answer: 'What comes through human language the other way' (*RT*, 154). And what comes through from the other way is, in conventional terms, the voice of God, or in Frye's terms, a divine current of energy that consolidates the arts of myth and metaphor so that the human and the divine interpenetrate (*RT*, 156)."[107]

Such a difference between the "conventional" definition of revelation and Frye's own accounts for my distinction (without division) between the Christian and spiritual dimensions of his critical theory. As suggested earlier, Frye's spiritual thinking is experiential and, consequently, draws from a wider array of religious sources than Christianity alone. The source of the idea of "interpenetration," for instance, which appears as a key concept in Frye's definition of revelation, is the *Avatamsaka Sutra*: "This sutra stresses the identity of all things or the interpenetration of all elements in the world, a paradox Frye found compelling."[108] Looking for a Christian equivalent, Frye noted: "'The Holy Spirit, [...] being everywhere at once, is the pure principle of interpenetration' (*LN*, 2: 562)."[109] As Denham remarks, however, "Frye also associates interpenetration with anagogy, kerygma, apocalypse, spiritual intercourse, the vision of plenitude, the everlasting gospel, the Union of Word and Spirit, the New Jerusalem, and atonement."[110] In this case, why choose to focus on kerygma when trying to approach the spiritual character of literature?

A theological concept originally borrowed from Rudolf Bultmann,[111] in Frye's use, kerygma becomes the means to study revelation as "the conveying of information from an objective divine source to a subjective human receptor" (*GC*, 29). In other words, Frye's delineation of a kerygmatic mode of language in *Words with Power* would seem to be where he comes closest to defining a kind of linguistics of revelation, the fundamental query behind his lifelong study of the Bible: "The linguistic idiom of the Bible [...] is not metaphorical like poetry, though it is full of metaphor, and is as poetic as it can well be without actually being a work of literature. It does not use the transcendental language of abstraction and analogy, and its use of objective and descriptive language is incidental throughout. It is really a fourth form of expression, for which I adopt the now well-established term *kerygma*, proclamation. [...] It is the vehicle of what is traditionally called revelation" (*GC*, 29).

Of particular interest to my study, however, is the fact that Frye did not restrict his theoretical effort to the theological terrain but rather seems to have been intent on bringing it to bear on literature. Though he was sometimes hesitant to acknowledge the kerygmatic power of literature,[112] critics now recognize that "the thrust of much of Frye's later work is to suggest that secular literature can be a source of revelation equally with scripture."[113] This involved for Frye both the recognition of the literary aspects of the Bible as well as of the metaliterary dimension within literature, the difference between the literary and kerygmatic revolving around the function played by metaphor, a key device in both modes: "In poetry anything can be juxtaposed, or implicitly identified with, anything else. Kerygma takes this a step further and says: 'You are what you identify with.' We are close to the kerygmatic whenever we meet the statement, as we do surprisingly often in contemporary writing, that it seems to be language that uses man rather than man that uses language" (*WP*, 116).

Discriminating between an ornamental and arbitrary versus an ontological and ecstatic use of the identifying process at the root of metaphor, Frye's analysis offers a linguistic theory of interpenetration. The gist of his critical effort thus seems to have consisted in trying to formalize the experience of spiritual revelation as the most expanded form of consciousness attainable by a human being[114] and the highest aim of language. As Frye himself noted: "Spirit is the initiative excluded from literature; for vision to be total, the Spirit must animate the Word (*LN*, 1: 271–2)."[115]

As might not seem apparent from this entry, however, Frye did "extend the non-objectifying discourse of the sacred to the secular, arguing that literary discourse preserves the structure of the sacred discourse without being addressed exclusively to God."[116] This is where I cross the path of (rather, I hope, than swords with) the philosophical debate on postmodernism and religion.

Deconstruction and Transcendence: From Theory as the Structure of Religious Experience to Practical Criticism. The Impetus behind This Project and Its Corpus

Despite appearances to the contrary, there is a profound congruence between this project and some of the major insights of deconstruction, particularly as expressed in Derrida's late work. So as to reach this conclusion, which might seem at present rather far-fetched, a few remarks regarding similarities between Frye and Derrida might be in order.

Indeed, following a curiously parallel course, the fame of both thinkers is related to a major work that seems poles apart from religious concerns, while their later theory actually increasingly revolves around them.[117] One could even claim that, for both, theory eventually becomes a way of giving shape to what is essentially a structure of religious experience. Indeed, for Frye, criticism, as a structure of knowledge, "is designed to reconstruct the kind of experience that we could and should have had."[118] In his own work, this ultimately takes the form of the kerygmatic, his theoretical formulation of the non-dual encounter between human and divine speech, the model of which is Christian

Revelation. This "pure speech," Garry Sherbert contends, is based for Frye on the suspension of the referentiality of language.[119] In a similar manner, John Caputo analyses Derrida's theoretical work as follows: "Deconstruction repeats the structure of religious experience [...] *sans* the concrete, historical religions; it repeats non-dogmatically the religious structure of experience, the category of the religious. It repeats the passion for the messianic promise and messianic expectation, *sans* the concrete messianisms of the positive religions."[120]

For both Frye and Derrida, then, theory appears as the means to give structural and verbal contours to the essentially non-verbal content of religious experience (as embodied spirituality rather than doctrinal message).[121] In this light, far from negating deconstruction, the present project could be read as its most exacting fulfilment. Besides, based as it is on the close reading of texts and the examination of their structure, prior to any theory, it even answers Paul de Man's familiar call in "The Return to Philology," only divested of his final requirement regarding "a principle of disbelief that is not so much scientific as it is critical."[122] On the contrary, the kind of spiritual criticism offered here would claim belief in the same sense that Caputo could say of deconstruction that it is "set in motion by an overarching aspiration, which on a certain analysis can be called a religious or prophetic aspiration, what would have been called in the plodding language of the tradition (which deconstruction has rightly made questionable) a movement of 'transcendence.'"[123] Only, as Caputo points out, transcendence in Derrida's work "means excess, the exceeding of the stable borders of the presently possible, [...] a prophetic, messianic bent [...], which is always and structurally to come,"[124] suggesting a reading of Derrida's theory as a process of transcendence remaining on the horizontal plane of immanence while still open to transcendence as the sudden vertical irruption of the *tout autre*.[125]

This brings us to Lars Sandbeck's illuminating essay on "God as Immanent Transcendence in Mark C. Taylor and John Caputo," where he compares their respective deconstructive presentations of God. In Sandbeck's words, both philosophers "present a God who is best described in terms of immanent transcendence," which "must be subdivided into two types according to [its] direction: [...] a process in which something or someone transcendent becomes immanent ('irruption') and the process in which something or someone immanent moves beyond itself ('surmounting'). Whereas irruption indicates a vertical 'downward' movement, surmounting points to a more horizontal, linear movement."[126] While Mark C. Taylor's philosophy of religion is premised on the former, Sandbeck contends, Caputo's would rather reflect the latter.

In turn, Sandbeck's analysis helps bring my project into focus. As a matter of fact, its aim is to draw a tentative chronological sketch of the relationship to transcendence of six famous American novels. Indeed, while *The Scarlet Letter* seems to (guiltily) suggest, in Mark C. Taylor's words, the possibility of "the death of God [as] the sacrifice of the transcendent Author/Creator/Master who governs from afar,"[127] Henry James's *The Europeans* celebrates His demise in the name of hedonism. Marking a turn away from ethical to aesthetic concerns, James's novel interestingly intersects with Taylor's analysis of imagination as immanent transcendence.[128] While pursuing this line of analysis exceeds the scope of the present project, the connection with Taylor's deconstructive theology serves to indicate both the relevance and the reason for the choice of *The Europeans* as probably James's least ambiguous novel regarding the happy character of this turn away from transcendence and ethics to immanence and creativity.[129] However, as this study purports to show, this nearly unadulterated bliss is cut short by modernist anxieties.

In this respect, the next two novels chosen, *The Great Gatsby* and *The Grapes of Wrath*, illustrate two opposed literary responses to the death of the God of transcendence in the modernist era: while Fitzgerald's novel appears to bemoan the loss of transcendence as the end of all idealisms, Steinbeck's epic reads like the literary formulation of a fully immanentized transcendence, where the evolution of the main characters is curiously consonant with Mark C. Taylor's deconstructive reading of self: "By breaking down the barriers between self-enclosed egos, communicating forces transform subjects into communicants. No longer possessive, the communicant seeks neither to secure his properties not to preserve his propriety. [...] The disappearance of the self in the communion of subjects expands the kenotic process of scripture. Kenosis is a self-emptying that becomes actual in the crucifixion of independent individuals."[130]

Indeed, Steinbeck's novel charts a path showing how, to paraphrase Walter Lowe reading Mark C. Taylor, "once [the] death [of the self] is no longer resisted but actively embraced, genuine openness to the other becomes possible [and] passion then becomes compassion."[131] In this light, *The Grapes of Wrath* may be read as the literary expression of a "radical Christology, [...] *thoroughly* incarnational,"[132] "signal[ing] the end of God's transcendence, [which] opens up a new form of transcendence, [...] human self-transcendence."[133]

Following this Christic thread, the last two novels under consideration, *On the Road* and *Beloved*, complete this suggested outline of a possible history of the link between American fiction and transcendence in a way that radicalizes the diverging directions taken by their two literary predecessors. A failed quest for a very secularized father, Kerouac's novel both echoes the Christic complaint on the cross and ridicules the quest for transcendence in its parodic portrayal of Dean Moriarty as a kind of mad Christ. In a very different context, Morrison's historiographic metafiction,[134] on the contrary, rewrites Margaret Garner's physical escape from slavery as psychological and spiritual emancipation.

As demonstrated above, the present work thus tries to follow the arguably contrasted route taken by American imagination in its relationship to transcendence. It is not and never could be comprehensive, but rather remains open to (and even calls for) a critical dialogue based on comparative analysis with other works of fiction. This being said, two points remain to be made.

The first concerns the paradoxical claim of an approach that will not situate itself at odds with deconstructive readings of religion and yet seems to construct a clear historical metanarrative of the link between American fiction and transcendence.[135] Beyond an easy objection as to the danger of a confusion between the spirit of deconstruction as a radically open discourse and incoherence, another more subtle distinction is to be made between our aforementioned heuristic principle of holism and critical dogmatic closure.

This brings me back to my choice of Frye as a theoretical model, whose project was also criticized as "totalizing." Yet, as Sára Tóth shows, Frye's totality curiously reads like the twin "other" to deconstruction:

> We may question the postmodern complaint against Frye's project being "totalizing." Frye's totality, as it were, is as mysterious and as absolutely beyond human control as its contrary, the kenosis of discourse in deconstruction. Both are impossible visions (it is as impossible to say all than [*sic*] to say nothing) yet necessary vantage points. As the vision of saying nothing safeguards difference and singularity, so the vision of saying all safeguards the possibility of understanding in the midst of diversity. Both aim at safeguarding a secularized sacred space within culture so as to provide a distance from our numerous and often aggressive ideologies.[136]

Safeguarding the possibility of understanding in the midst of diversity would be one aspect of the impetus, rather than metanarrative, animating this project. Another is its structural symbol – the cross – an imprint of Frye's theory[137] and an apt symbol for my broader design: the attempt to overcome the dichotomy between immanence and transcendence. As Sandbeck forcefully argues in his analysis of the concepts of imagination and event in Taylor's and Caputo's respective deconstructive philosophies of religion, these two concepts "are interpretable as two different instances of immanent transcendence" but "neither [...] seems to be very 'Christian'":

> Taylor's God as imagination represents the Dionysian God of paganism, Caputo's God as event represents the transcendent God of messianic Judaism [...] These labels [...] are, it must be noted, used [...] as heuristic devices serving to highlight different ways of interpreting God as immanent transcendence. Whereas 'paganism' represents a position that emphasizes God's immanence, and "Judaism" represents a position that emphasizes God's transcendence, "Christianity" represents [...] an attempt to overcome the very dichotomy between immanence and transcendence, that is, to emphasize equally God's immanence and transcendence.[138]

In Sandbeck's analysis, "a more specific 'Christian' understanding of God as immanent transcendence" would insist on the centrality of the Holy Spirit as "the resurrected 'body' of Christ."[139] In similar fashion, this project could be described as the effort to follow the evolution of the relationship between American literary imagination and a progressively immanentized transcendence understood not as the inevitable erasure of transcendence but as a possible "overcoming or reconciliation of opposites, the reconciliation between Father (Transcendence) and Son (immanence)"[140] through the literary word as Spirit.

This is where I will part company with deconstruction[141] and return to Frye's inquiry into the complex interrelatedness between the Bible and Western literary imagination.

American Literature and the Quest for Kerygmatic Power

Marked as it is by Puritan belief and dogma, the literature of the United States appears as an ideal testing ground for Frye's conception of the

Bible as the "great code" of Western secular literature. According to him, the latter reflects the Bible's core structure, defined as follows:

> The Bible is held together by an inner core of mythical and metaphorical structure: mythical in the story it tells of the redemption of man from between the beginning and the end of time; metaphorical in the way that its imagery is juxtaposed to form an "apocalyptic" picture of a cosmos constructed according to the categories of human creative energy [...]. How [this poetic unity] got there will doubtless always be something of a mystery. [...] We can only [...] hold to our central principle: the Bible is not a work of literature, but its literal meaning is its mythical and metaphorical meaning. (*WP*, 102)

The challenge would then consist in using Frye's theoretical cross to examine the six novels selected. This will involve probing their plots for traces of a mythical concern with redemption, which might then be related to a specific construction of space measured against the Bible's metaphorical picture of the cosmos. The underlying query being the kind of mechanism that gives language its potentially revelatory power both in a sacred text like the Bible and in the secular arena of literature, such an analysis will then logically also address the issue of the dominant verbal mode in the text under study. Such an approach consciously assumes Frye's heuristic principle of coherence:

> There is a distinctive theoretical implication in my position, [...] closer to what the word *theoria* implies, a conception originally ([*Anatomy of Criticism*], 1957) directed against the assumption that criticism must be either parasitic on literature or an extension of another discipline. The implication for me was that criticism is a coherent but not inexhaustible subject. [...] Coherence is a preliminary intuition or assumption about criticism: it does not prescribe any programs or predict any goals, but merely turns the engine on to enable us to get started. It is what is called a heuristic assumption, adopted for the sake of seeing what comes out of it. What comes out of it, however, is criticism itself. (*WP*, xvii)

My assumption is that what comes out of the study of the biblical subtext in American fiction is American fiction itself. The intimate and passionate relationship that the United States has had to the Bible, as purveyor of a common cultural identity, is to be held responsible for this. Tied to a long line of theological and historical texts marked by Puritanism and its traditional distrust for imagination and artistic creativity, burdened by the cultural models of Old Europe, American literature owes its birth to a definite spirit of emancipation.[142] As signalled by the title of one of its founding texts, *The Scarlet Letter* (1850), a "hellfire story" in its author's own words, it also bears the guilt of such rebellion.[143] However, remorse at fuelling his ancestors' Puritan disgust for "a writer of story-books" is not only what animates Hawthorne's exclamation.[144] His phrase also suggests his terrified awareness of the power of the letter to rival the Word of God. Red-tinted, the sinful A fantastically embroidered on his heroine's breast is an apt if romantic representation of the WASP literary imagination, which sears the human heart for signification. For, beyond the open defiance of the Puritan dogmatic law, based on a narrow, "literal" reading of the Bible,[145] the writer's art is aimed at the depths of the human soul, through its human capacity to falter and fall. In this daring probing of the human mind, it faces the deepest fears of the Puritan psyche pertaining to transcendence when it finds itself confronted with the unexpected revelation of the kerygmatic power of the letter.

On perusing this study, the reader might justifiably be surprised to find none of Frye's numerous literary analyses included. As suggested before, the present work is no synthesis of Frye's practical criticism,[146] but rather, wishes to test Frye's *theoria* on a ground relatively less tread by its author: American fiction. True, Frye did state his high esteem for the literature from the United States and produced perceptive criticism of some of its most prominent authors, notably Poe, Eliot, Pound, and Wallace Stevens but also James, Melville, and Emily Dickinson. However, as suggested by most of the preceding names, the bulk of his critical work addresses poetry, a lifelong dedication initially focusing on the great English romantics who made his reputation as a critic: Milton, Keats, Shelley, and of course, mainly, Blake.

More than trying to build upon Frye's remarks on American fiction, then, the present work is oriented by one of his key heuristic principles: *Aufhebung*. Commenting upon it, Denham notes that "sometimes Frye speaks as if interpenetration takes the form of a Hegelian synthesis, or at least the dialectical transition described by Hegel as an *Aufhebung*, a term used to embody the idea that oppositions can be transcended without being abolished":[147] "We have then in *Aufhebung* a triple meaning – a canceling, a preserving, and a lifting up – and it was this threefold meaning of the term that Frye appropriated for his own ends."[148] Returning to this concept at the end of his own study, Denham suggests that the way Frye did appropriate *Aufhebung* was by making it a structuring device in both *Words with Power* and *The Double Vision*. Indeed, in both cases, Frye seems to have ended his chapters using that process, moving beyond the oppositions under study in an attempt to reach towards the spiritual vision granted by the resulting higher awareness. If applied to literary history, such a process suggests the possibility of looking at the history of literature as reflecting a secularizing progress by no means antithetical with the development of a spiritual consciousness, the *Aufhebung* of both being a transformed awareness of secularity. This appears all the more interesting in the cultural context of the United States because it is shaped by the pastoral myth of the American Dream and its suggested vision of history as a quest for an Edenic "New World." Indeed, according to Frye, if in our secular age, "the earthly paradise, the natural and original home of man, represented in the Biblical story by the Garden of Eden, [...] has disappeared as a place, [it] is to a degree recoverable as a state of mind." In fact, for Frye: "Even if there are no paradises, lost or hidden, no angels, no divine presence, and no hell, there is still the range of human mentality, which could be immensely more powerful and efficient than it normally is, or fall far below even its average performance now. We can understand this best, perhaps, by thinking of each level of this imaginative cosmos as a way of experiencing the primary categories of consciousness, time and space" (*WP*, 175). In other words, the West's gradual secularization and consequent increasing interest in man's mental universe rather than God's symbolic one makes biblical cosmology relevant in a whole new way: psychological rather than religious, the secular journey goes all the way from an experience of total alienation (the former hell) to one of temporal and spatial immediacy (the equivalent of the former Heaven). When applied to the mythic representation of the history of the United States as shaped by a quest for Eden, this suggests a vision of this history as conditioned by a quest for the higher levels of consciousness. This view, in turn, brings us to Frye's vision of the cyclicality of cultural process, which he saw as characterized in the twentieth century by a descent into modernist irony, followed by a subsequent ascent towards spiritual vision, an evolution best represented by Eliot's poetry. On this issue, Glen Robert Gill's introduction to *Northrop Frye on Twentieth Century Literature* deserves quoting at length:

> For Frye modernism represented a rotation of the Spenglerian cycle of culture [...]. The preponderance of ironic (or what Frye frequently calls "demonic") symbolism in modern literature was obviously a consequence of

> its suspicion if not dismissal of the imagination [...]. Frye [...] deduced that what ultimately distinguished Romanticism from modernism was the latter's scepticism toward the possibility of the subject-object union that made imaginative creation or spiritual revelation, what Frye would later call *kerygma*, possible [...]. The second half of Frye's career, which saw him increasingly theorizing the spiritual significance of literature, was an effort to hasten another turn of the Spenglerian wheel, ideally creating such a consciousness of its cyclicality that it would on its next turn acquire a third dimension and become the spiral ascent that was his later apprehension of real cultural process.[149]

When applied to Eliot's work, Frye's vision of the spiralling progress of spiritual consciousness in twentieth-century literature becomes apparent:

> When Frye approaches the imagery of Eliot's work, he finds it [...] to be thoroughly committed to ascent within a pre-romantic cosmology. The cyclical imagery of *The Waste Land* [...] belongs to the poet's "infernal vision" or phase, his articulation of an interminable "nightmare life in death" witnessed or narrated by hollow men and women like Prufrock, Gerontion, Tiresias [...]. Eliot's real goal is revealed in his "purgatorial phase," which begins with *Ash Wednesday* and culminates in *Four Quartets* [...]. Frye's reading of *Four Quartets* shows it to involve an ascent through four fulfilling states [...]. Likewise his interpretation of *Four Quartets* [...] sees its constituent poems as paralleling each other in a similar form: a reflexive withdrawal from the axis of linear time and a descent to a vacant "dark night of the soul," followed by an ascent through the world of ordinary experience to an incarnational moment that restores innocence and invites one still higher into a concluding vision of divine plenitude. Through such ascents, Frye writes, Eliot strives to depict the "human tragedy ... consumed in the divine comedy."[150]

My approach to American fiction is clearly consistent with this vision of literary history since the nineteenth century, one marked by what might be termed spiritual emancipation: from the Romantic rebellion against the tyrannical authority of a traditionally omnipotent God through the modernist descent into alienation and despair, American fiction seems to be ascending back from the demonic pit, though in radically altered imaginative forms in terms of its relationship to transcendence.

The Task of the Literary Critic: A Tentative Conclusion

For Frye, kerygma is the transforming power of literary language: "The literary language of the New Testament is not intended, like literature itself, simply to suspend judgment, but to convey a vision of spiritual life that continues to transform and expand our own. That is its myths become, as purely literary myths cannot, myths to live by; its metaphors become, as purely literary metaphors cannot, metaphors to live in. This transforming power is sometimes called kerygma or proclamation" (*The Double Vision*, 17–18).

In its effort to follow the track of this transforming power in the novels under study, this work hopes to fulfil the kerygmatic function that Frye saw as the task of criticism:

> In "The Responsibilities of the Critic," the important essay of 1976 and almost a manifesto of the second half of his career, Frye had in fact suggested a role for the critic in connection with kerygma. In this address, originally given at Johns Hopkins University and twice reprinted, he focused on the prophetic authority of literature and suggested that the critic's task is to identify it. Characteristically, he emphasized that "this act, I have so often urged, is not an act of judgment but of recognition [...]. The door to our Eden is still locked, but [the critic] has a key, and the key is the act of recognition."[151]

One hope of the present work is that it will answer Frye's call and do justice to his theory, which he reputedly hoped would serve as "a kind of lumber room to which people would go to find what they needed for their own building projects." While this is probably an apt metaphor in the present case, in the end, I would endorse the observation that "what we find [...] is that our sense of Frye's own accomplishment – the nature of the working materials themselves – is revised or refined by the writers he illuminates."[152] As a concluding wish, in Frye's own words again, all I can do now is "to hope that somehow, somewhere, and for someone, th[is] struggle to unify and relate, because it is an honest struggle and not because of any success in what it does, may be touched with a radiance not its own."[153]

1 *The Scarlet Letter*: Puritan Imagination and the Kerygmatic Power of Sin

I Sinful Redemption

Mythos as Story in The Scarlet Letter

In *The Great Code*, Frye insists on grounding his definition of myth in its literary context: "As a literary critic I want to anchor the word in its literary context; so myth to me means, first of all, *mythos*, plot, narrative, or in general the sequential ordering of words. As all verbal structures have some kind of sequence, [...] all verbal structures are mythical in this primary sense, a sense that is really a tautology" (*GC*, 31).

One might question the usefulness of such a definition, as underlined by its author himself, were it not for the whole context of Frye's gradual construction of the notion. For the preceding rather neutral descriptive outline is but the basis of a global vision of myth as a verbal structure with a specific ideological and spiritual function. From an ideological standpoint, myth conveys a system of belief expressed in metaphorical terms, as analysed in the first chapter of *The Great Code*. In a symbolic or spiritual sense, Frye contends that its aim is to transcend history, holding the author's and reader's time in direct communication (*WP*, 60–1). However seemingly far apart, these two possible delineations of the notion are rooted in its fundamental literary structure, which aims at producing a final *anagnorisis*, a term Frye borrows from Aristotle to name the final simultaneous understanding of any *mythos* or story, when the sequential ordering of words suddenly gives way to a global understanding of the whole. In this fundamental structural sense, the anagnorisis produced by mythos might run the whole spectrum from the simple discovery of the murderer at the end of a detective story to the actual experience of a Revelation in its strongest sense.

Central in the American canon of romantic literature, Hawthorne's *Scarlet Letter* appears to be capitalizing on this revelatory power of mythos. A mere observation of the storyline leads to the final chapter, significantly entitled "The Revelation of The Scarlet Letter," a most theatrical moment when the highly esteemed Reverend Arthur Dimmesdale reveals his secret sin, imprinted on his chest in the shape of a letter A. Carefully placed in the last chapter as the purport of the whole story, this final revelation is one only for "the horror-stricken multitude" made up of the minister's parishioners. Still, even to the reader, who has been held privy to the secret torment of the minister from the beginning of the novel, it does appear carefully staged as a paradoxical scene of Transfiguration: "With a convulsive motion, he tore away the ministerial band from before his breast. It was revealed! But it were irreverent to describe that revelation. For an instant, the gaze of the horror-stricken multitude was concentred on the ghastly miracle; while the minister stood, with a flush of triumph in his face, as one who, in the crisis of acutest pain, had won a victory. Then, down he sank upon the scaffold!" ("The Revelation of the Scarlet Letter," 308).

Aside from the repeated references to the sacred character of the revelation, its symbolic location on the scaffold, immediately preceding Dimmesdale's death, casts the scene as a repetition of Christ's Crucifixion in expiation for mankind's sins. Indeed, this interpretation has been carefully prepared by the rest of the plot, which is animated by the central biblical myth of redemption: in fact, the whole story is that of the Christlike Way of the Cross undertaken by the two central characters, Reverend Dimmesdale and Hester Prynne, one of his parishioners, illicit and secret former lovers, who are going to bear the burden of their sinful guilt with such heroism as to be explicitly turned into saints. The sign of this conversion, the letter A embroidered on Hester's dress, evolves in the course of the text from referring to her adultery to variously meaning Able, as the symbol of her helpfulness and power to sympathize (194) and even Angel. Referred to as having "the effect of the cross on a nun's bosom [as] it imparted to the wearer a kind of sacredness" (195), the scarlet letter reads as the Christic symbol of Hester's conversion from sinner into saint.[1] This conversion is first and foremost one in the eyes of the beholders, as the townspeople gradually develop "a species of general regard in reference to Hester Prynne" due to "the blameless purity of her life during all these years in which she had been set apart to infamy" (192). Yet, the conversion is also actual for Hester Prynne, who develops a rather preternatural capacity for sympathy with her fellow sufferers' sins, as a consequence of her own inner ordeal: "[Hester] felt or fancied [...] that the scarlet letter had endowed her with a new sense. She shuddered to believe, yet could not help believing, that it gave her a sympathetic knowledge of the hidden sin in other hearts" ("Hester at Her Needle," 106).

When Dimmesdale's inner experience is described, the similarity to Hester's is quite striking,[2] which seems to confirm the redemptive reading of the story in *The Scarlet Letter*: "This very burden [of crime or anguish] it was that gave [Arthur Dimmesdale] sympathies so intimate with the sinful brotherhood of mankind; so that his heart vibrated in unison with theirs [...] and sent its throb of pain through a thousand other hearts, in gushes of sad persuasive eloquence. [...] The people knew not the power that moved them thus. They deemed the young clergyman a miracle of holiness" ("The Interior of a Heart," 172). Viewed as the type of a profound inner conversion, the scarlet letter might appear to lose all transgressive character, were it not for Dimmesdale's own theatrical insistence at the end:

> "People of New England!" cried he, [...] "ye, that have loved me! – ye that have deemed me holy! – behold me here, the one sinner of the world! [...] The Devil knew it well [...] but he hid it cunningly from men, and walked among you with the mien of a spirit, mournful, because so pure in a sinful world! Now, [...] he bids you look again at Hester's scarlet letter! He tells you, that, with all its mysterious horror, it is but the shadow of what he bears on his own breast, and that even this, his own red stigma, is no more than the type of what has seared his inmost heart!" ("The Revelation of the Scarlet Letter," 308)

Despite such insistence, Dimmesdale's proclaimed guilt and final revelation of it through the exposure of his chest still reads as a redemptive act, with devilish Chillingworth's expressed dismay at having lost his prey.[3] The minister would thus be enacting both a personal and collective redemption, as the scarlet letter's secret power is repeatedly linked to its capacity of exposing the sins hidden in people's hearts:

> Sometimes the red infamy upon [Hester's] breast would give a sympathetic throb, as she passed near a venerable minister or magistrate, the model of piety and justice [...]. "What evil thing is at hand?" would

> Hester say to herself. Lifting her reluctant eyes, there would be nothing human within the scope of view, save the form of this earthly saint! Again, a mystic sisterhood would contumaciously assert iself, as she met the sanctified frown of some matron, who, according to the rumour of all tongues, had kept cold snow within her bosom throughout life. ("Hester at Her Needle," 107)

Such a global redemptive reading would, however, both clash with Dimmesdale's emphatic final self-condemnation and leave the fundamental moral ambiguity on which the novel appears to rest unaccounted for. From the start, the narration is careful to stress the interrelatedness of sin and saintliness, as for instance, in the symbolic passage where Hester is first introduced: "Never had Hester Prynne appeared more ladylike, in the antique interpretation of the term, than as she issued from the prison. Those who had before known her, and had expected to behold her dimmed and obscured by a disastrous cloud, were astonished, and even startled, to perceive how her beauty shone out, and made a halo of the misfortune and ignominy in which she was enveloped" ("The Market-Place," 67). Both sinner and saint, the adulteress is even explicitly compared to the Virgin Mary: "Had there been a Papist among the crowd of Puritans, he might have seen in this beautiful woman, [...] and with the infant at her bosom, an object to remind him of the image of Divine Maternity; [...] something which should remind him, indeed, but only by contrast, of that sacred image of sinless motherhood, whose infant was to redeem the world" ("The Market-Place," 70).

From the beginning, the interweaving of the two supposedly opposed moral categories is thus insisted upon, whether through the characterization of the two protagonists as saintly sinners, the setting of the story in a "utopia of human virtue and happiness" whose first glimpse we have is of its "prison-door" (59), or the development of the mythos towards the apex of the final confession on the part of the community's most highly esteemed minister. Imprinted on the front cover, as the title of the novel, and concluding the text in the shape of the device carved on Hester and Arthur's common tombstone ("On a field, sable, the letter A, gules," 318), the letter A seems thrust forward as the symbol of that oxymoronic morality. Still, should Hawthorne's novel be read as boiling down to a moral fable about two Puritan transgressors on their way to redemption through the conversion of their sin by the daily martyrdom of their hearts and conscience?

As the main two female characters in the novel, Hester and Pearl, suggest, the novel is much more subversive than that. As pointed out by French critic Jacques Cabau, one explicit dimension of its subversion is political. Hester not only is a transgressor of the Puritan laws but grows into a full humanist outlaw, with "a freedom of speculation, then common enough on the other side of the Atlantic, but which our forefathers, had they known it, would have held to be a deadlier crime than that stigmatised by the scarlet letter" (197). In Cabau's words: "This is not about redeeming sin through suffering. Sin makes one grow, opens new human perspectives. Sin is a revolutionary act, castigating oppressive and obsolete institutions and demanding fulfilment for the human being. It is also an act of intelligence, nourished by truth."[4]

Besides, there is also a symbolic and poetic side to the subversion. Cabau analyses it through the paradoxical symbolism associated to colours and light in the novel, weaving a pattern of sin and rebirth. This is also epitomized by Pearl, who is the scarlet letter come alive and who will eventually reap the fruit of the seeds of disorder sown by her mother. She will go away, marry, and be happy, fulfilling the transformation of the letter from symbol of sin into the free expression of nature and life, which she is seen to embody throughout the book. In that respect, her answer to the venerable minister questioning her about her creator is significant:

> "Canst thou tell me, my child, who made thee?" [...]
>
> After putting her finger in her mouth, with many ungracious refusals to answer good Mr Wilson's question, the child finally announced that she had not been made at all, but had been plucked by her mother off the bush of wild roses that grew by the prison-door. ("The Elf-Child and the Minister," 136)

Presented, in realistic terms, as the product of the "perversity, which all children have more or less of" (135), Pearl's rejoinder also reminds the reader of the "wild rose-bush" at the threshold of the prison in the narrative portal that the two-page first chapter acts as. Seen as a token of the "deep heart of Nature" for condemned criminals (60), the wild bush is an apt metaphor for Pearl's transgressive character. As a spirit of nature, the little elf stands outside the world of Puritan morality. Hers is a free life force, a "jet of flame" (124) that evades the Puritan hierarchical world order, subjected to a transcendent and authoritative Creator. Claiming that she has not been made at all is no jest but shows her to manifest a life force that is not to be restricted to "the first column of the Westminster Catechisms" (135).[5] Branded as "the scarlet letter endowed with life" (124), she reveals the full nature of sin in the book: an act of creation that would equal the creative Word of God.

Mythos as Structure and Strategy: Sin and Creation

This further dimension of transgression in the novel, which might account for the lurid gleam it insistently casts through the omnipresence of the scarlet letter, implies a discussion of the much-debated prologue. A good fifty pages long, "The Custom-House" acts as a heavy frame for the story, which it introduces in retrospect. Actually, the story is presented as the reconstruction of Hester Prynne's past: "She had flourished during the period between the early days of Massachusetts and the close of the seventeenth century" (43). Throughout the prologue, the narrator thus appears at pains to establish the historical character of the story, while simultaneously stressing its legendary aspect: "Aged persons, alive in the time of Mr Surveyor Pue, and from whose oral testimony he had made up his narrative, remembered her […]. It had been her habit, from an almost immemorial date, to go about the country as a kind of voluntary nurse, […] by which means […] she gained from many people the reverence due to an angel" ("The Custom-House," 43). Suspense then builds up in this prologue, carefully designed to present the story as a mystery to be unveiled, which its heavy theatrical frame yet seems to postpone indefinitely.

The question thus arises as to the reason for such a dual insistence on the historical and legendary character of the story to come. This would appear to serve the narrator's romantic strategy well, with its quest for a meeting point between "the Actual and the Imaginary […], where each might imbue itself with the nature of the other" (47). Still, this does not thoroughly account for the feeling of suspense so artfully evoked by those preliminary pages nor for the prominence the narrator grants a number of venerable Puritan ancestors, among them late "Jonathan Pue, Surveyor of His Majesty's Customs for the Port of Salem" (40). In fact, the ambivalent feelings Hawthorne's narrative persona entertains regarding those Puritan ancestors, as both guardians of his American identity and figures of tyranny, hardly justify these noble characters' omnipresence in the prologue, except for the historical weight they give to the story to come: "Prying further into the manuscript, I found the record of other doings and sufferings of this singular woman, for most of which the reader is referred to the story entitled 'The Scarlet Letter'; and it should be borne carefully in mind that the main facts of that story are authorized and authenticated by the document of Mr Surveyor Pue" ("The Custom-House," 43). Indeed, one might wonder at the narrator's strange insistence on being "very little more" than the editor of a tale, whose circumstances of discovery are the subject matter of so many preparatory pages: "It will be seen, [...] that this Custom-House sketch has a certain propriety [...] as explaining how a large portion of the following pages came into my possession, and as offering proofs of the authenticity of a narrative therein contained" ("The Custom-House," 8).

Considering the Puritan natural distaste for "a writer of story-books" (16), such circumlocutions may be read as the narrator's respectful acknowledgment of his ancestors' diffidence. Still, bearing in mind the Puritan rejection of art on the basis of its competition with the creative power that should be God's alone, one better understands the narrator's efforts to ground his creation in some sort of historical reality, when his professed and sinful aim is to resurrect the past: "My imagination was a tarnished mirror. [...] The characters of the narrative would not be warmed and rendered malleable by any heat that I could kindle at my intellectual forge. They would take neither the glow of passion nor the tenderness of sentiment, but retained all the rigidity of dead corpses, and stared me in the face with a fixed and ghastly grin of contemptuous defiance" ("The Custom-House," 46).

As revealed by those lines, what the narration is after, in the end, is what no Puritan mind could have withstood: the "kerygmatic" power of words, which Frye refers to in the title to his second study of the Bible and literature, *Words with Power*, an allusion to Jesus, whose "word was with power" (Luke 4:32). In this context, the pseudo-historical character of the story appears as a necessity if characters are really to be brought back to life, "reality" being the key to the kerygmatic, as will be explored in the examination of the main verbal mode in the novel.

The global narrative strategy animating *The Scarlet Letter* thus appears as one that stresses the historical character of the story the better to mythologize it.[6] This apparent paradox dissolves when one considers Frye's analysis of the "two directions of development [of poetic myth]" (*WP*, 45), which address, respectively, "primary" (physical) and "secondary" (ideological) concerns of human life:

> One [direction of development] is toward the acceptance of the secondary concern: thus the concern for life may extend to a concern for posterity, for

> immortality [...]. The other direction is toward the metaphorical, as the concern for food and drink develops into the Eucharist symbolism of the New Testament. The difference is that the metaphorical or "spiritual" direction is thought of as fulfilling the physical need in another dimension of existence: it may require sublimation, but it does not cut off or abandon its physical roots. (*WP*, 45)

In *The Scarlet Letter*, both these directions of poetic myth – the ideological concern with posterity and immortality and the spiritual concern with communion – are made manifest in the narrator's description of his introductory "sketch" as authored by late Mr Surveyor Pue, "writing from beyond the grave" ("The Custom-House," 57), and his own reaching out for the redemptive communion subsequently described through his main characters. In Charles Feidelson's words: "The scarlet letter [...] gives Hawthorne a token of duration but also includes him, alienated as he is, in the enduring reality it radiates. [...] He is in communion; he belongs in the succession of Hester Prynne, who first wore the letter, and of Surveyor Pue, on whose mind it was so deeply branded. [...] He is redeemed."[7] Hawthorne's romantic writing thus undoubtedly mythologizes history with some ideological intent considering the harsh criticism of Puritans' moral intolerance implicit in Hester's life story. Still, the underlying narrative impulse goes in the metaphorical-cum-spiritual direction indicated by Frye in the sense that it fulfils the more "primary" need to partake of transcendence by evoking life in a narrative act of communion. When this is combined with the novel's subversive questioning of the Puritan conception of transcendence, as will be examined, *The Scarlet Letter* reads as very sinful indeed.[8]

II Beyond Moral Space

In *The Scarlet Letter*, fictive space is divided into two places: the little seventeenth-century settlement of Boston, where most of the plot unfolds, and the forest bordering it. In keeping with the Puritan mindset, this spatial division is symbolically constructed as a Manichean one opposing the little town as the place of law, introduced through its cemetery and prison – two locations symbolic of the "fallen world of alienation" (*WP*, 169) – and the wild space of the forest, where four of the twenty-three chapters are located. In these four chapters, Hester Prynne breaks a seven-year-long silence with her secret former lover, Reverend Arthur Dimmesdale, to disclose the identity and sinful influence of the man who has been living with him: Roger Chillingworth, her former husband.

These four chapters are the one moment in the whole novel and life of the heroine when she actively seeks to escape from the tyranny of Puritan law by offering to go away with Dimmesdale. Fittingly, the episode takes place in the forest, introduced from the start as "so black and dense […] that, to Hester's mind, it imaged not amiss the moral wilderness in which she had so long been wandering" (220). Repeated allusions to the dark and evil aspect of the place eventually culminate with Pearl's query, when she "half earnestly, half mischieviously" questions her mother about the devilish "Black Man" supposedly haunting it (222). Still, as if to undermine its sinful character as a wild place, the forest is also presented as a "primeval" wilderness (220), where Hester will remind the minister of the sacred character of their "sin," guided by the heart:

> "What we did had a consecration of its own. We felt it so! We said so to each other. Hast thou forgotten it?"
>
> "Hush, Hester!" said Arthur Dimmesdale, rising from the ground. "No; I have not forgotten!" ("The Pastor and His Parishioner," 235)

In this postlapsarian Eden, where the former lovers cannot help lingering, for "no golden light had ever been so precious as the gloom of this dark forest" (236), Hester will encourage Arthur to walk deeper into the wilderness to his freedom and happiness and "begin all anew" in her company (237–9), a sermon whose effect is to bring about Arthur's resurrection:

> The decision once made, a glow of strange enjoyment threw its flickering brightness over the trouble of his breast. It was the exhilarating effect […] of breathing the wild, free atmosphere of an unredeemed, unchristianized, lawless region. […]
>
> "Do I feel joy again?" cried he […]. "Oh, Hester, thou art my better angel! I seem to have flung myself – sick, sin-stained, and sorrow-blackened – down upon these forest leaves, and to have risen up all made anew, and with new powers to glorify Him that hath been merciful! This is already the better life! Why did we not find it sooner?" ("A Flood of Sunshine," 243)

Following this new catechism of natural life, Hester throws away the scarlet letter and instantly recovers her youth and beauty, while nature echoes this rejuvenation with "a sudden smile of heaven": "Her sex, her youth, and the whole richness of her beauty, came back from what men call the irrevocable past, and clustered themselves with her maiden hope, and a happiness before unknown, within the magic circle of this hour. And as if the gloom of the earth and sky had been but the effluence of these two mortal hearts, it vanished with their sorrow. All at once, as with a sudden smile of heaven, forth burst the sunshine, pouring a very flood into the obscure forest" ("A Flood of Sunshine," 244).

The primeval Eden thus recovered stands in sharp contrast with the biblical one, traditionally represented as under a close celestial guardianship. On the contrary, the sympathetic nature hosting Arthur and Hester's reunion is a "wild, heathen Nature [...], never subjugated by human law, nor illumined by higher truth" (245). Squarely placed outside the realm of religious law represented by the Puritan settlement, the natural space of the forest offers a way out of the tyranny of moral authority, for its only ruling power is the same life force that pervades the whole of creation. This echoes the opening of the narrative with its description of the wild rose-bush beside the prison, which had allegedly "sprung up under the footsteps of the sainted Ann Hutchinson as she entered the prison door [...] in token that the deep heart of Nature could pity and be kind to [the condemned criminal]" (60). Likewise these chapters illustrate the deep bond between Pearl, the "elf child," and "the mother-forest," which, together with "these wild things which it nourished, recognized a kindred wildness in the human child" (247). Conflating the myth of edenic harmony with the poetic convention of pathetic fallacy, the text thus rewrites the Puritan moral universe governed by transcendence into a world ruled by the companion forces of life, love, and sympathy: "Love, whether newly-born, or aroused from a death-like slumber, must always create a sunshine, filling the heart so full of radiance, that it overflows upon the outward world" ("A Flood of Sunshine," 245).

As the expression of the light that permeates Creation, love is an ontological force clearly situated outside the Puritan realm of morality. As such, it is not subject to moral rules for it does not belong to that order of existence. This, in turn, accounts for the consistently unconventional and even transgressive behaviour of Pearl, the embodiment of this life force of love that defies moral laws. Seen from a Puritan perspective, this is a very subversive message indeed. From the perspective of the century to come, however, Hawthorne's text is a creative act that opens up an immanent, secular space of possible redemption in the here and now, the minute the flow of the creative power of love is released. This is what happens with Pearl at the end of the novel. As soon as Dimmesdale publicly acknowledges her as his daughter and the fruit of his adultery, she discards her strange, demonic insensitivity to him:

> "My little Pearl," said [Dimmesdale], feebly "dear little Pearl, wilt thou kiss me now? Thou wouldst not, yonder, in the forest! But now thou wilt?"
>
> Pearl kissed his lips. A spell was broken. The great scene of grief, in which the wild infant bore a part had developed all her sympathies; and as her tears fell upon her fathers' cheek, they were the pledge that she would grow up amid human joy and sorrow, nor forever do battle with the world, but be a woman in it. ("The Revelation of the Scarlet Letter," 309)

As evidenced by the rumours of Pearl's subsequent happy married life away from New England, as opposed to Hester's final return and residence there until her death to complete her penitence, such redemptive experience remained inconceivable to seventeenth-century stern Puritans. To the nineteenth-century nascent United States of America, however, it is the promise of a new world order, no longer fettered to the tyrannical rule of a transcendent authority. To put it in Frye's perspective, Hawthorne's novel reflects the pivotal role played by a number of cultural and scientific factors in the nineteenth century to desacralize the traditional biblical vision of the cosmos as divided into four hierarchical levels, man's residence being wedged between Heaven and Hell (see Figure 1).

In the nineteenth century, Frye contends, the top level was cut off, "leaving man, who was assumed to be the highest product of evolution, with nothing above him unless he surpassed himself, as he was urged to do in Nietzsche" (*WP*, 174). Nevertheless, Frye adds, "there is no reason for the metaphorical structure to disappear from literature when its application to authority or the physical world does" so that "what we have now is a structural model of intensified consciousness, once linked to various physical phenomena" (*WP*, 174) (see Figure 2).

In the context of *The Scarlet Letter*, one could argue that Hawthorne brings to the fore a horizontal construction of space, opposing the Puritan settlement to the wild forest and suggesting the necessary transition from one to the other – a transgression in the literal sense – if one is to pass from one level of consciousness, burdened by moral rules, to one more fundamentally attuned to the law of life and love. In Frye's second chart, such transition could be read as the elevation from level three (the

Figure 1.

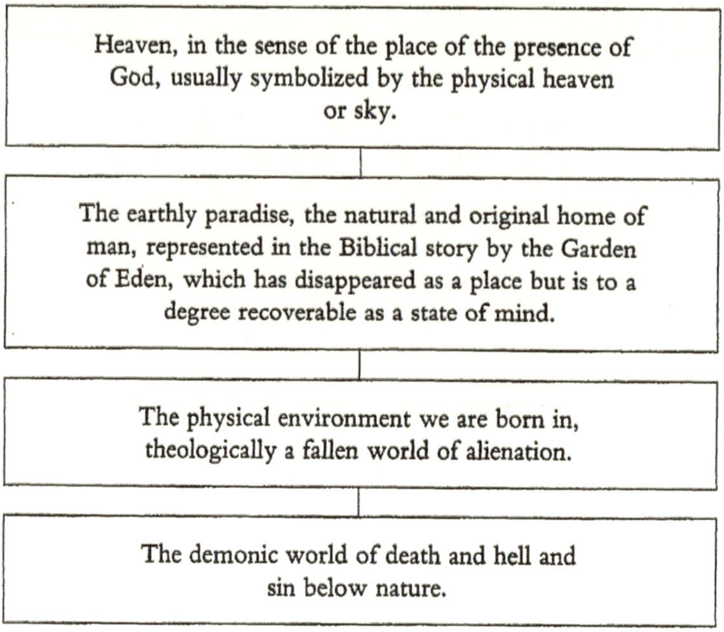

Heaven, in the sense of the place of the presence of God, usually symbolized by the physical heaven or sky.

The earthly paradise, the natural and original home of man, represented in the Biblical story by the Garden of Eden, which has disappeared as a place but is to a degree recoverable as a state of mind.

The physical environment we are born in, theologically a fallen world of alienation.

The demonic world of death and hell and sin below nature.

Source: *WP*, 169.

fallen world of experience) to level two: there, space becomes man's "natural" abode, and time that of an inner exuberance, perfectly in keeping with Arthur and Hester's experiences of resurrection and rejuvenation in the forest. In turn, Frye's analysis of the "unfallen mode of experience" accounts for Arthur, Hester, and Pearl's feeling of edenic harmony in the forest: "In the unfallen, paradisal, angelic or other modes of experience more intense than the ordinary one, time would exist without the sense of external compulsion that we feel in being continually dragged into the future with our faces toward the past. Such an existence would be a *musical* one, in harmony with nature, in counterpoint with other living beings, and in itself a pulsating inner exuberance" (*WP*, 176).

Read in this light, Hawthorne's novel opens up a new relationship to transcendence. No longer viewed as belonging to a realm of existence totally cut off from human beings, transcendence becomes a quality of experience human beings might access provided they are willing to go

Figure 2.

Cosmic Level	Time	Space
Heaven	Time as total "now" or real present	Space as total "here" or real presence
Unfallen world	Time as exuberance or inner energy (music, dance, play)	Space as home or "natural place"
Fallen world of experience	Time as "then" (linear and cyclical)	Space as "there" (objective environment)
Demonic world	Time as pure duration and power of annihilation	Space as alienation

Source: *WP*, 179.

beyond the confining limits of ordinary morality. A risky step for a Puritan mind, this transgression is necessary if one is to reach the ontological ground of human life.

III Sin and Kerygma

From Puritan Allegory …

What is it about artistic creation that Puritans should have deemed so sinful? As regards *The Scarlet Letter,* part of the answer undoubtedly lies in the subversive nature of its plot. Part of it also has to do with the potential power of language.

Looked at it from Hawthorne's viewpoint, the Puritans' relationship to reality appears mediated by their understanding of supernatural transcendence as the source of meaning, which is then to be interpreted:

> Nothing was more common, in those days, than to interpret all meteoric appearances, and other natural phenomena that occurred with less regularity than the rise and set of sun and moon, as so many revelations from a supernatural source. Thus a blazing spear, a sword of flame [...] prefigured Indian warfare. [...] It was, indeed, a majestic idea, that the destiny of nations should be revealed, in these awful hieroglyphics, on the cope of heaven. [...] The belief was a favourite one with our forefathers, as betokening that their infant commonwealth was under a celestial guardianship of peculiar intimacy and strictness. ("The Minister's Vigil," 186–7)

As Paul Ricoeur explains, such an interpretive act characterizes the allegorical mode of relationship to meaning.[9] In *The Great Code*, Frye calls it metonymic language, of which allegory is a particular form:

> The basis of expression here is moving [...] to a relationship that is rather metonymic ("this is put for that"). Specifically, words are "put for" thoughts, and are the outward expressions of an inner reality. But this reality is not merely "inside." Thoughts indicate the existence of a transcendent order "above," which only thinking can communicate with and which only words can express. Thus metonymic language is, or tends to become, analogical language, a verbal imitation of a reality beyond itself that can be conveyed most directly by words. [...] Allegory [...] is a special form of analogy, a technique of paralleling metaphorical with conceptual language in which the latter has the primary authority. (*GC*, 8)

In the Puritan community of *The Scarlet Letter*, such language is used for ideological purposes, as exemplified by the way Hester is turned into the very illustration of the notion of sin: "Throughout [the accumulating days and added years], giving up her individuality, she would become the general symbol at which the preacher and moralist might point, and in which they might vivify and embody their images of woman's frailty and sinful passion. Thus the young and pure would be taught to look at her, with the scarlet letter flaming on her breast [...] as the figure, the body, the reality of sin" ("Hester at Her Needle," 97).

Trying to ascertain what relationship to language this implies, one may follow Frye's analysis of verbal modes in *Words with Power*. His progression from the less to the most inclusive mode rests on his conception of the inclusiveness of a mode as being linked to the quality of awareness it relates to: whereas the descriptive mode addresses the senses and the conceptual/dialectic one focuses on reason, the rhetorical mode targets emotion, while the imaginative impacts a greater part of the psyche including the unconscious. In this perspective, *The Scarlet Letter* shows the Puritan dominant verbal mode to be rhetorical, as its dialectic impulse does not remain confined to the rational but aims at supporting the community's ideological system of belief. As made obvious by the heavy theatrical mise en scène of the whole episode when Hester emerges from the prison to be exposed to public infamy and urged to reveal the name of her partner in sin, in this Puritan world, "the tactics of ideology are incorporated in works of rhetoric, or oratory, where the aim is to persuade and create a response of *conviction*" (*WP*, 17; original emphasis):

> Discerning the impractible state of the poor culprit's mind, the elder clergyman, who had carefully prepared himself for the occasion, addressed to the multitude a discourse on sin, in all its branches, but with continual reference to the ignominious letter. So forcibly did he dwell upon this symbol, for the hour or more during which his periods were rolling over the people's heads, that it assumed new terrors in their imagination, and seemed to derive its scarlet hue from the flames of the infernal pit. ("The Recognition," 86)

In Hester's society, reality thus disappears behind theological rhetoric, just as the young woman gradually "gives up her individuality" to become the mere embodiment of the concept of sin.

... to Romantic Kerygma

When attention is paid to characterization in *The Scarlet Letter*, Hawthorne's narrative strategy might seem to follow a curiously similar path. Pearl, for instance, is described as the literal embodiment of the fruit of sin: "The child could not be made amenable to rules. In giving her existence a great law had been broken; and the result was a being whose elements were perhaps beautiful and brilliant, but all in disorder" ("Pearl," 111)

Here a crucial distinction is to be made between Puritan rhetoric and the type of verbal mode Hawthorne's novel aims at. Indeed, Pearl's disorderly character is no mere allegorical translation of her parents' transgression but the result of her physical and spiritual intimacy with her mother before being born: "Hester could only account for the child's character [...] by recalling what she herself had been during that momentous period while Pearl was imbibing her soul from the spiritual world, and her bodily frame from its material of earth. The mother's impassioned state had been the medium through which were transmitted to the unborn infant the rays of its moral life" ("Pearl," 111).

Pearl's close relationship of empathy with her mother accounts for her way of being. Likewise, just as Arthur derives his special gift of eloquence, quite distinctive from the rhetorical strategies of his colleagues, from his intimate sympathy "with the sinful brotherhood of mankind" (172), the secret behind Hester's artful embroidery, expressed in her daughter's remarkable attire as well as in the flaming letter A on the breast of her own gown, lies in the identity between "the object of her affection and the emblem of her guilt and torture":

> It was the scarlet letter in another form: the scarlet letter endowed with life! The mother herself – as if the red ignominy were so deeply scorched into her brain that all her conceptions assumed its form – had carefully wrought out the similitude, lavishing many hours of morbid ingenuity to create an analogy between the object of her affection and the emblem of her guilt and torture. But, in truth, Pearl was the one as well as the other; and only in consequence of that identity had Hester contrived so perfectly to represent the scarlet letter in her appearance. ("The Governor's Hall," 124)

Sympathy thus gives rise to art, whether it takes the form of superordinate eloquence or fanciful embroidery. The artistic analogy takes root in life and manifests the meeting point between the real and the symbolic, just as Pearl, the creative offspring of Arthur and Hester's love, is the living symbol of their union: "In her was visible the tie that united them. She had been offered to the world, these seven past years, as the living hieroglyphic, in which was revealed the secret they so darkly sought to hide – all written in this symbol – all plainly manifest – had there been a prophet or magician skilled to read the character of flame!" ("The Child at the Brook-Side," 249).

In *Philosophie de la volonté*, vol. 2, *Finitude et culpabilité*, Paul Ricoeur analyses the symbol as a type of analogy that cannot be objectified or intellectually considered from the outside but that takes us to the symbolic level of signification through a process of assimilation that depends on our having first experienced (not just understood) the primary, literal level.[10] This is highly reminiscent of Frye's analysis of the symbol in *Words with Power*:

> Originally, a symbol was a token or counter, like the stub of a theater ticket which is not the performance, but will take us to where the performance is. It still retains the sense of something that may be of limited interest or value in itself, but points in the direction of something that can be approached directly only with its help. A symbol may be purely arbitrary ("extrinsic," as Carlyle calls it), but as a rule it has or develops some analogous or other connection with what it points to, so that it can expand in that direction, taking us with it. Practically all techniques of meditation, for example, work with symbols, verbal or pictorial, that expand toward an identity, however defined, with what they symbolize. (*WP*, 109)

When he first comes in contact with the cloth of the scarlet letter, this is just the kind of direct relationship to symbolic meaning that Hawthorne's narrator seems to experience:

> My eyes fastened themselves upon the old scarlet letter, and would not be turned aside. Certainly there was some deep meaning in it most worthy of interpretation, and which, as it were, streamed forth from the mystic symbol, subtly communicating itself to my sensibilities, but evading the analysis of my mind.
>
> When thus perplexed [...] I happened to place it on my breast. It seemed to me [...] then, that I experienced a sensation not altogether physical, yet almost so, as of burning heat, and as if the letter were not of red cloth, but red-hot iron. ("The Custom-House," 42)

Spurred on by the experience into writing the story connected to the letter, the narrator then expands on the difficulties of his task in a way that reveals his groping for the meeting point between life and imagination: "On Hester Prynne's story, therefore, I bestowed much thought. It was the subject of my meditations for many an hour, while pacing to and fro across my room [...]. My imagination was a tarnished mirror. It would not reflect, or only with miserable dimness, the figures with which I did my best to people it. The characters of the narrative would not be warmed and rendered malleable by any heat that I could kindle at my intellectual forge" ("The Custom-House," 45–6).

In the process, his frustration opens up onto a meditative moment, when he exposes the mechanism of romantic creativity: "Moonlight, in a familiar room, falling so white upon the carpet [...] is a medium the most suitable for a romance writer to get acquainted with his illusive guests. [...] Thus, therefore, the floor of our familiar room has become a neutral territory, somewhere between the real world and fairy-land, where the Actual and the Imaginary may meet, and each imbue itself with the nature of the other" ("The Custom-House," 47).

Once again, Hawthorne's narrative project intersects with Frye's analysis with respect to the issue of illusion and its relationship to reality:

> As for illusion, its central importance in imaginative writing needs little emphasis. It would be difficult to take such a scene as the blinding of Gloucester in *King Lear* without the realization that it was not really happening. But the situation is more complicated than that, because what is physically absent is spiritually present. We suggested earlier, in connection with the imagery used in *The Tempest*, that the play is a reality created out of illusion, in the teeth, so to speak, of what we usually call reality, a reality which itself eventually dissolves into illusion, leaving not a rack behind. Such created reality is neither objective nor subjective, though it preserves elements of both. (*WP*, 131)

Such created reality, which Frye also calls "the positive illusion which is a potential [...] that can be actualized by a creative effort," as opposed to the negative one "that merely fails to be an objective reality" (*WP*, 131), also happens to be the main characteristic of what Frye calls the kerygmatic mode: "The initiative excluded hitherto from the imaginative and the poetic, the principle that opens the way into the kerygmatic, is the principle of the reality of what is created in the production and response to literature. Such a reality would be neither objective nor subjective, but essentially both at once, and would of course leave the old opposition of idealism and materialism a long way behind" (*WP*, 128).

The most inclusive of all verbal modes, the kerygmatic addresses human consciousness at its deepest, which Frye refers to as "soma pneumatikon" or spiritual body, borrowing the term from the First Epistle to the Corinthians: "Paul distinguishes the *soma psychikon*, which is mortal, from the *soma pneumatikon*, the spiritual body (I Corinthians 15:44). This is also a body (Paul means that it *is* a body, not that it *has* one). We possess it in this life also, and it is the element in us that enables us to understand the scripture and other aspects of revelation (2:14)" (*WP*, 124; original emphasis).

In other words, the gist of the narrative effort in *The Scarlet Letter* seems to be directed at passing from the allegorical mode typical of religious rhetoric to the kerygmatic power of romantic symbolism, which depends on a conjunction of life and imagination.[11] Such conjunction is the secret behind the power of sympathy held by the greatest sinners and artists in the book, Arthur and Hester, as well as by their progeny, Pearl, from whose "ever-creative spirit [...] the spell of life went forth and communicated itself to a thousand objects, as a torch kindles a flame wherever it may be applied" (116). Now, this same conjunction subverts the whole Puritan ideological system of morality by suggesting life to be a creative force manifesting outside the limits of the ordinary categories of right and wrong. This amounts to replacing the Puritan moral logic with an ontological one, putting life on an equal footing with love and creativity, and accounts for both the power of the letter, as the symbol of language, and its fundamental "innocence," as testified by its semantic evolution from "adultery" to "angel."

On all levels of its conception, then, whether considered from the angle of its mythical and metaphorical structure or dominant verbal mode, to take up Frye's categories, *The Scarlet Letter* appears to invalidate the whole Puritan moral order. This is a way of accounting for the sinful character of the letter, so dramatically conveyed by its scarlet hue. Besides, this sheds new light on the contradictory character of the whole narrative mise en scène in "The Custom-House," which brings the narrator to the fore, while he insists on his being "the editor, or very little more" of the whole tale (8). Such narrative timidity, arguably, expresses a very Puritan reluctance at asserting authorship when the sole creator is God; however, it might also be interpreted as Hawthorne's need for a warrant when confronted with the openly kerygmatic power of his romantic imagination. Being "at the service" of his own tale rather than its deliberate author might, then, be a way of voicing the dual emotions of fear and humility aroused by contact with the force of kerygma. The fictive narrator would thus appear to be dramatizing the kerygmatic experience, when "a Word not our own, though also our own, proclaims and a Spirit not our own, though also our own, responds" (*WP*, 118).[12]

In this way, besides explicitly unveiling the power at the root of all "great" literature, Hawthorne's fictive narrator appears to be expressing the author's awareness of his century's decisive though still incipient shift away from a "vertical," hierarchical relationship with transcendence to a secularized and internalized one, where God's Word is no longer a distant decree to be deciphered on the cope of heaven but rather a revelation to be experienced "within." This is the time of the Transcendentalists and their well-known quest for intimacy with the divine but also of Nietzsche's famous words, heralding the West's unprecedented global secularization in the twentieth century, a new page in the history of human consciousness. For God is dead, indeed, yet maybe more as the idea of estranged transcendence than as the actual experience of redemptive sympathy. This is what the following study of some literary classics from the United States hopes to unveil, taking the symbolic route of redemptive initiation through the crossing of the modernist desert to a perceived progressive "return" of transcendence in such apparently dissimilar fictive projects as Steinbeck's epic fiction, Kerouac's hallucinated pilgrimage, or Morrison's fulfilled inner quest. A prerequisite to such a birth of transcendence as an immanent experience, however, James's fiction is first to be examined, for it completes the total break away from the God of metaphysics and morality that Hawthorne's still partly Puritan imagination may have been unable to achieve.

2 Henry James's *The Europeans*: Secularity and the Descent of the Word

The complex history of Hawthorne's literary legacy to James has long been documented.[1] This has mostly, however, consisted in pointing out the similarities and differences in their craft in terms of the usual romance versus realism opposition, each writer being a recognized master of one or the other of these modes. The point of entry for a discussion of their respective literary genius is thus their conception of art's relationship to reality, a point James himself made in his famous essay on Hawthorne. For James, Hawthorne's main shortcoming arises from the limitations of the romance mode itself, which account for his failing to "render exactly or closely" either the "actual facts of the society that surrounded him" or the details of his characters' psychology.[2]

Importantly, though, as Robert Emmett Long also points out, what James saw as Hawthorne's artistic limitation was to be linked to his predecessor's Calvinist imagination: "One feature of the cultural conditioning of Hawthorne and Melville that worked against a commitment to realism was the Calvinist imagination, which places the individual and his spiritual condition at the center of the universe and tends to regard the physical world as a symbolic chart containing concealed meanings that are relevant to him. Hawthorne and Melville have their roots in the theology of the seventeenth century, in writers like Bunyan, and hence the tendency of their imaginations is toward emblem, fable, and allegory."[3] In this light, James's criticism of Hawthorne in the name of realism reveals a decisive shift in American literary imagination away from the former Puritan concern for transcendence. Accordingly, Long notes that "of Hawthorne's religious and metaphysical background James says relatively little," preferring to focus on "his social milieu, the small, insular democracy that produced him."[4]

In his study of Henry Adams and Henry James entitled *The Emergence of a Modern Consciousness*, John Carlos Rowe points to precisely just such a shift in American literature at the end of the nineteenth century. Growing estranged "from an earlier transcendental and logocentric vision," Rowe contends, Adams and James express the turn-of-the-century American writer's rejection of "any transcendental level for human thought." The crisis in modern thought that they make manifest is thus not solely to be viewed in social and historical terms but in epistemological and ontological ones as well.[5]

One inevitable consequence of such a disappearance of transcendence from the horizon of literary imagination is a focus on human subjectivity and interpersonal relationships. Rowe aptly quotes J. Hillis Miller's assertion that "when God vanishes, man turns to interpersonal relations as the only remaining arena for the search for authentic selfhood. Only in his fellow men can he find any longer a presence in the world which might replace the lost divine presence."[6] The question then arises as to what becomes of the biblical *mythos* that Frye sees as the "great code" of Western literature. Does it simply vanish from the realm of literary representation or does it remain, albeit in altered form?

Turning to James's *The Europeans* (1878) provides an interesting perspective on this issue. A novel belonging to the end of the period generally considered as James's formative years as a writer, *The Europeans* is emblematic of its author's lifelong preoccupation with the confrontation between innocence and experience. This statement at once suggests how indebted to the Puritan concern for evil James actually was. Nonetheless, his treatment of this recognizably Puritan theme shows the distance taken from its traditionally religious character. Indeed, the Jamesian encounter between good and evil characteristically takes the shape of a human encounter between characters originating, respectively, from the New and the Old Worlds. In other terms, James's famous international theme mediates what used to be a strictly religious matter. The literary focus has shifted away from a privileged concern for the relationship between man and God to an examination of interpersonal relationships as governed by what used to be religious morality, now divorced from any reference to the transcendent. In what follows, we shall see how one of the key aspects of *The Europeans* is the way it secularizes the religious.

I From Ethics to Aesthetics: The Fall into Secular Modernity[7]

Europeans in America: The Snake(s) in Eden?

Though couched in realistic terms, the plot in *The Europeans* reads like a secular version of the biblical story of temptation. Indeed, the eponymous Europeans appear as intruders challenging the moral order of the New World characters.[8]

Set in the 1840s, the story deliberately evokes "a quintessentially New England Puritan atmosphere,"[9] a prelapsarian time for American consciousness before the crucial divide of the Civil War which, according to James, acted as a fall from innocence: "The Civil War marks an era in the history of the human mind. It introduced into the national consciousness a certain sense of proportion and relation, of the world being a more complicated place than it had hitherto seemed, the future more treacherous, success more difficult. [...] The good American, in days to come, will be a more critical person than his complacent and confident grandfather. He has eaten of the tree of knowledge."[10]

Accordingly, the initial description of the Wentworths' house on a beautiful spring Sunday is of a "big, unguarded home" whose front door "stood open with the trustfulness of the golden age" (51). For their part, coming from Europe as representatives of its elaborate civilization, Felix and Eugenia will stand in sharp contrast with the New England characters. The novel thus initially seems to introduce a dualistic opposition between Europe and America through these two casts of characters embodying, respectively, civilized refinement and Puritan pastoral simplicity. Viewed in this light, the arrival of Felix and Gertrude in the midst of the Wentworth family heralds inevitable corruption, which seems initially confirmed. Indeed, the first meeting between the European brother and sister and their American cousins is narrated as a seduction scene, the seduction theme being introduced through Eugenia's determination to "please":

> Felix ushered his sister into the gate. "Be very gracious," he said to her. But he saw the admonition was superfluous. Eugenia was prepared to be gracious as only Eugenia could be. [...] When she desired to please she was [...] the most charming woman in the world. Then he forgot that she was ever anything else; that she was sometimes hard and perverse; that he was occasionally afraid of her. Now, as she took his arm to pass

> into the garden, he felt that she desired, that she proposed, to please, and this situation made him very happy. Eugenia would please. (62)

"With her ugly face and her beautiful smile" (63) hiding her aforementioned occasional perversity, Eugenia seems to partake of the original tempter's duplicity. In fact, throughout this initial encounter, both her brother's smile and her own are consistently contrasted with the Wentworths' Puritan gravity, "pregnant [...] with a sense of grand responsibility" (63). The American moral sense is thus at once opposed to the European concern for social appearances. Indulging in flattery, Eugenia commends her cousins' good looks, much to Charlotte's dismay, who "had never yet heard her personal appearance alluded to in a loud expressive voice" (64), while Felix's sally regarding the "adorable" character of his American female cousins is "received in perfect silence, [...] the silence of expectation, of modesty" (69). Besides, in a fitting remark in this temptation scene, Eugenia soon states her intention "to *know* [her American relatives] well" and have them *know* her (65; emphasis added) as the explicit goal of her coming to New England.

As Eugenia's emphatic declaration suggests, sinful knowledge thus appears as the unavoidable consequence of this morally debatable visit, whose transgressive character is suggested by Charlotte Wentworth's fanciful vision of Eugenia's maid coming to stay with them and "flitting through the sacred penetralia of that large, clean house" (76). As a matter of fact, the Europeans' presence will cause a breach of Puritan morals, as when Felix, wishing to undertake his uncle's portrait, is faced with his very Puritan refusal:

> "I should like to do your head, sir," said Felix to his uncle one evening [...]. "I think I should make a very fine thing of it. It's an interesting head; it's very mediaeval."
>
> Mr Wentworth looked grave; he felt awkwardly [...]. "The Lord made it," he said. "I don't think it is for man to make it over again." (88)

This association of the European visitors with art is a constant feature of their opposition to their American hosts, whether it be Mr Wentworth or the significantly called Mr Brand, the young clergyman associated to the family whose name bespeaks his attachment to the stern Puritan morality and who emulates Mr Wentworth's position by claiming he knows nothing of art (158). If both Felix and Eugenia are artists, it is not, however, quite in the same way. Contrary to Felix's self-proclaimed identification as an "amateur" and "bohemian" painter, Eugenia's art is more covert. For her, life is artful and she lives her life as an actress would perform her role. This is made explicit in her parting scene with her brother near the end of the novel:

> "Is the play over, Eugenia?" asked Felix.
> She gave him a sharp glance. "I have spoken my part."
> "With great applause!" said her brother.
> "Oh, applause – applause!" she murmured. And she gathered up two or three of her dispersed draperies. (192)

Eugenia's artfulness adds deceit to Felix's artistry and is actually the reason why the Wentworths' close friend, Robert Acton, will not propose to her. The son of a dying lady who is presented as a reader of Emerson's lofty transcendentalist philosophy, Acton will never be able to reconcile himself with Eugenia's duplicity. In turn, her failure to entice either him or the Wentworth heir into marrying her raises the issue of the victory of evil in this apparent allegory of temptation.

In this respect, it would seem that Felix, as "a highly successful comedian" whose "affectation" of "eternal gaiety" (153) wins the heart of Gertrude Wentworth, fares better than his sister. Initially, his developing romance with Gertrude is explicitly frowned upon on moral grounds. Just as distressed as Mr Brand, Gertrude's moral guide and Puritan suitor, Charlotte Wentworth exclaims over her sister's obvious change under Felix's influence: "You *are* wicked; you *are* changed!" (130). This, in turn, confirms her father's sense of disintegrating values, expressed in his stern rejoinder to Acton's enquiry regarding the Wentworth household on his return from Newport in the last quarter of the novel: "'If we have ever had any virtue amongst us, we had better keep hold of it now,' he said. He was not quoting" (141).

Indeed, throughout the novel, intercourse with his nephew and niece never fails to hurt Mr Wentworth's Puritan sensitivity. While he fears that "he should not be able to like his distinguished, delicate, lady-like niece" (86), Felix's constantly happy disposition, though easier to relate to, still feels "almost vicious" (87) to him. Besides, conversing with Felix always seems to lead him astray. After "one of the various forms of idleness" (90) that would appear to be commended by his nephew's initial suggestion of having him sit for his portrait, the conversation they have when Mr Wentworth finally resolves to do so centres on vices: as a solution to Clifford Wentworth's momentary "love of liquor,"

Felix suggests lust in the guise of his own sister's help to make Clifford "a gentleman." Besides, this follows a question about the risk of jealousy on the part of Clifford's fiancée, causing Mr Wentworth's "vague sense of jealousy being an even lower vice than a love of liquor" (116). Inevitably, his reaction to the proposed union between his daughter Gertrude and Felix will be one of "severe reticence" (183) on "moral grounds" (186).

In short, at heart, the confrontation between art and morality reveals the fundamental opposition between the European visitors and their American cousins. A wholly Puritan narration would have made it the encounter between sin and virtue. In James's novel, it is dramatized as the conflict between pleasure and duty, introducing a decisive shift away from ethics to aesthetics as the narrative focus passes from conscience to consciousness.

Confused Morals

In fact, the allegorical dualism opposing the Europeans to the Americans that seems to shape the novel is deeply questioned by the characters' interpersonal relationships, which expose a psychological logic redistributing roles in terms of a prelapsarian versus postlapsarian cast of characters.

Felix's unconditional contentment, first, squarely places him in the prelapsarian category, while his surname ("Young") makes him a natural inhabitant of the Wentworths' golden age New England.[11] As it happens, his own account to his sister of the Wentworths' welcome during his first visit explicitly makes him a sort of prodigal son:

> That evening, at dinner, Felix Young gave his sister, the Baroness Münster, an account of his impressions. [...] "I suppose, at least, they didn't turn you from the door," she said. [...]
>
> "Turn me from the door!" Felix exclaimed. "They took me to their hearts; they killed the fatted calf." (59)

This deep-seated affinity between Felix and his American relations, far from being a mere boast, will prove true not only in his romantic involvement with Gertrude but also in his moral scruples about it. Belying his apparently amoral offhand manners, his reluctance to openly "make love to" Gertrude is based on his "joyous" wish to "have a good conscience" by pleasing everyone (154) and not making himself guilty of "an abuse of hospitality" (175). As a prodigal son, however, his constant, joyful disposition will remain an implicit comment on the excessive austerity of his relatives' Puritan morality.

In complete opposition to her brother's unflagging joyfulness, Eugenia is defined by her restless irritation, which makes her impatient with her brother's good humour, considered as mere childishness. In turn, Felix's significant rejoinder to such a charge symbolically sets her up as a fallen creature:

> "One would suppose that you, madam, [...] were a thousand years old."
> "I am – sometimes," said the Baroness. (44)

The allegorical frontier that seemed so neatly to separate the Europeans from their American relatives thus shifts, revealing the rift between the European brother and sister as well as the hidden affinities with their American cousins, subverting the Manichean opposition between European-cum-Old World vice vs American-cum-New World Puritan virtue. Gertrude, for one, before she meets Felix, appears to be prey to much the same irritated restlessness as Eugenia. In fact, her restlessness is a matter of moral concern to her kin, something she senses and gives voice to by deliberately calling herself "wicked" (50). As in the case of Felix and Eugenia, lack of understanding thus appears to characterize Gertrude's relationships with her family, which once more brings the European/American divide into question. Besides, hers is a disagreement with her surrounding ethos that hinges on the very terms that seemed to define the European/American contrast: sensual pleasure versus moral duty, or a concern for aesthetics rather than ethics. This is apparent from the start, in the symbolic passage involving Gertrude and her sister Charlotte where, after discussing Gertrude's mood, the two young women turn to the topic of Charlotte's way of dressing. The sisters' exchange is highly revealing as regards their differing interest in aesthetics:

> "You should draw [your scarf] differently over your shoulders. [...] You should look differently behind." [...]
>
> Charlotte, by a movement of her elbows, corrected the laxity that had come from her companion's touch. [...] "It doesn't matter now. Indeed, I don't think it matters,' she added, 'how one looks behind."
>
> "I should say it mattered more," said Gertrude. "Then you don't know who may be observing you. [...] You can't try to look pretty." [...]

"I don't think one should ever try to look pretty," she rejoined earnestly. (48)

The conversation introduces the opposition between appearances and genuine reality that is at the core of the European/American divide, only this time Gertrude and Charlotte are standing one on either side. Their opposing reactions to the Puritan credo will later find expression in their encounter with Eugenia, for whom Gertrude will soon act as an interpreter to her own family. For, just as she guesses Eugenia's need for "privacy and pleasure" (73) when it comes to deciding whether to invite her to stay at the Wentworths', she instantly sympathizes with Mrs Münster's urge to "dispose anomalous draperies over the arms of sofas and the backs of chairs" (79) in the little white cottage they eventually make available for her. While Gertrude starts wondering "What is life, indeed, without curtains?" (79), her sister, for her part, stops short of "proposing to come and help [the Baroness] put her superfluous draperies away" (79).

Besides, the Manichean contrast between European vice and American innocence is further questioned by another American figure, who seems curiously conversant with Eugenia's worldliness. Robert Acton, whose name suggests his own familiarity with the game of social appearances, is described as "a man of the world" (61). Endowed with a "natural shrewdness [that] had a reach of which he had never quite given local circles the measure" (99), he is explicitly posed as Eugenia's American counterpart. Just as both Felix and Gertrude prophesy Robert and Eugenia's mutual attraction, so Robert will match Eugenia's manners with his own show of courtesy, and her capacity for duplicity with his pretended "humorous view of Madame Münster" (100) to hide his actual interest in her.[12] Eugenia, for her part, though initially presented as the villain of the story, will surprisingly come out as the wronged one in this comedy where she ends up the unmarried outcast, "walk[ing] homeward, alone, in the starlight, asking herself a question. Was she to have gained nothing – was she to have gained nothing?" (173).

Lastly, another feature of this Jamesian rewriting of the Puritan morality is the ambivalent treatment of supposedly "good" characters. Not only is the villain of the story not to be condemned wholesale, the angelic figures are not so unquestionably saintly: as Gertrude remarks, even Mr Brand, purportedly "as good as gold" (50), is not beyond self-indulgence. When he offers to unite Gertrude, his nearly betrothed, with Felix, whom he so strongly initially objected to, the young woman's analysis of his feelings blurs the opposition between Puritan duty and pleasure: "'He wanted to be magnanimous; he wanted to have a fine moral pleasure. [...] He thought it would be beautiful. At last he made up his mind that it was his duty. [...] He felt exalted; he felt sublime. That's how he likes to feel'" (188).

Taken from the psychological angle, Puritan morality thus sounds conspicuously close to a disguised form of aesthetic pleasure. James's psychological treatment of traditionally religious issues allows him a subtle shift away from ethics to aesthetics.

From Ethics to Aesthetics

What characterizes James's critical dramatization of Puritan Manichean morals in this encounter between Europeans and Americans is the total absence of any transcendent warrant. In the absence of God, morality becomes a purely human – and relative – matter, a question of subjective viewpoints, a cultural rather than moral issue. By being subjected to individual judgment, ethics are subtly devalued and replaced by psychological and aesthetic criteria.

This is most apparent in the scene where the European visitors meet their American relatives and where Mr Wentworth's Puritan rigidity, from his nephew's viewpoint, is likened to a funereal type of behaviour:

> Felix had observed on the day before [Mr Wentworth's] characteristic pallor; and now he perceived that there was something almost cadaverous in his uncle's high-featured white face. But so clever were this young man's quick sympathies and perceptions that he had already learned that in these semi-mortuary manifestations there was no cause for alarm. His light imagination had gained a glimpse of Mr Wentworth's spiritual mechanism, and taught him that, the old man being infinitely conscientious, the special operation of conscience within him announced itself by several of the indications of physical faintness. (63)

This external and descriptive stance regarding "the special operation of conscience within" is indicative of a narrative strategy that will consistently shift the reader's focus away from ethics to aesthetics. This shift is given prominence in the story through the central role that Felix acquires as an educator. Being himself described as a great admirer of "the beauty of virtue – a form of beauty that he admired with the same vivacity with which he admired all other forms" (114), his gradually replacing the young clergyman Mr Brand as Gertrude Wentworth's spiritual mentor is indicative of the novel's conversion of ethical concerns into aesthetic ones.

To start with, Felix first meets Gertrude in her house, where "this innocent Sabbath-breaker" (46) has stayed while the rest of her family has gone to church. Significantly giving the beauty of the actual blue sky as an excuse for staying away from religious service and its allegorical portrayal of Heaven, Gertrude will find herself playing host to Felix in a very symbolic manner: by bringing him wine and "a big round cake" (55). A thinly veiled parody of the religious service taking place at the same time, the scene highlights the secular, epicurean felicity of Felix, as he "sat there, with his glass in one hand and his huge morsel of cake in the other – eating, drinking, smiling, talking" (55). It also suggests that the young "Sabbath-breaker" will be a much more faithful attendant to Felix's lay sermons, as she soon proves to be when she offers to come and sit for her portrait. Gertrude's offer is a transgressive act performed in direct response to her own father's refusal to have his likeness taken and completes her fortunate fall: taking her sessions as an opportunity to question Felix about what he thinks of his new acquaintances, she will imbibe his view of life as "opportunity" rather than "discipline" (93),[13] and grow increasingly estranged from her family's ethos of duty. In that sense, Felix acts as a beneficent temptor, who will enable the young woman to come into her own.[14] In the light of her newly acquired knowledge, she will openly confront Mr Brand's admonitions regarding Felix's frivolous character:

> "That is probably what I like him for. I am frivolous myself."
>
> "You are trying [...] to lower yourself."
>
> "I am trying for once to be natural!" cried Gertrude passionately. "I have been pretending, all my life; I have been dishonest; it is you who have made me so!" [...] "One has a right to be frivolous, if it's one's nature. No, I don't care for the great questions. I care for pleasure – for amusement. Perhaps I am fond of wicked things; it is very possible!" (128)

Wickedness, in this context, loses all moral character to become synonymous with subjective differing from the communal credo. Gertrude's paradoxical claim evidences the relativity of moral judgment, as wickedness, in her case, is seen to produce honesty, when being "good" actually made her closer to the Baroness's duplicity.

James's Religion of Consciousness

The Europeans might thus be read as a psychological parody of morality plays, which accounts for both the persistence of the allegorical structure in the novel and the systematic disruption of its clearcut moral dichotomy. In the context of James's criticism of the Puritan moral straitjacket, this choice of a strategy makes perfect sense. More, however, than simply arguing for a realistic complexification of moral matters, James's subversive tactics would seem to yank the carpet away from under the moralist's feet, by altogether removing morality from the stage of the reader's concerns. To be sure, the comic spirit that the author deliberately intended for this novel to relieve the gloom of his preceding fiction accounts for what might be felt as an easy dismissal of moral weight.[15] However, by directing the reader's attention away from morality to psychology, James does more than question Puritan ethics. By emptying the usual moral allegory of its substance, he ushers in a new, secular age. "A secular man who felt no shame, anxiety, or doubt about his secularism, [...] at ease in a world viewed humanistically and agnostically,"[16] James creates a fictive world where the moral debate, though central from a structural viewpoint, is conspicuously cut off from any transcendent source: "Christianity, Transcendentalism, and Spiritualism were rejected without travail by a man whose full faith in the powers of the human consciousness sufficed as the only religion he knew or needed."[17]

The Europeans makes James's "religion of consciousness" manifest.[18] For in lieu of the moral conflict at the core of Puritanism, we find a confrontation between psychological faculties, most notably imagination and reason, as respective qualities of the European, artistic mind as opposed to the American, Puritan one. To a Puritan mind such as Charlotte Wentworth's, imagination is "a dangerous and irresponsible faculty" (75), while Mr Wentworth is described as evidencing "no imagination at all" (187). To Felix and Eugenia, on the contrary, "one's reason is dismally flat. It's a bed with the mattress removed" (189). In this respect, Gertrude's "peculiar temperament" (186), which is never called sinful by her relatives but is still thought of as "requiring a special line of development" (187) best provided by Mr Brand's spiritual guidance, is characterized by her excitability and flights of fancy. She will read the *Arabian Nights* rather than go to church, and much of the pleasure she derives from sitting for her portrait comes from the "great many stories" (94) Felix tells her about his life.[19]

Besides, however, projecting Gertrude "in a fantastic world" where reality looks like romance (94), her imagination also appears to be linked to another highly valued faculty: intelligence. Often linked to observation, imagination is consistently praised in the novel as a character's capacity to comprehend others. Gertrude has it, which makes her intuit the best way to accommodate Eugenia and earns her Acton's praise as "the cleverest girl in the world" (74).

As a clever woman, Madame Münster is also described as endowed with a "lively perception and refined imagination" (77). Her wit is actually constantly admired by another clever character, Robert Acton, something that undoubtedly plays a major role in the reader's eventual feeling of a failure of poetic justice when Eugenia is sent on her way, alone, while all the other characters happily pair off. In turn, this feeling, which diminishes the interpretation of Eugenia as "what Northrop Frye calls the *pharmakos* – the rascal inimical to the well-being of society who is driven out in the comic resolution,"[20] bears testimony to the subtle displacement operated by the novel away from moral to psychological concerns: for a strictly moral conclusion would not have caused the feeling of tragic pity that her eviction produces, nor consequently given the novel's last sentence ("and Robert Acton, after his mother's death, married a particularly nice young girl," 194) its touch of subtle irony. At heart, the sense of tragic pity comes from the nearly heroic grandeur Eugenia acquires through her dignified, clever demeanour, while that of unfulfilled poetic justice is due to her inability to secure the desired husband, despite all her intelligence. Indeed, this breaks the tacit rule of psychological affinity that seems to govern the concluding marriages and leaves the reader with a feeling of unfulfilled promise and wasted worth.[21]

To sum up James's strategy in *The Europeans*, the image of the empty shell might provide an apt metaphor: for he retains the structure of Puritan morality while divesting it of all moral meaning. Nowhere is this clearer probably than in Felix's professed ambition to "do [the Wentworths] good" by "cheering [them] up" (61). To this "healthy nature," for whom "it is beside the matter to say that he had a good conscience; for the best conscience is a sort of self-reproach" (94), Puritan morality is simply irrelevant.[22] Doing the Wentworths good is no moral undertaking on his part but rather targets the psychological consequences of a bad conscience. For him, his American relatives "look as if [they] were undergoing martyrdom, not by fire, but by freezing" (61) and "he would often wish, suddenly, that they were not all so sad" (81).

The religious vocabulary is still there but the redemption offered by the young artist, whose sallies are often called irrelevantly profane, is purely psychological and secular. Redemption, for him, is a matter of morale more than morals and amounts to "stimulating [one's] aesthetic consciousness" (118), as in the case of Clifford Wentworth, whose "higher education" (119) – in manners rather than morals – he spontaneously entrusts to his shrewd sister.

Often taxed with excessive levity and consequent lack of profundity, Felix comes as close to the allegorical as James could reasonably make him in an overall realistic context.[23] His undeniable superficiality should, however, be gauged less in the light of failing technique in the context of the author's interest in "deeper psychology" than in terms of James's disengagement with Puritan morality and entrance into a modernist concern for form, which Felix's amoral and artistic temperament represents. Nonetheless, rather than focusing on this formal modernism, usually observed in James's later fiction, the present analysis is concerned with the modern relationship to transcendence that already gives this early novel its topic and form. Indeed, James's rewriting of the classic Puritan allegory into a psychological one reveals an evolution characteristic of modernity:

> David Rapport Lachtermann was surely correct to discern, apart from all the semantic vagaries of its meaning, a common shape to modernity. [...] For Lachtermann the modern marks its beginning via "the identification of mind as essentially constructive." [...] [N]ow consciousness is thought to construct the phenomenal world. [...] This emphasis on the constructive mind tends to eliminate any mind-independent account of ontology (a feature which helps to give modernity its characteristic immanence).[24]

Quite strikingly, when *The Europeans* is regarded as a response to Puritan allegory, nothing seems to lie outside the scope of the characters' mutual psychological investigations: no transcendent sense of evil animates Robert Acton when he muses about Eugenia's dishonesty, trying to decide whether to propose to her, and the Baroness's final departure is no divine curse but simply "the supreme exhibition of a character to which the experience of life had imparted an inimitable pliancy" (193). To put it in Nietzsche's words in the same period of time, James's fiction does demonstrate that God is dead indeed, both as "the moral God, the God of consciences"[25] and as the Transcendent: "The death of the God of morality necessarily brought with it the death of the God of metaphysics. […] It is these moral determinations that in the end have turned against the idea of God"[26] In this respect, Mr Wentworth's characteristic frigidity is curiously reminiscent of the Enchanter's self-description in *Thus Spoke Zarathustra*: "I played the role of the *Penitent of the Spirit* … the man who freezes on contact with his bad conscience,"[27] and suggests the convergence of views between Nietzsche and James regarding the alienating effects of Christian morality. If, however, as the novel's images suggest, such morality brings a deathlike life rather than redemption, a term ironically reserved for a purely secular usage when it designates Clifford's "higher education" by Eugenia, what remains to be seen is the consequence of such a comprehensive secularizing process in terms of spatial representation. What of the metaphorical biblical cosmos?

II From the Figurative to the Literal: James's Rewriting of Religious Space

From Europe to America: Rewriting The Pilgrim's Progress

Just as the plot of *The Europeans* rests on the structure of the Puritan allegory the better to challenge its moral ethos, so its representation of space rewrites that of *The Pilgrim's Progress*.

To start with, the fundamental spatial opposition underlying James's novel is that of Europe and America. For though Europe is not featured directly, as the story takes place in New England, the Europeans' surprised vision of America suggests by contrast everything that Europe is not: a pastoral paradise. While "the stony pastures, the clear-faced ponds, the rugged little orchards" give Eugenia the feeling of a place that is "all very good, very innocent and safe," out of which "something good must come" (78), Felix also derives "a greater sense of luxurious security" than he has ever had from the "pastoral roughness" (80) of his new surroundings. Besides, more than one allusion is also made to the way the Wentworths' household harks back to some golden age, whether it be when their house is first described with its front door open "with the trustfulness of the golden age" (51) or when Felix muses on the "fresh-looking abundance about [the fare set before him] which made him think that people must have lived so in the mythological era, when they spread their tables upon the grass, replenished them from cornucopias, and had no particular need of kitchen stoves" (80). All in all, the America/Europe opposition boils down to the nature/culture one, as further suggested by the "uncastled landscape" of rural New England, which is explicitly opposed to the "wonderful Schloss," "sculptured gables and gothic churches" (104) of Eugenia's original Silberstadt. In this context, the Europeans' voyage to the New World would seem to bear a distinctive redemptive quality as a return to the simplicity of nature. This "return to nature" is testified to by Eugenia herself in a letter to a friend (78), while its redemptive quality is apparent in the narrator's description of her visit as a "pious pilgrimage" enabling her to "come into those natural relations which I knew I should find here. Over there I had only, as I may say, artificial relations" (102). In this sense, Boston would be the Celestial City for the European pilgrims – and so Eugenia does call it "a paradise" (100) – while many allusions are made to the "primitive" and "wild" character of the American scenery, suggesting its primeval, edenic quality (103).

Still, however cogent this allegorical subtext equating New England with Eden and the Europeans' visit with a pilgrimage, it is challenged in a number of ways. First, the pilgrim's spiritual conversion is no part of Eugenia's plans, for she has elected to travel to New England "to make her fortune" (42). In the process of becoming the "repudiated wife" of a German prince, the "redemption" she looks for in America, both regarding herself and her penniless, single "bohemian" brother, is financial and affective, giving the word its literal rather than religious meaning.[28] In turn, this literal dimension of a traditionally figurative quest exposes the significance of James's imaginative relationship to space, as it subverts the figurative representation of both the Puritan and the romantic traditions. Actually, James's narrative challenges the fairy tale quality of his own story through Eugenia,[29] who is not only rejected by her princely husband but will fail to find a spouse even in the more modest social circle of her American relatives. Gertrude and Felix's love story could indeed easily have passed for one, from the moment of their meeting when, engrossed in the *Arabian Nights*, Gertrude looked up and "beheld, as it seemed to her, the Prince Camaralzaman standing before her" (52) to their final union, which makes them "imperturbably happy [...] far away" from Gertrude's Puritan origins (194). Ending with such a conclusion, especially in the context of the other happy marriages mentioned, the novel could have been interpreted as a romantic revision of the Puritan morality tale. By serving as a foil, Eugenia's disappointed ambitions prevent such a monolithic reading and suggest James's narrative as more than a simple romantic comedy questioning Puritan morals. Rather, it is the figurative representation of space, a feature of both romantic and Puritan fiction, which appears to be at stake.

From Allegory to Phenomenology: A Work in Progress

The incipit of the novel clearly aims at destabilizing any coherent figurative reading of space. Alternately presented as dismal and delightful, gloomy and comical, depending on whether Eugenia's or Felix's point of view is taken, Boston still initially appears as a postlapsarian place: "A narrow grave-yard in the heart of a bustling, indifferent city, seen from the windows of a gloomy-looking inn, is at no time an object of enlivening suggestion; and the spectacle is not at its best when the mouldy tombstones and funereal umbrage have received the ineffectual refreshment of a dull, moist snow-fall" (33).

Through an effective delaying technique, however, the text subtly shifts the narrative focus away from its apparent object of interest – external space – to the actually eagerly awaited piece of information: the identification of its subjective observer. James's characteristic interest in viewpoint at once diverts the reader's attention away from a final interpretation of space by emphasizing its subjective character, while Felix's alternate and opposed vision of the same place completes the realistic deconstruction of any potential single figurative construct. James would thereby seem to evince the "commitment to considering the phenomena *as* they present themselves" that Merle Williams sees at the heart of both James's fiction and the phenomenological enquiry.[30]

The Europeans, however, rests on no simple erasure of biblical allegorical cosmology. Rather, its representation of space relies on both allegorical and realistic strategies. This is apparent in a few passages such as the interview between Gertrude Wentworth and Mr Brand, as they walk back across the fields to the Wentworths' house after Gertrude's visit to Robert Acton's mother. In their progression across the fields, Gertrude and Mr Brand halt at several gates that they must open to continue their walk. Though part of an overall realistic scene, these are still given an obvious allegorical function as representative of how much of an obstacle the disagreeable ardour of Mr Brand's suit is in Gertrude's path to freedom and happiness:

> [Gertrude] felt guilty and uncomfortable, and yet she was vexed with herself for feeling so. But Mr Brand, as he stood there looking at her with

> his small, kind, persistent eyes, represented an immense body of half-obliterated obligations that were rising again into a certain distinctness.
>
> "You have new interests, new occupations," he went on. "I don't know that I can say that you have new duties. We have always old ones Gertrude," he added.
>
> "Please open the gate, Mr Brand," she said. (96)

In the context of her companion's thinly veiled allusion to her neglect of him – the consequence of Felix's recent arrival – as undutiful for a future wife, Gertrude's "cowardly and petulant" request that he open the gate for her to pass through amounts to a clear act of transgression. The two characters' walk then becomes illustrative of Gertrude's determination to overcome the obstacles represented by the Puritan life her father and sister intend for her through her marriage to Brand even though, as she claims, "it doesn't make them happy" because "no one is happy here" (97). In a direct echo to this scene, Gertrude's subsequent conversation with Felix about her unwillingness to marry the young theologian also has a natural setting, as Felix has taken her rowing across a pond. Once again, Gertrude's response to her companion's query endows the realistic scenery with definite allegorical overtones:

> "If it were settled that you were to marry Mr Brand [...] I should feel more at liberty."
>
> "More at liberty?" Gertrude repeated. "Please unfasten the boat."
>
> [...] "I could tell you how much I admire you, without seeming to pretend to that which I have no right to pretend to." (123)

An obvious invitation for Felix to overcome his own reservations about "making love" to her, Gertrude's request turns the boat into a means of conveyance to the desired freedom. This inevitably makes Felix's rowing across the lake resonant with allegorical implications, as Gertrude's melancholy dissipates with their steady progression across the water. Though explicitly produced by Felix's proposed solution to preclude her marriage with Mr Brand, the dissipation of Gertrude's distress cannot but ring as the soul's joyful liberation on safely getting to the Celestial City after crossing the last obstacle: the river of sorrowful death.

Nevertheless, this allegorical dimension of James's story once more comes out as the underlying subtext that is consistently being rewritten. In James's novel, this subtext substitutes psychology for religion and is both recognizable as a traditional spiritual allegory yet disconnected from the religious content it used to convey. In this way, marital happiness replaces spiritual felicity as the goal of Gertrude's quest, and space loses its allegorical quality as the representation of the various stages in the soul's spiritual conversion. Instead, it becomes the reflection of psychological states, as in the above-mentioned episode between Gertrude and Mr Brand, where the latter does, indeed, stand as an obstacle in a landscape whose description bears the unmistakable mark of Gertrude's infatuation with her artistic cousin: "In the western sky the great picture of a New England sunset, painted in crimson and silver, was suspended from the zenith" (95).

Throughout the novel, places are thus divested of their potential allegorical and moral meaning to reflect the characters' psychology. Opposite the Wentworths' conventlike dwelling (77), for instance, Eugenia and Felix's "little white cottage among the apple trees" (80), "pitifully bare" as it is (79), could read as the perfect allegorical expression of the refined Europeans' redemptive stay in the Puritan Eden, whose moral purity is suggested by the "unspotted" character of the Wentworth household (77). Textual emphasis, however, falls less on such a moral interpretation as on the transformation of the house by Eugenia's maid to better fit her mistress's theatrical disposition:

> [Augustine] began to hang up *portières* in the doorways; [...] to dispose anomalous draperies over the arms of sofas and the backs of chairs. The Baroness had brought with her to the New World a copious provision of the element of costume; and the two Miss Wentworths, when they came over to see her, were somewhat bewildered by the obtrusive distribution of her wardrobe. [...] But what Charlotte mistook for an almost culpably delayed subsidence, Gertrude very presently perceived to be [...] the most romantic intention. "What is life, indeed, without curtains?" she secretly asked herself; and she appeared to herself to have been leading hitherto an existence singularly garish and totally devoid of festoons. (79)

Standing midway between Eugenia's festooned house and the Wentworths' monastic one, Robert Acton's is that of a man both sharing the Wentworths' honesty "and withal, [...] not absolutely simple" (108–9): accordingly, though reminiscent of the Wentworths' "clean-faced house" (62) when it is described as "fresh and clean as a well-kept dairy" (108), his own dwelling still appears to Eugenia's trained eyes as "more redundantly upholstered and expensively ornamented" than Mr Wentworth's (107). The main three houses of the story thus express a world view where places reflect people's character rather than abstract moral values.

This, in turn, reflects what Frye analyses as the transformation of the traditional biblical cosmos into mental states: "Even if there are no paradises, lost or hidden, no angels, no divine presence and no hell, there is still the range of human mentality, which could be immensely more powerful and efficient than it normally is, or fall far below even its average performance now. We can understand this best, perhaps, by thinking of each level of this imaginative cosmos as a way of experiencing the primary categories of consciousness, time and space" (*WP*, 175).

This internalization of the formerly allegorical projection of space is most obvious when one has a look at James's handling of the theme of the journey, as in the passage where Charlotte Wentworth's Puritan mind is contrasted with her sister's: "Gertrude's imagination seemed to [Charlotte] to be fairly running riot. [...] [F]or the moment, it seemed to threaten to make her sister a strange person who should come in suddenly, as from a journey, talking of the peculiar and possibly unpleasant things she had observed. Charlotte's imagination took no journeys whatever; she kept it, as it were, in her pocket, with the other furniture of this receptacle – a thimble, a little box of peppermint, and a morsel of court-plaster" (75–6). The spiritual journey of former moral allegories becomes that of imagination, Charlotte's reservations hinting at its danger: defamiliarization. The spiritual nature of the initiation journey has thus become psychological with Europe and America acting as cultural poles mediating this mental transformation, which replaces the spiritual conversion formerly operating between Heaven and Hell. In this new context, Gertrude, who, in a traditional morality, would have held the part of the sinner challenging the Puritan dichotomic moral order, becomes the true quester, just as willing to challenge the stability of her family's conception of life as her sister appears unprepared to do so. This speaks volumes for the change in world views that James's fiction reflects: not only is the verticality of biblical cosmology questioned – as in Hawthorne's *Scarlet Letter* with its suggestion of an ontological redemption to be achieved on earth rather than a spiritual one in Heaven – its very structure, resting on the antithetic moral absolutes represented by Heaven and Hell, crumbles. Just as America cannot be all Arcadian innocence lest it remain the diminutive and stifling space represented by Charlotte's pocket, neither can Europe be equated with corruption. The contrast between the two spaces is no cause for anathema but a simple matter of cultural difference. As Gertrude puts it, going to visit Eugenia in her New England house "will be like going to Europe" because "she will do all kinds of little things differently. [...] She will have a boudoir. She will invite us to dinner – very late" (75). One may thus understand why this deceptively simple assertion causes her sister to tax her imagination with "running riot," for it threatens their Puritan moral order with relativity. Accordingly, the novel concludes on no arrival in a unique edenic haven. If Eugenia retires to "the elder world" (193) after her unsuccessful stay in the new one, so do "imperturbably happy" Gertrude and Felix, suggesting that Europe is no unequivocal place of sadness and corruption. America, for its part, also appears to provide a perfectly adequate shelter for the other three couples' conjugal felicity. Besides, the characters' final happiness carries no overtone of moral reward but rather emphasizes the natural gaiety resulting from the union of like minds. In a passage representative of the subversion of biblical cosmology in the novel, Felix has a conversation with Mr Brand where he makes the young theologian's moral certainties into a simple matter of outlook: "'I was just making a note of that sunset. I never saw such a blaze of different reds. It looks as if the Celestial City were in flames, eh? If that were really the case I suppose it would be the business of you theologians to put out the fire. Fancy me – an ungodly artist – quietly sitting down to paint it!'" (158–9).

What is destroyed in the Celestial City's fire is more, however, than a representation of the world: it is also a whole attitude to the word.

III The Secular Word

Language and Truth: Europe vs America

The crux of the actual opposition between what Europe and America, respectively, represent for James is probably best reflected in Eugenia's and Charlotte's contrasted relationship to language. In a telltale passage where Charlotte and Gertrude discuss the actual meaning of one of Eugenia's apparent compliments to the Wentworths, their European cousin's manipulation of words stands out as so antithetical to Charlotte's conception of the transparent relationship of language to truth as to require Gertrude's interpretation to her baffled sister:

> "One goes into your house as into an inn – except that there are no servants rushing forward," [Eugenia] said to Charlotte. And she added that

> that was very charming. Gertrude explained to her sister that she meant just the reverse; she didn't like it at all. Charlotte enquired why she should tell an untruth, and Gertrude answered that there was probably some very good reason for it which they should discover when they knew her better. "There can surely be no good reason for telling an untruth," said Charlotte. "I hope she does not think so." (83)

Likewise, the problematic communication between Robert Acton's mother and Eugenia originates in the two ladies' obverse relationship to language: while the Emersonian disciple is clearly puzzled by the "fibbing" manner of her brilliant European guest (109), her straighforward remark that Eugenia's permanent stay in America would be "so pleasant" for her son leaves the Baroness with the feeling that "she would never know what such a woman as that meant" (167). In a way, the fundamental distinction *The Europeans* would seem to operate is between literate and illiterate characters, depending on their respective capacity or inability to decipher double meaning. In this respect, the American characters unexpectedly prove to be the knowledgeable ones. For just as Eugenia is at a loss to comprehend Mrs Acton's discourse, her own brother's disposition is "a frequent source of wonder to her" (153), while he is said never to know "how she would take things" (62). On the contrary, Gertrude reads Eugenia so well as to be able to correctly interpret her stated wish to be "taken in" by the Wentworths (70) as not literal. Likewise, both Robert Acton and his sister Lizzie will become adept at understanding that "everything the Baroness says is to be taken the opposite way" (136). In other words, the divide between the two attitudes to language apparent in the novel is not so much cultural as generic, as will now be seen.

The Drama of Complex Meaning

One consistent feature defining Eugenia's social behaviour is theatricality. Her behaving like an actress is visible in her initial mise en scène (45) of her first appearance before the Wentworths, when she sends her brother to "announce her" (56). She then arranges her "little salon" with "its becoming light and its festoons" (83) before eventually "gather[ing] up two or three of her dispersed draperies" once she perceives that "the conditions of action on this provincial continent [are] not favourable to really superior women" (192–3). Besides, the narrative voice also makes the theatrical nature of Eugenia's part in the novel explicit both through various comments and a specific narrative strategy. One instance of this is the way the fictive characters are referred to as "the little circle of spectators who have figured in our narrative" (193), while the readers themselves are placed in a spectatorial position. This starts from the very first lines, where the delayed presentation of the fictive viewpoint makes the readers just as much spectators of gloomy-looking Boston as the lady actually supposed to contemplate it. The strategy then expands to the whole novel, where the various characters' interactions, particularly with Eugenia, are presented as a series of scenes in a play, with Robert Acton one of its most devoted spectators. His having to leave Boston for a few days even causes him some frustration, for "he felt as if he had been called away from the theatre during the progress of a remarkably interesting drama. The curtain was up all this time, and he was losing the fourth act; that fourth act which would be so essential to a just appreciation of the fifth. In other words, he was thinking about the Baroness" (139).[31]

In turn, such consistent emphasis on theatricality makes what may justifiably be considered as the novel's whole point, for it exposes a new relationship to language and meaning, especially when the novel is viewed as a direct heir to Puritan moralities. With their clear dramatization of vices and virtues, moralities rested on an allegorical strategy implying an unambiguous relationship between their literal and figurative levels of meaning. The trace of such a transparent conception of language can be felt in Eugenia's ironical remark about Charlotte's generous proposal to act as her usherer into Boston circles: "'There are half a dozen places,' she said; 'a formidable list. Charlotte Wentworth has written it out for me, in a terrifically distinct hand. There is no ambiguity on the subject; I know perfectly where I must go. Mr Wentworth informs me that the carriage is always at my disposal, and Charlotte offers to go with me, in a pair of tight gloves and a very stiff petticoat'" (101).

The metonymic relationship between Charlotte's stiff dress and lack of ambiguity is an implicit comment on the rigidity of Puritan discourse, whose insistent clarity puts Eugenia off. A brilliant adept in the art of conversation, she is described as never saying anything wholly untrue nor wholly true (78). Her art being that of ambiguity, drama serves her purpose well. The gap it introduces between person and persona, being and role, involves a complex relationship to truth. As Eugenia views social relationships as a form of theatrical performance, the ensuing divorce between words and meaning creates a gap that makes art and deception correlatives.

The Literal and the Figurative: a Study of Verbal Modes in The Europeans

The basic cause for problematic communication between Europeans and Americans is the New England characters' Puritan lack of familiarity with figurative language. During one of her conversations with Felix, even Gertrude, who is so intuitive when it comes to understanding Eugenia's actual wishes and motives, "quite failed to understand the figurative meaning which her companion appeared to attach" to his self-description as a "bohemian" (93). As for Eugenia, her manipulation of literal and figurative levels of language is so complex as to obscure her meaning even for her own brother, so that the narrator ends up having to act as her interpreter in the delicate matter of her unstated wish that Felix should help her marry Robert Acton: "There were several ways of understanding her: there was what she said, and there was what she meant, and there was something, between the two, that was neither. It is probable that, in the last analysis, what she meant was that Felix should spare her the necessity of stating the case more exactly, and should hold himself commissioned to assist her by all honourable means to marry the best fellow in the world" (156).

Felix, however, will altogether fail her in this mission, taking Eugenia's apparent wish that he should not speak of her to Robert Acton to be literal. In this way, Eugenia will ironically end up the deceived one, as not only Acton but also Clifford Wentworth, her "second bowstring" (132), eventually marry someone else. The final marriages would thus seem to consecrate the triumph of transparent language: if Acton will not propose to Eugenia because "she is a woman who will lie" (171), Felix manages to win Gertrude's hand when he overcomes his scruples to "really express" himself and "tell the whole truth" (175) regarding his feelings for the young woman. In turn, his frankness will lead both to his own marriage and to that of Charlotte and Brand's Puritan hearts.

Felix's frankness, however, is no Puritan honesty. Turning to the issue of verbal modes in the novel, one is struck by Felix's considerable verbal skill, which is contrasted with Mr Brand's eloquence and its lack of "brilliant imagery" (121). Felix, on the contrary, resorts to verbal tactics that characteristically turn the tables on his Puritan interlocutors by appealing to what they most repress: their feelings. Nowhere is this strategy more obvious than in his interview with Mr Brand, where he undertakes to manoeuvre the young theologian into giving up his interest in Gertrude in favour of her sister Charlotte. As their conversation proceeds, Mr Brand's righteous composure is seen to dissolve gradually under the emotional impact of Felix's revelation regarding Charlotte's supposed feelings for him. Unable to "simulate nor dissimulate" (162), the "innocent young man" goes through "a mixture of sensations" (161) that will prove capital in his subsequent complicity with Felix's project to marry Gertrude, as the young artist rightly surmised.

In terms of the verbal modes delineated by Frye, Felix's strategy would then rank as belonging to the rhetoric, which aims at "creat[ing] a response of conviction" (*WP*, 17) through a strong appeal to emotion. Interestingly, the emotion it creates is the "initiative excluded from" the "dialectic" or "conceptual" mode that precedes the rhetoric in Frye's delineation of verbal modes as instruments of ever expanding consciousness. For Frye, what characterizes the "conceptual" or "dialectic" mode is its appeal to reason in its search for "whatever objective truth words can give" (*WP*, 9). As a consequence, the impersonal and objective quality of the dialectic mode is an ideal, but as Frye objects, "the impersonal leaves out the personal, and one wonders if the personal can be left out indefinitely" (*WP*, 12).

Now, defined in those terms, the "dialectic" or "conceptual" mode would appear to characterize the Puritan way of thinking. Indeed, Frye's analysis of this mode's impersonal quality sounds curiously consonant with Felix's observation regarding his cousins' self-effacement for fear of being selfish (124), which explains why Gertrude's excitability is looked upon very unfavourably. Felix's secular education would then seem to consist in opening up his Puritan cousins' minds to some degree of self-knowledge, effecting a transition from a conceptual to a more rhetorical way of thinking by acknowledging "subjective desire or energy" (*WP*, 12) rather than mere intellectual compulsion.

While Felix's rhetoric does seem to have this joyful, liberating effect concerning Gertrude, who ends up emphatically asserting her right to be "natural" (184), Eugenia's refined manipulation of figurative language creates a much more problematic relationship to truth. As has been observed, her constant theatrical duplicity subverts the transparency between the literal and figurative levels of language that was the hallmark of Puritan language, as expressed in moral allegories. Such transparency, which was at the service of moral meaning, placed emphasis on the signified rather than the signifier, recalling Ricoeur's claim that once the figurative meaning of an allegory has been deciphered, the allegory ceases to be of any use.[32] Conversely, in the name of manners, Eugenia's art of conversation privileges the signifier at the expense of the signified, while constructing no necessary link between the two. Meaning and truth consequently become highly problematic as they may not be construed from the words themselves. Nevertheless, her dramatic temperament combines with the novel's spectatorial narrative strategy to suggest that meaning and truth might have to be tracked down in the observation of appearances rather than through words. In the context of Frye's verbal modes, this would correspond to the strategy of the "descriptive mode."

Though "the last historically to become fully mature" (*WP*, 4), its initial position in Frye's sequence indicates that the descriptive mode is the less inclusive one in terms of the aspects of consciousness it encompasses: "In the descriptive mode [...], we follow the Lockean procedure in which perception leads to reflection [...]. It is in the reflection stage that one normally begins writing, and the word contains the metaphor of the mirror, what is reflected in thought being the wordless data of sense perception" (*WP*, 7). In this mode, "words or signifiers are, in theory, being subordinated to what they signify, servomechanisms to the information they convey" (*WP*, 4). A good description of the linguistic mechanism at work in "realistic" writing, the descriptive mode seems to reflect James's spectatorial strategy. Still, the "objective truth" that is usually "the overriding criterion" of this mode (*WP*, 5) paradoxically becomes subjective in James's novel, since observation is directed at the characters' motives. In the end, this descriptive strategy reveals that the Puritan quest for truth is redirected rather than abandoned, with truth being sought in the confusing world of appearances and subjectivity rather than in a pure, transcendent one. That aesthetics, rather than ethics, should be the means in this quest is indicative of James's modernity. This also suggests a revision of the usual understanding of modernity's characteristic secularity, as less an outright rejection of transcendence than a refusal of a form of transcendence alienated from humankind. In this sense, James's secular art might, paradoxically, be calling for a descent of the Word, as it both rejects the God of transcendence and still looks for meaning in the confusion of appearances. James's secular aesthetic quest would then seem not so far removed from the kenotic movement of Spirit that Thomas Altizer deems characteristic of modern secularity:

> We must recall that the modern historical consciousness is little more than two hundred years old, and that it was born by means of an eclipse of the transcendent realm, an eclipse resulting in the birth of a unique sense

> of historical particularity [...] as being wholly detached from a universal order or law. [...]
>
> As the God who *is* Jesus becomes ever more deeply incarnate in the body of humanity, he loses every semblance of his former visage, until he appears wherever there is energy and life.[33]

Even if my point is not to support Altizer's radical Christianity through a study of American literature, his analysis regarding the paradoxically Christian character of nineteenth-century atheism bears scrutiny in the light of James's artistic response to Puritan morality in *The Europeans*. For Altizer,

> Nietzsche's protest against Christianity, like Blake's and Hegel's, is most fundamentally directed against the Christian God [...] [as] the transcendent enemy of the fullness and the passion of man's life in the world. [...]
>
> Standing upon the threshold of what he believed to be a new age of humanity, the nineteenth-century prophet identified the God of Christianity as the deepest obstacle to liberty and joy.[34]

As "the embodiment of an infinitude of man's self-hatred and guilt,"[35] the transcendent God Nietzsche claimed dead is clearly the real source of Gertrude's rebellious outcry against her family: "Why do they try to make one feel guilty? Why do they make it so difficult? Why can't they understand?" (178). Her breaking away from her Puritan family through her marriage to Felix is not, however, synonymous with the final suppression of all religious sensitivity. For, though her departure spells the death of the Puritan transcendent God of morality as unequivocal authority, it does not erase the quest for meaning dramatized through Eugenia. In this perspective, the instability of meaning that Eugenia embodies makes sense in the context of a fictive world questioning the traditional transcendent warrant of absolute truth and meaning. His disappearance would even seem to account for James's characteristic elusiveness of meaning, variously analysed as confusion, ambiguity, or complexity.[36] More importantly, though, as we have tried to show, such elusiveness bears testimony less to the absence of the Word in secular modernity than to the problematic hermeneutics resulting from Its incarnation.

3 Fitzgerald's *The Great Gatsby*: Modernism and the Death of the Word

If there is one clear portal to the twentieth century, it is a passage through the death of God, the collapse of any meaning or reality lying beyond the newly discovered radical immanence of modern man, an immanence dissolving even the memory or the shadow of transcendence. With that collapse has come a new chaos, a new meaninglessness brought on by the disappearance of an absolute or transcendent ground, the very nihilism foreseen by Nietzsche as the very next stage of history.[1]

A measure of the achievement of the preceding writers under study is their ability to give literary expression to the Word, or to put it differently, to give, respectively, a romantic and realist expression to the process called incarnation. In more or less morally confining contexts, depending both on the time they wrote and on that in which they situated their story, these two writers dramatized the death of the God of transcendence, though with differing implications: for Hawthorne, still very much entangled in Puritan morality, the consequent ontological redemption to be achieved on earth remains postponed to a future time, "when the world should have grown ripe for it" (*The Scarlet Letter*, 317). For James, the disappearance of transcendence is liberating for the human self but raises problematic hermeneutic issues. In both cases, however, redemption is relocated in the here and now and, though individual, is to be achieved through interpersonal relationships, particularly romantic ones. Whether in the case of Hester Prynne and Arthur Dimmesdale or in the encounter between the Europeans and their American cousins, male/female relationships are clearly privileged as the site of an inner conversion that is both an emancipation from the God of transcendence and morality and a "process of ontological opening."[2]

Before, however, such ontological opening can happen, the American "modern man" is faced with a radical loss of bearings in his fast-industrializing society, where he "may no longer follow the prevailing beliefs of [his] time and [is] yet unable to formulate satisfactory new ones."[3] In the modern United States, the prevailing ethos is "the Success Myth and the conceit it engendered in the individual,"[4] the secular version of the Puritan dogma of predestination:

> According to Franklinian doctrine (Calvinism distilled through Poor Richard), a man's worth, or, if one prefers, God's election of man, is determined and demonstrated by his material success. [...] Man was not a man until he had proven himself by owning the world. In terms of identity one was no longer born of woman into a society where one found purpose and a place. Instead, one symbolically gave birth to himself by becoming "worth his weight in gold." Material facts were their own justification. No matter how savagely fortunes were achieved, mere possession of wealth and resources proved to Robber Barons that it was right and just that they should own the world. Materialism, capitalist variety, finds its roots in the dogma of predestination. Possession of the world reflects election.[5]

It is no wonder, then, that the disappearance of the God of transcendence – which used to act as the ultimate justification for the "American superiority complex"[6] evidenced in the colonists' ruthless and righteous fight for power and later expressed through the myth of the self-made man – should both expose a hubristic American ego as well as produce total despair in "the American of sensibility."[7] No wonder either that this disappearance should lay bare "the dominant idealist-materialist poles" of the American mythic construction of history,[8] which the same critic sees as originating in Puritanism:

> The dominant idealist-materialist poles of the American myth circuit yield up a common source in the opposite, yet complementary Puritan dogmas of Antinomianism and Arminianism. The Antinomian conviction that ultimate being and power lay in God as omnipresent, immanent, unchanging Spirit led to an idealism, pervasive in American romanticism, that viewed reality and experience as states removed from finite time, states existing in the mind and/or the eternal kingdom of paradise. The Arminians, with their denial of predestination and of the immediate, subjective experience of God, and their doctrine that man earns, even

> demands, grace as a reward for his works, are prophets of Ben Franklin, Horatio Alger, John D. Rockefeller, and of the self-made man psychology of success and personality.[9]

Divested of its religious garment, this "schizophrenic" division between idealism and materialism appears endemic to the American world view,[10] and it might account for the canonical status acquired by one of the novels most explicitly dramatizing it: Fitzgerald's *The Great Gatsby* (1926).

I The Fall of the "Son of God"

Materialism vs Romanticism: Allegorical Drama or the Jamesian Touch?

The Great Gatsby is by no means the only Jazz Age novel to record the anguish linked to modernity. It is worthwhile remembering, however, that the author of *The Waste Land* (1922), emblematic of the modern angst, credited Fitzgerald's novel with being "the first step forward in the American novel since Henry James."[11] If the nature of this "step forward" remains undefined in Letha Audhuy's essay, which concerns itself with the intertextuality operating between Eliot's *Waste Land* and *The Great Gatsby*, the statement remains provocative in the way it relates the master of American realism and precursor of modernism to the iconic writer of the "Roaring Twenties." Often a matter of thematic study,[12] this relationship has also been considered from the point of view of form, as in Brian Way's "The Great Gatsby." In this essay, Way studies Fitzgerald's dramatic mode of fiction in the novel in the light of James's explicit advocacy of dramatic form as the secure basis on which a novel should rest:

> The power of a great novel often depends, more than anything else, upon the firmness and suitability of its underlying structure. [...] Henry James wrote in his Preface to *The Awkward Age* [...]: "The dramatist has verily to *build*, is committed to architecture, to construction at any costs; to driving in deep his vertical supports and laying across and firmly fixing his horizontal, his resting pieces." If a novel is to have this secure basis, it should be written, like a play, in scenes. [...]
>
> The most striking formal characteristic of *The Great Gatsby* is its scenic construction.[13]

Even if the use of drama serves different purposes in James's and Fitzgerald's fiction, as will be seen, it may still provide a good leading thread in the exploration of Fitzgerald's representation of modernity and its link with the biblical *mythos* of redemption. In fact, the dualistic structure of the novel, opposing the materialist Buchanans to the idealistic Gatsby, is strangely reminiscent of the Manichean strategy of moralities.[14] The difference would seem to rest in the fact that the characters embody opposite attitudes to life rather than moral qualities, a characteristic making Fitzgerald's narrative strategy close to James's in *The Europeans*. A major difference between the two novelists, however, is their handling of narrative viewpoint. Whereas James makes it a point never to "'go behind' the action so as to analyse and comment upon it,"[15] Fitzgerald reintroduces narrative judgment via his first person narrator, Nick Carraway: "He is both stage manager and chorus, recreating situations in all their actuality, and at the same time commenting upon them."[16] To a certain extent, he thus appears as Fitzgerald's central realistic device as well as moralizing agent, making the novel a veiled allegory of the encounter between (evil) materialism and (pure) romanticism.[17]

Beneath the story's surface realism, the novel's underlying structure appears to rest on the traditional Puritan body/spirit dichotomy. This is obvious in the way Tom Buchanan and Jay Gatsby are each introduced.[18] Whereas Tom's distinctive feature is his body, "a body capable of enormous leverage – a cruel body" (13), Gatsby first appears to Nick as a barely visible "figure" in the night, "emerg[ing] from the shadow" of the neighbouring mansion (27). While Nick meets Tom in broad daylight, on his "sunny porch," the circumstances of Nick's first glimpse of Gatsby, alone in the dark and suddenly inexplicably stretching out his arms in the direction of a green light seaward, construct a romantic aura of mystery. When Tom is defined by his "sturdy physical egotism" (27), Gatsby's frailty is suggested by the trembling Nick thinks he perceives in his gesture, while Gatsby's "vanishing" in the night even hints at his insubstantiality. Besides, whereas Tom's face, with its "two arrogant eyes [that] had established dominance over his face" (13), bespeaks the agressivity that seems to define him, Gatsby's smile, with its "quality of eternal reassurance in it" (55) suggests profound, even Christlike sympathy: "It was one of those rare smiles with a quality of eternal reassurance in it [...] It faced – or seemed to face – the whole eternal world for an instant, and then concentrate on *you* with an irresistible prejudice in your favour. It understood you just so far as you wanted to be understood, believed in you as you would like to believe in yourself, and assured you that it had precisely the impression of you that, at your best, you hoped to convey" (54). Furthermore, this central, dualistic opposition between Tom and Gatsby is further confirmed in the way the female characters they are associated with are presented. Tom's mistress, Myrtle Wilson, is described as a "thickish figure of a woman [who] carried her flesh sensuously as some women can" (31).[19] By contrast, Daisy Buchanan, the object of Gatsby's romantic adoration, first appears to Nick, in company with her friend Jordan, as an ethereal creature, "buoyed up" on an "enormous couch" "as though upon an anchored balloon": "They were both in white, and their dresses were rippling and fluttering as if they had just been blown back in after a short flight around the house" (14).

Interestingly, no further physical description of Daisy is offered, but for her "bright eyes and bright passionate mouth" and the way she looks up into Nick's face "promising that there was no one in the world she so much wanted to see" (15), in a manner heralding Gatsby's own open welcome of Nick.

In other words, the narration carefully constructs the main characters around this clearcut division between down-to-earth physicality and romantic ethereality. In this light, the Buchanans appear as a gross case of misalliance that poetic justice is sure to mend.

Romantic Love and Redemption

More than a mere matter of poetic justice, though, romantic love holds a definite promise of redemption in the novel, as evidenced in the passage relating Gatsby and Daisy's first kiss before he left to war and she got married. In fact, the extract is constructed as a romantic conflation of the Fall/Incarnation process. At first, Gatsby's romantic attachment for Daisy is seen as barring his access to transcendent Heaven: as he is about to kiss Daisy, Gatsby has a sudden vision of a ladder, clearly reminiscent of Jacob's ladder to Heaven, which he may not ascend if not alone: "Out of the corner of his eye Gatsby saw that the blocks of the sidewalks really formed a ladder and mounted to a secret place above the trees – he could climb to it, if he climbed alone, and once there he could suck on the pap of life, gulp down the incomparable milk of wonder. [...] He knew that when he kissed this girl [...], his mind would never romp again like the mind of God" (118).

He embraces his own fall out of love, however, in a gesture metaphorically related to the Incarnation, or the coming together of Spirit and flesh: kissing Daisy, he "wed his unutterable visions to her perishable breath" and "the incarnation was complete" (118). Gatsby's renunciation of transcendence for the sake of romantic love is thus likened to Christ's kenosis,[20] as He espoused the human condition out of love for humanity. To this extent, Gatsby's fall is redemptive and his desperate struggle to win Daisy back is a quest for eternity through romantic love. To him, Daisy's voice is "a deathless song" (103) and meeting her again after five years evokes in Gatsby all the feelings of mystic rapture: "consumed with wonder at her [actual and astounding] presence" (99), he stares at the external world "as though [...] none of it was any longer real" (98), while he and Daisy are "possessed by intense life" (103).

More than an individual obsession, Gatsby's infatuation is thus endowed with a redemptive quality. In turn, this suggests that Gatsby's demise has symbolic implications far exceeding personal melodrama or tragedy. As a "son of God" (105), he embodies potential spiritual liberation and his death should all the more be construed as a good omen as "[Wilson] murders Gatsby at 3:00 pm, the hour another man-god had died."[21] Like Him, too, Gatsby takes on someone else's fault (Daisy's accidental killing of Myrtle Wilson) and dies for it, while the actual murderer is set free. The mode of Gatsby's death, however, clearly cancels out all hope of redemption.

Merciless Money: The Death of the God of Incarnation

In fact, Gatsby's actual death only comes as the completion and actualization of a most devastating one: his figurative murder, caused by the exposure of his glamorous social persona as a sham:

> In chapter six, the exposure starts with Nick's unveiling of Gatsby's true identity:
>
> James Gatz – that was really, or at least legally, his name. [...] The truth was that Jay Gatsby of West Egg, Long Island, sprang from his Platonic conception of himself. He was a son of God – a phrase which, if it means anything, means just that – and he must be about His Father's business, the service of a vast, vulgar, and meretricious beauty. So he invented just the sort of Jay Gatsby that a seventeen-year-old boy would be likely to invent, and to this conception he was faithful to the end. (105)

The debunking of Gatsby's quasi-divine status starts here, as his greatness, carefully constructed until then, suddenly comes crashing down in the revelation of its wholly artificial character. However, what is being exposed goes beyond individual deceit. More importantly, it is the symbolic and even spiritual dimension of Gatsby's glory that is shown to be groundless. His identity as a "son of God" is but a projection of his own ego, while his mission on earth appears restricted to the worship of false appearances ("meretricious beauty"). As a parody of Christ, he is less concerned with the Holy Spirit than with his Father's "business" – which turns out to be shady dealings with dubious individuals – and his "faithfulness" is that of an actor conscientiously playing his role "to the end." The only function of the mythic substratum on which Gatsby's persona is built thus seems to be the revelation of its parodic status in the glamour of the 1920s affluent America. In those highly selective circles, the new God is money ("business"),[22] and Eden is the world of the rich, which Gatsby realizes as a young, penniless soldier visiting Daisy's parents' house, "overwhelmingly aware of the youth and mystery that wealth imprisons and preserves" (155). So, if Gatsby is a "swindler," as Tom Buchanan claims in an effort to shatter the image of his wife's lover (140), his imposture is but a reflection of the wider society's sham, made apparent through the novel's theatrical narrative.

The "Roaring Twenties": The Death Masquerade

Structured around Gatsby's wild summer parties viewed from Nick's outsider/insider's position, the novel both displays and exposes its hero's "extravaganza" (154) as a way of revealing the theatrical and empty character of social relationships. An obvious stage, with its blazing lights and orchestra, Gatsby's mansion becomes the grand setting of a social comedy where "men and girls came and went like moths among the whisperings and the champagne and the stars" (45):

> The lights grow brighter as the earth lurches away from the sun, and now the orchestra is playing yellow cocktail music, and the opera of voices pitches a key higher. Laughter is easier by the minute [...]. The groups change more swiftly, swell with new arrivals, dissolve and form in the same breath; already there are wanderers, confident girls who weave here and there [...] become for a sharp, joyous moment the center of a group, and then, excited with triumph, glide on through the sea-change of faces and voices and colour under the constantly changing light. (46)

The emphasized theatricality of the social exchanges at Gatsby's amply makes Brian Way's point that "*The Great Gatsby* [...] is best regarded as a social comedy," not only as "a mode of writing which is satirical and moral," because Fitzgerald's writing "rises to a level of rich absurdity where comedy is not subordinated to a satirical or moral point, but is itself the point."[23] Whereas Way insists on the "Dickensian," "irresistibly joyous and liberating sense of the ridiculous which Fitzgerald conveys," as a way of expressing the "creative ludicrousness of life itself,"[24] the theatricality of Gatsby's parties would seem rather to stress the absurd component of the social comedy taking place. In those parties, false enthusiasm rules social intercourse between people "who never knew each other's names," whose "hair bobbed in strange new ways and [whose] shawls beyond the dreams of Castile" suggest actors' costumes (46). Impromptu shows suddenly interrupt the lively surrounding chatter and laughter when, for no reason, an unknown guest "seizes a cocktail out of the air, dumps it down for courage and, moving her hands like Frisco, dances out alone on the canvas platform" (47). Enjoyment for its own sake seems the rule of the game and the throngs, usually uninvited, flooding to Gatsby's are described as "conduct[ing] themselves according to the rules of behaviour associated with an amusement park" (47). Still, the spectacular character of those parties reveals the artificial dimension of the apparent general merriment. "Spilled with prodigality, tipped out at a cheerful word" (46), laughter is actually "vacuous" (53), and once Gatsby's theatre is deserted, "a sudden emptiness seem[s] to flow […] from the windows and the great doors, endowing with complete isolation the figure of the host" (62).

As a matter of fact, the same loneliness haunts the world outside Gatsby's, as Nick feels when in New York: "At the enchanted metropolitan twilight I felt a haunting loneliness sometimes, and felt it in others – poor young clerks who loitered in front of windows waiting until it was time for a solitary restaurant dinner" (63). The theatre of social relationships is thus not restricted to Gatsby's garden parties. All intercourse, particularly in the case of romantic involvement, appears afflicted with the same artificiality and attending duplicity. Nick's flirt, Jordan Baker, turns to the world a "bored haughty face" to conceal something, as "most affectations conceal something," for she is "incurably dishonest" (64); Tom Buchanan's mistress, Myrtle Wilson, the wife of a nondescript garage mechanic, starts putting on a ladylike show the minute she reaches the New York flat Tom rents for them. Still, of course, Daisy Buchanan herself, with her romantic ethereality hiding her actual craving for sex and money, is the greatest sham of them all.

Metonymically characterized by her seductive voice, a major romantic asset, Daisy turns out to be a "golden girl" (126), who breaks down in front of Gatsby's many "such-such beautiful shirts" (99), while rushing back to the safe harbour of her husband's wealth once he proceeds to demonstrate the dubious foundation of Gatsby's. Besides, while her "thrilling" voice is eventually exposed as "full of money" (126) in one of Gatsby's perceptive remarks to Nick, the exclusive and eternal character of Gatsby's Platonic love for her holds no weight when faced with Tom's open allusions to his and Daisy's sexual complicity:

> "There's things between Daisy and me that you'll never know, things that neither of us can ever forget."
>
> The words seemed to bite physically into Gatsby.
>
> "I want to speak to Daisy alone," he insisted [...]
>
> "Even alone I can't say I never loved Tom," she admitted in a pitiful voice. "It wouldn't be true." (139)

Deeper affinities than would have seemed at first thus link the southern belle to her aggressive husband, whose slaveholder's mentality – expressed in his assertion that "it's up to us, who are the dominant race, to watch out or these other races will have control of things" – she echoes, whispering "We've got to beat them down," "winking ferociously toward the fervent sun" (19).

A fierce struggle for life thus animates the materialist Buchanans. Contrary to James, the theatricality that Fitzgerald shows as affecting social intercourse points to no complex elusiveness of meaning but rather to a pervasive sense of vacuity and meaninglessness. Behind the social masquerade and devotion to money as the means to the only elevation now sought, there is only fear of death. In a telltale comment as to the main reason for her affair with Tom, Myrtle Wilson states: "I was so excited that when I got into a taxi with him [...] all I kept thinking about, over and over, was 'You can't live forever; you can't live forever.'" (42)

Clinging to life is found to be the basic urge in the novel, only, in a world both devoid of a transcendent source of life and fast killing the God of incarnation, the attempt is like clutching thin air. Or dust, rather.

II The Wasteland

Demonic Space: Rewriting Biblical Creation

The spatial structure of the novel perfectly reflects the postlapsarian, unredeemable society it is supposed to represent. Broken unity, first, marks the Eden of the rich, divided as it is between the Buchanans' world of established wealth and Gatsby's own gaudy, newly rich empire. An apt image conveys this sense of a broken primeval identity: that of the two eggs where their respective houses are located:

> On that slender riotous island which extends itself due east of New York, [...] there are, among other natural curiosities, two unusual formations of land. Twenty miles from the city a pair of enormous eggs, identical in contour and separated only by a courtesy bay, jut out into the most domesticated body of salt water in the Western hemisphere, the great wet barnyard of Long Island Sound. They are not perfect ovals – like the egg in the Columbus story, they are both crushed flat at the contact end – but their physical resemblance must be a source of perpetual wonder to the gulls that fly overhead. To the wingless a more interesting phenomenon is their dissimilarity in every particular except shape and size. (11)

A traditional symbol of cosmic unity, the motif of the egg is significantly related both to the theme of the twin and to the figure of *the* American quester, the discoverer of the New World: Christopher Columbus. The pattern of the American quest (through the allusion to Columbus) as a quest for primeval unity (the cosmic egg) is thus firmly imprinted on the fictional landscape, divided from the start between the Buchanans' East Egg and Gatsby's West Egg. At once defined by their similarity, as seen from above, or difference, as seen from below, they expose the contending forces of transcendence and immanence, whose struggle constructs a dualistic fictive universe striving for unity, as best illustrated by Gatsby's characteristic stretching of arms in the direction of the green light at the end of Daisy's dock. However, reduced to the imagined vision of birds, transcendence is obviously doomed in this postlapsarian world of division, as evidenced by the disclosure of the setting behind the rich stage of the American wealthy:

> About half-way between West Egg and New York the motor road hastily joins the railroad and runs beside it for a quarter of a mile, so as to shrink away from a certain desolate area of land. This is a valley of ashes – a fantastic farm where ashes grow like wheat into ridges and hills and grotesque gardens; where ashes take the forms of houses and chimneys and rising smoke and, finally, with a transcendent effort, of ash-grey men, who move dimly and already crumbling through the powdery air. (29)

In this parodic version of the biblical story of Creation, Fitzgerald depicts a place not only inhabited by death – as represented by the ashes making up the natural and human landscape – but from which the figure of the Creator is conspicuously absent. In this world of death, no transcendent Spirit infuses Creation with life. The creative process is actually inverted for, rather than descending from the heavens, it appears to come from below, as ashes "grow into ridges" and "take the forms" of houses and men. Transcendence manifests as an autonomous, self-creating "effort" on the part of nothingness (ashes) to take human shape, while the parody of God's omniscience completes that of His creative powers in the famous paragraph describing the fading placard overlooking the valley: "The eyes of Doctor T.J. Eckleburg are blue and gigantic [...]. They look out of no face, but, instead, from a pair of enormous yellow spectacles [and] dimmed a little by many paintless days, under sun and rain, brood on over the solemn dumping ground" (29). A "waste land" (30), overlooked by a short-sighted God in the shape of an old advertisement, whose handicapped omniscience George Wilson, the main inhabitant of the valley of ashes, will still turn to at the time of his wife's death, such is the face of the society hiding behind the glittering mask of the wealthy. Totally cut off from divinity, it is the "demonic world" described by Frye as the modern equivalent of hell, where space is totally alienating and time "pure duration [...] with no significant alteration [...], only repetition of the same thing, or the same kind of thing" (*WP*, 177–8). The description of the "obscure operations" of the anonymous "ash-grey men" who "swarm up with leaden spades and stir up an impenetrable cloud" when "occasionally a line of grey cars crawls along an invisible track, gives out a ghastly creak, and comes to rest" (29) seems perfectly to fit this definition. Sometimes, however, the pointlessness and meaninglessness of their incessant activity breaks through the thin partition screening their alienation from the world of superficial wealth and happiness and exposes this selfsame alienating loss of meaning as also plaguing the rich. This is apparent in Daisy Buchanan's exclamation: "What'll we do with ourselves this afternoon? [...], and the day after that, and the next thirty years?" (124). Echoing the woman in the second part of Eliot's *Waste Land*,[25] Daisy's question is followed by her own sudden suggestion to go to New York. Totally purposeless, as her husband remarks, this suggestion still initiates one of the many commuting trips illustrating a basic restlessness in the novel.

The Disoriented Quest

If we take up Audhuy's suggestion that Eliot's *Waste Land* is "the informing myth" in *The Great Gatsby*, her remark that "the central myth of

The Waste Land" is that of the Grail story bears scrutiny.[26] In fact, this remark appears supported by Nick Carraway's narrative comment regarding the nature of Gatsby's romantic attachment for Daisy: "[Gatsby] had intended, probably, to take what he could and go – but now he found that he had committed himself to the following of a grail. He knew that Daisy was extraordinary, but he didn't realize just how extraordinary a 'nice' girl could be. She vanished into her rich house, into her rich, full life, leaving Gatsby – nothing" (155).

Rather than a close study of the thematic relationship between the Grail legend and Fitzgerald's novel, which is the point of Audhuy's essay, the aim of the present study is to expose the deconstruction of the pattern of the quest in the novel. For, not only is Nick's remark proleptic regarding the impending failure of Gatsby's romantic quest, the very nature of Gatsby's endeavour, as a meaningful and dedicated line of conduct, contrasts with the restlessness and vacuity of the other characters' actions.

A first point to be made is the connection established in the novel between movement and death, as made obvious in the climactic episode of Myrtle Wilson's accidental killing caused by Daisy's fast driving. But even before this event, a number of apparently minor suggestions build up a network of allusions linking death to travelling, as, for instance, when Nick and Gatsby drive to New York. Looking at the city "from the Queensboro Bridge," Nick reflects that, seen from there, "the city [...] is always the city seen for the first time, in its first wild promise of all the mystery and the beauty in the world" (74–5). This characteristic quester's vision is, however, quickly followed by that of "a dead man [...] in a hearse heaped with blooms" (75). Coming as it does in a moment when the two characters are travelling west from Long Island to New York, the scene is to be related to the motif of the failure of the American Dream often observed in the novel,[27] which is explicitly expressed at the end.

The well-known visionary passage concluding the novel, first, makes Gatsby's dream that of the American Pilgrim fathers and even that of the whole human race,[28] a romantic quest for lost origins that is essentially doomed as "the orgastic future [...] year by year recedes before us" (188). But, not only is the Pilgrim's Progress fated, it has actually become meaningless. Not only is the quester killed, the very questing spirit itself has gone.

Indeed, no trace of the pioneering spirit that used to animate the Pilgrim Fathers' voyage and relentlessly push the settlers west can be found in the Buchanans' peregrinations: "Why they came East I don't know. They had spent a year in France for no particular reason, and then drifted here and there unrestfully wherever people played polo and were rich together. This was a permanent move, said Daisy over the telephone, but I didn't believe it – [...] I felt that Tom would drift on forever seeking, a little wistfully, for the dramatic turbulence of some irrecoverable football game" (12).

Besides, Nick's coming east, though for apparently no flimsy reason since he comes looking for work, is also motivated by the restlessness he owns up to on his return from "the Great War" (9). Like the Buchanans, too, he plans his residence in the east to be permanent, yet goes away once Gatsby dies.

In other words, the Pilgrim's and pioneer's quests are over. Both Jay Gatsby, the romantic lover who hankers for the green light at the end of Daisy's dock, as "Dutch sailors" had once been enraptured by the "fresh, green breast of the new world" (187), and his parodic alter ego, George Wilson, who locks his adulterous wife up, planning to take her west, fight for love and lose it together with their lives. And just as the Celestial City has given way to the Big Apple,[29] and the promise of the wild West to the comfortable safety of Nick Carraway's Middle West family home, the romantic quest, modelled after the Christian one, has lost direction. Either the princess withdraws to her wealthy castle or – as in the case of Jordan Baker – "the uncertainty of her [...] movements between hotels and clubs and private houses ma[kes] her hard to find" (161). Shiftlessness and restlessness have thus replaced all moral and spiritual direction and yet the basic struggle for life remains. In the context of a world devoid of creative transcendence, however, and destroying "the idea that energizes the living, not the idea of God but the idea of Christ – God made incarnate,"[30] such a struggle seems hard put to succeed. And just as the quest fails for lack of a genuine object, its narration fruitlessly tends towards fully meaningful revelation.

III From Kerygma to Rhetoric: Words without Word

One passage most clearly revealing the redemptive aim of the narration in the novel is the description of Nick's reaction to Gatsby's tale of the first time he kissed Daisy:[31] "Through all he said, even through his appalling sentimentality, I was reminded of something – an elusive rhythm, a fragment of lost words, that I had heard somewhere a long time ago. For a moment a phrase tried to take shape in my mouth and my lips parted like a dumb man's [...]. But they made no sound, and what I had almost remembered was uncommunicable forever" (118).

Couched in images likening this memory of romantic fulfilment to Christ's kenosis, Gatsby's tale triggers a Platonic process of reminiscence in Nick that reflects back on the spiritual motivation of his own narrative. His mediation of Gatsby's story then appears as an attempt to recapture the ideal, transcendent truth manifesting in Gatsby's tale, a redemptive intention that is at once shown to fall short of its aspiration. Nick's description of Gatsby's narration is, however, a comment on the "appalling sentimentality" of his own romantic tale and the rhetorical quality of his own imagery as actually a tool to try and retrieve the lost power of the Word.

This gap between narrative aim and means undoubtedly accounts for the dispute over the literary value of Fitzgerald's novel, which has provoked opposed reactions depending on whether critical attention was brought to bear on its "inflated rhetoric," as Ron Neuhaus put it in "Gatsby and the Failure of the Omniscient 'I,'" or on its sense of romantic possibility, the focus of Richard Lehan's book-length study, *The Great Gatsby: The Limits of Wonder*. Rather than entering such a tricky battlefield, the present study is more interested in the narrative process whereby the book's admittedly bombastic rhetoric tends towards the promise of kerygmatic revelation that gives the romantic turn of mind its fundamental power of attraction.

Interestingly, in his sequence of ever more inclusive verbal modes, Frye places the rhetoric in between the dialectical or conceptual mode – with its exclusive appeal to "the conscious mind and sense of objectivity" and its quest for truth "within the verbal order [it] is constructing" (*WP*, 9) – and the literary, "in which ordinary consciousness is only one of many possible psychic elements, the fantastic and the dreamlike having conventionally an equal status" (*WP*, 22). In other words, stopping short of the irrational border that marks out the literary domain properly speaking, the rhetorical mode still involves more than the impersonal neutrality of the conceptual one, as it is based on the personal vision of the locutor: "In oratory an identification of speaker, speech and audience is what is aimed at. That is, the 'I,' who is the writer or speaker, is identifying himself with the 'we' he is addressing [...]. Such an identification would be impossible if the audience's attention were diverted to the objective" (*WP*, 17).

This, in part, would seem to answer critical objections to the use of a first person narrator in the novel as marring the occasional omniscience Fitzgerald still resorts to:[32] in *The Great Gatsby*, the basic verbal mode is rhetoric because the narration tries to make the reader identify with Nick the better to support the romantic outlook Nick is mourning in his materialistic society. Nevertheless, this leaves open the question of how his "inflated rhetoric" is to create such an identification. Before examining this apparent contradiction, a preliminary analysis of the rhetorical apparatus at work in the novel is necessary.

Rhetoric in The Great Gatsby

Apart from the focus on the subjectivity of the orator, the other characteristic defining the rhetorical mode according to Frye is its division of style and content: "In rhetoric, style and content, the oratorical tricks and the persuasive message, are separable and this assumption of separability is often carried into literature by critics who are thinking in rhetorical terms. [...] Literature [...] does not say things: literary works communicate in mythical wholes, and if a distinction of style and content seems to be essential, it means that the writer has not escaped from the rhetorical orbit" (*WP*, 27).

The Great Gatsby has definitely not left the rhetorical orbit; still this should not be assessed in terms of success or failure but rather looked at as significant of its narrative strategy and relationship to transcendence.

When it comes to examining narrative strategy in *The Great Gatsby*, Michael Leff's method of rhetorical criticism proves illuminating.[33] Though Leff's concern is with political texts of historical significance, his method of textual criticism is perfectly adapted to the study of a literary text.[34] Focusing on the rhetor's construction of self, his target audience and the enactment within the text of the relationship between the two, Leff defines three features that distinguish the rhetorical approach to argumentation: embodiment, enactment, and evocation."[35] "Embodiment arises from what the text says, from the assertions and appeals that it makes. Enactment arises from what the text does. To understand this distinction, we need to think of an argumentative text not just as an inert product but also as a field of action that constructs representations and relationships as it unfolds – as a microcosm of the social world to which it is addressed. In this sense, texts construct a persona for the author, a persona for the audience, and a relationship (or a set of relationships between the two)."[36]

In *The Great Gatsby*, the first person narrator appears as the central rhetorical tool in the text, a way for Fitzgerald of constructing a narrative persona that will, in turn, enable him to project a persona for his readership and a specific relationship with it serving his purpose: romantic eulogy.

Taking up Leff's notion of "rhetoric embodiment" is useful to realize Nick Carraway's "instrumental function."[37] From the start, Nick poses as a trustworthy confidant and witness, privy to many people's secrets owing to his rare capacity to "reserve all judgements" (7). An attitude to life derived from his own father's advice to refrain from criticizing others, who may not have had the same "advantages" (7), Nick's supposed a priori neutrality is an implicit argument for the objective realism of his following tale about Gatsby. Besides, as the very embodiment of reserve, he can hardly be charged with rhetorical excess. In short, Gatsby's "greatness," which his tale is about, is no subjective construct but the product of observation and close intimacy with the object of the story. Besides, presenting himself in this way, Nick also projects the reader's persona as an intimate confidant, all the more privileged as the reserved character of his informant is bound to make his revelations priceless. Nick's self-portrayal thus both underlines his narrative reliability and suggests the extraordinary nature of his tale. If one were to take up Gatsby's persona as "the Son of God" for a point of departure, rhetoric embodiment in the novel would seem to place Nick in the position of the apostolic witness and the reader in that of the Christian disciple.[38]

In this light, nothing short of supreme truth seems to be the aim of the narration. Turning to the "rhetorical enactment" in Nick's introductory self-portrait, in other words, to what the narrative does rather than says, a somewhat contradictory picture emerges: while claiming reserve and self-restraint in expression, Nick curiously resorts to a high-flown and even pompous style. Though partly consistent with his nearly oxymoronic self-description as "unusually communicative in a reserved way" (7), his characterization of Gatsby as endowed with a "responsiveness [that] had nothing to do with that flabby impressionability which is dignified under the name of the 'creative temperament'" (8) or his own admission that, after Gatsby's death, he "wanted no more riotous excursions with privileged glimpses into the human heart" (8) still jar with his self-presentation as a moderate person. Even more intriguing, however, is the total meaninglessness of the sequence of pleonastic images used to convey his disappointment with humanity in the wake of Gatsby's personal tragedy: "Conduct may be founded on the hard rocks or the wet marshes, but after a certain point I don't care what it's founded on" (8).

Nonetheless, if one takes Leff's notion of rhetorical enactment as a basis, Fitzgerald's text appears to enact a rhetoric of emptiness that might prove more meaningful than it has usually been taken to be.

"Signs Are Taken for Wonders"

Commenting on George Wilson's blind (or rather short-sighted) belief in the false god of commercialism or materialism represented by the eyes of Dr T.J. Eckleburg that, Wilson is confident, "see everything" (166), Letha Audhuy is reminded of a line from Eliot's "Gerontion" – "signs are taken for wonders" – and remarks: "Here, Fitzgerald's joke is to make an actual sign (board) into a wonder."[39] Seeing the shocked reaction of the other character involved in the scene where Wilson solemnly affirms Eckleburg's omniscience, one may express qualifications as to the funny side of the situation. Wilson's attitude does make an important point, however, for it manifests the idolatry of a society so enamoured with appearances as to worship parodies of transcendence. In that sense, as "a son of God – a phrase which, if it means anything, means just that – " (105), Gatsby embodies this parody of transcendence. As the narrator suggests, Gatsby's divine persona is just an empty "phrase," a surface signifier with no signified, a word without Word. Nick's parenthetical comment implies that Gatsby is but the rhetorical embodiment and enactment of a society's empty aspirations, living on a stage whose curtains only hide vacuity, alternately represented by his own sham identity or the wasteland between rich Long Island and commercial Manhattan.

In this perspective, Gatsby comes out as a rhetorical tool, which accounts for the often-criticized vagueness of his characterization and fully supports Audhuy's assertion that, "Gatsby was an idea, not a character."[40] Furthermore, the mode of his characterization, best rendered by Neuhaus's phrase "inflated rhetoric," is reminiscent of the creative process enacted at the beginning of chapter 2: like the ashes' "transcendent effort" to take the form of ash-grey men, Fitzgerald's hyperbolic prose artificially insufflates sham divinity into Gatsby. The result is a very unsavoury sense of deficient realism for the reader, which should be less construed as failed artistry on the part of the author than as the narrative consequence of the broken bond with transcendence enacted in the plot.[41]

This is where Fitzgerald would seem to take up where James left off: as the enactment of the reign of empty signs – expressed through

Fitzgerald's occasionally meaningless hyperbolic style – *The Great Gatsby*'s theatrical structure brings the disquieting complexification of meaning evidenced in James's use of drama to its apex, producing such a complete divorce between words and reality, signifiers and signifieds, as to result in reverence for signs totally devoid of meaning. "Material without being real," signs procure the illusion of meaning while their actual disconnection from life makes them empty. This is the ultimate linguistic manifestation of the death of the son of God, who used to stand for the force of the incarnate Word.

Rhetorical Evocation and Kerygma

Such a disconnection between words and reality at once brings to mind Frye's definition of kerygma, the vehicle of revelation: "The initiative excluded [...] from the imaginative and poetic, the principle that opens the way into the kerygmatic, is the principle of the reality of what is created in the production and response to literature. Such a reality would be neither objective nor subjective, but essentially both at once, and would of course leave the old opposition of idealism and materialism a long way behind" (*WP*, 128).

Based as it is on this very opposition between materialism and idealism, *The Great Gatsby* seems very far from creating the kerygmatic reality inhabited by revelation that Frye describes. In the novel, the subjective and objective worlds are so severed as to render the one heartless and the other immaterial – spiritless dust taking natural forms.[42] Once again, Michael Leff's notion of "rhetorical evocation" helps us understand the nature of the revelation at stake in the novel: "Evocation operates at a higher level of generality than embodiment and enactment, since it refers to the representation and apprehension of the situation as a whole. [...] Walter Jost and Michael Hyde explain that evocation occurs through the realization of a pattern within a set of accumulated particulars. This realization must be vivid, and it must grasp something as 'a whole within which everything else makes sense,' and it is achieved through persuasion."[43]

Such a vivid realization of "a whole within which everything else makes sense" would seem precisely enacted in Nick's final vision of the significance of Gatsby's quest in the broader context of the human quest for a lost Eden with such historical consequences as the discovery of the "New" World. In turn, the relationship of deep sympathy with the reader, rhetorically enacted from the start – a kind of discipleship duplicating that between Nick and Gatsby – culminates in the final "we":

> Gatsby believed in the green light, the orgastic future that year by year recedes before us. It eluded us then, but that's no matter – tomorrow we will run faster, strech out our arms further … And one fine morning –
>
> So we beat on, boats against the current, borne back ceaselessly into the past. (188)

Enacting the bond of sympathy with the reader that the whole narrative has been working towards, this final passage operates the identification between orator and audience that Frye signals as characteristic of the rhetorical mode. It also produces the evocation that Leff sees as the third feature of rhetorical argumentation, when "it summons up recognition of the situation both as an integral whole and as something that fits within our cultural inheritance."[44] This, in turn, recalls Frye's remark that, in the rhetorical mode, what was still unconscious, or to put it in his own terms, what remained the initiative excluded in the dialectic/conceptual mode, now becomes the focus of rhetorical argumentation: "the great frameworks of accepted (and by the great majority unexamined) assumptions that we call ideologies" (*WP*, 16). In the case of Fitzgerald's novel, Nick's romantic eulogy demonstrates the far-reaching consequences of the American new cult of materialism: destroying humanity's idealistic quest for Eden as the symbolic place and state of primeval, redemptive unity, it is also killing its vital spirit and "creative passion" (103), suppressing the very possibility of kerygma as life-giving verbal power and reducing language to an inflated rhetoric desperately tending towards its own impossible transcendence.

4 Immanent Christianity in *The Grapes of Wrath*

Seeking a definition of modernism, Warren French, interestingly, turns to *The Great Gatsby* as a good representation of the ironic "double realm of values" that he finds characteristic of modernist literature:

> Asked to exemplify the presentation in fiction of this "double realm of values" that characterizes the "ironic vision," one would tend to turn first to Nick Carraway's paradoxical opening comment about the title character in F. Scott Fitzgerald's *The Great Gatsby*: "When I came back from the East last autumn I felt that I wanted the world to be in uniform and at a sort of moral attention forever. ... Only Gatsby ... was exempt from my reaction – Gatsby, who represented everything for which I have an unaffected scorn." Because Nick Carraway is *able to perceive* that Gatsby embodies the extreme opposites of complete innocence and complete corruption rather than merely look at him and the world in terms of some "uniform" set of values, Fitzgerald's novel has come to be recognized and will probably remain unchallenged as the supreme fictional embodiment of its age.[1]

Drawing from Kierkegaard's definition of irony as "a synthesis of ethical passion, which infinitely stresses within the mind, the personal integrity of the individual, and of culture, which as one of the finite forces operating upon the individual, infinitely abstracts externally from the personal ego,"[2] French focuses on Marston LaFrance's interpretation of Kierkegaard's statement. LaFrance takes this to mean "that the individual endowed with this 'ironic vision' has 'a perception or awareness of a double realm of values.'"[3] Though acknowledging that this kind of double vision "did not suddenly spring into being in the dying days of the pre-modernist, Victorian period," French argues that "what distinguishes the Modernist period from others is the special, exalted value that was placed then upon this particular ironic vision":[4] "What in an earlier period of 'faith' might have been a serious liability cutting the possessor off from 'societal bonds' to his detriment became during the first two-thirds of the twentieth century a characteristic so highly prized that those lacking it fell into critical disrepute."[5]

The last remark is of special interest to my purpose. Indeed, French's remark about faith as precluding such a modernist ironic attitude conversely suggests modernism to rest on a detachment based on lack of faith. When applied to *Gatsby*, this may sound a most apt suggestion in the light of the stark opposition in the novel between Gatsby's outdated romantic devotion and the Buchanans' wholly materialistic values. At one and the same time, then, what made the strength of the modernist turn of mind – its ability to see through value systems – also seems to be its essential weakness: an inability to believe, an impediment to full – which does not mean uncritical – selfless dedication.

Spiritual desolation is thus the price modernist awareness has to pay, as symbolized by Fitzgerald's wasteland and its short-sighted God. With Steinbeck's *Grapes of Wrath*, though, American fiction seems to start moving away from such a sense of waste and emptiness, founded, as is made clear in *Gatsby*, on the negation of man's spiritual aspirations, be they expressed in romantic terms. As underlined by French, "although [Steinbeck's] early novels [...] are almost models of the alienated Modernist sensibility [...], Steinbeck had abandoned it by 1938 before the publication of what remains his most monumental work": *The Grapes of Wrath*.[6] In French's view, with this turning-point novel, Steinbeck "was to transcend the ironic detachment of Modernism with a new affirmative conception of individual regeneration"[7] and even go as far as to herald postmodernism: "There is a widespread feeling [...] that whatever direction Post-Modernism takes, the growing emphasis will be [...] on consciousness-raising techniques and the implications for a bankrupt industrial culture of transcendentalist philosophies, especially of Eastern origin. Should this speculation indeed prove true, John Steinbeck may be seen on the strength of *The Grapes of Wrath* and *Cannery Row* as one of the significant prophets of Post-Modernism."[8]

French's analysis, written in 1976, will require qualifications in the light of a certain nihilistic doxa permeating subsequent critical approaches of postmodernist texts. Nevertheless, his point remarkably anticipates Frye's contention, fourteen years later, regarding the fundamental function of literature: "In our day the intensifying of consciousness, in the form of techniques of meditation and the like, has become heavy industry. I have been somewhat puzzled by the extent to which this activity overlooks or evades the fact that all intensified language sooner or later turns metaphorical, and that literature is not only the obvious but the inescapable guide to higher journeys of consciousness" (*WP*, 28). Such a higher journey of consciousness seems precisely what *The Grapes of Wrath* was meant to take us on.

I "New Christianity" in *The Grapes of Wrath*

From Anger to Wrath: The Resurrection of True Christian Spirit in The Grapes of Wrath

It is noteworthy that the more criticism moved away from an instinctive reaction to the ideological content of the novel as an indictment of capitalism, the more responsive it grew to its religious symbolism. As early as 1941, Frederic Carpenter concluded his essay "The Philosophical Joads" asserting that *The Grapes of Wrath* "develops a new kind of Christianity – not otherworldly and passive, but earthly and active."[9] Nearly fifty years later, Stephen Railton echoes Carpenter, insisting that John Joad's final "conversion from guilt to wrath is Steinbeck's way of insisting that his faith is a newer testament. To be saved, the nation needs to be converted, yet it will have to leave Christianity as well as capitalism behind. The novel's very last scene tries to build a bridge between the realm of the spirit, where individuals find their home, and the world of action, where men and women can help each other."[10] If both critics stress the call to action that Steinbeck's new Gospel puts forward, Railton also points out that the "solution to the economic and political problems that inspired [Steinbeck] to write the novel in the first place" is "essentially religious and mystical."[11] Inner change is the basis of social salvation:[12] "It is offstage, in solitude, alone with his own consciousness that each man somehow arrives at the new faith that Steinbeck is preaching to us, becomes the New Man who can redeem the waste land."[13] A direct response to Fitzgerald's modernist alienation, Steinbeck's "un-christian wisdom" means to "carry his readers beyond the New Testament to a new revelation."[14] The critic also emphasizes the stark contrast between the revolutionary effect of Casy's death and the traditional meekness often preached in churches. Still, his suggestion that this would be an instance of the "un-christian and anti-christian values" of the novel seems to overlook the whole point of the narrative strategy, which Railton nevertheless observes as operating for the characters: arousing the saintly wrath famously epitomized in Jesus' driving the merchants away from the temple. Indeed, His literal and symbolic command[15] not to "make my Father's house an house of merchandise"[16] could sum up the vindictive spirit animating Steinbeck's novel – a most genuine Christian spirit. Nonetheless, for this true Christian spirit to emerge collectively, much has to be gone through individually in order to achieve the "new, self-less sense of self" that the critic observes as the aim of the main characters' conversion in the novel. This conversion is one from anger to wrath, which separates Tom's groundless, drunken act of violence at the start of the novel from his final murder as a response to Casy's brutal death, for which Ma "can read no fault on [him]" (392). No simplistic endorsement of violence, the novel merely acts out Casy's discovery of man and God's essential bonding: "'I figgered about the Holy Sperit and the Jesus road. I figgered, "Why do we got to hang it on God or Jesus? Maybe," I figgered, "maybe it's all men an' all women we love; maybe that's the Holy Sperit – the human sperit – the whole shebang. Maybe all men got one big soul ever'body's a part of." Now I sat there thinkin' it, an' all of a suddent – I knew it. I knew it so deep down that it was true, and I still know it'" (27).

Indeed, if human and Holy spirits are one, God's wrath manifests through men, as suggested by the use of the biblical image usually attached to divine fury to characterize the migrants' rebellious spirit slowly developing:[17] "In the souls of the people the grapes of wrath are filling and growing heavy, growing heavy for the vintage" (349). For men, however, to become such true vehicles of divine wrath as to be found "without fault before the throne of God" (an image from Revelation, strangely echoing Ma's absolution of Tom), a deep inner conversion to the essential spirit of Christianity has to occur – a conversion to brotherhood as selfless sympathy, actively preached by the novel's moral guide: Casy.[18]

Casy's Unreligious Christianity

Casy's personal realization of the essential connection between man and God has been called Emersonian. It also, however, echoes Jesus' famous revelation regarding God's kingdom as being within:

> And when he was demanded of the Pharisees, when the kingdom of God should come, he answered them and said, the kingdom of God cometh not with observation:
>
> Neither shall they say, Lo here! Or, lo there! For, behold, the kingdom of God is within you.[19]

Just as Jesus' remark commands his listeners to turn inside if they will find God, Casy's sudden realization comes from personal experience rather than literal adherence to the Book. In fact, he had to go beyond the text of the Gospel to find out truth for himself: "It's like me. I wouldn't take the good ol' gospel that was just layin' thereto my hand. I got to be pickin' at it an' workin' at it until I got it all tore down" (24).

In a telltale image, trying to explain his new revealed faith to Tom, Casy "spread out his hand and looked at his palm as though he were reading a book" (25). In the new unwritten text of his hand, the gospel he reads out to Tom confronts the central Puritan equation between sin and sexual desire:

> He laid two fingers down in his palm in rhythm, as though he gently placed each word there side by side. "I says, 'Maybe it ain't a sin. Maybe it's just the way folks is. Maybe we been whippin' the hell out of ourselves for nothin'. [...] Before I knowed it, I was sayin' out loud, 'The hell with it! There ain't no sin and there ain't no virtue. There's just stuff people do. It's all part of the same thing. And some of the things folks do is nice, and some ain't nice, but that's as far as any man got a right to say.'" (26)

Casy's "unreligious" view (26), which produces this a-moral conclusion, paradoxically leads him back to Jesus' central teaching of love, at the same time as he disclaims all allegeance to Him: "I says, 'What's this call, this sperit?' An' I says, 'It's love. I love people so much I'm fit to bust, sometimes.' An' I says, 'Don't you love Jesus?' Well, I thought an' thought, an' finally I says, 'No, I don't know nobody name' Jesus. I know a bunch of stories, but I only love people.'" (26)

Shedding the burden of sin and theological doctrine makes Casy free to experience Christian love as an overwhelming feeling opening up the doors to the mystic revelation of the essential bond between the human and Holy spirits. In other words, Casy's new faith is less un-christian as "unreligious" for a preacher, as he himself acknowledges (26), a reconfiguration of Christian faith along lines dictated by personal, immediate rather than doctrinal revelation. Still, as Tom remarks, "You can't hold no church with idears like that" (27). What people want is to "feel swell": "'Jumpin' and yellin'. That's what folks like. Makes 'em feel swell. When Granma got to talkin' in tongues, you couldn' tie her down. She could knock over a full-growed deacon with her fist'" (27).

Trance rather than true transformation is what people have been used to and what Casy's new faith turns away from. In the paradoxical position of the preacher no longer able to preach the usual way, his often-noted position as the moral guide in the novel, whose gospel Tom will eventually convert to, still makes his unorthodox gospel of sympathy a religious model. As suggested by the ineffectual character of Tom's baptism – he admits it made no difference in his life and was just a moment when he "had fun" (27) – or the superstitious character of Rose of Sharon's angry lack of compassion for her brother after he kills Casy's murderer, both dramatic religious practices and superstitious fears of sin have to be dropped before the true spirit of Christianity may manifest.

Sympathy as Theme and Structure in The Grapes of Wrath

Far from being restricted to Casy, this Christian spirit of active sympathy is the novel's central *mythos* in the literary, ideological, and spiritual senses Frye gives to the word. Not only does it shape its plot,[20] it is the novel's political message – which Railton calls "Pilgrim's Politics" – and animates its structure. As Railton notes, "you and I, the novel's readers, are the converts whom [Steinbeck] is after."[21] However, "recount[ing] the story of the Joads' conversions" and "letting the Joads' lives and characters speak for themselves" may not render complete justice to Steinbeck's narrative art.[22] If it did, the novel would remain basically didactic and rhetorical, as Railton does suggest. Defining the kind of conversion Steinbeck is after, the critic asserts: "The novel owes its power to Steinbeck's urgent but painstaking intention to enact the revolution he apparently foresees. [...] Working a profound revolution in our sensibilities is his *rhetorical* task."[23] Still, I would argue, Steinbeck's unquestionably rhetorical strategy goes further than Fitzgerald's in that the novel's structural principle is not theatrical. Steinbeck's aim does not boil down to exposing the spectacle of the Joads' misery. As the strongly religious connotation of the word "conversion" suggests, beyond spectatorial empathy and probable catharsis – Fitzgerald's strategy – Steinbeck strives for communion, which Casy's Christlike retreat into "the wilderness" provides a model for: "'There was the hills, an' there was me, an' we wasn't separate no more. We was one thing. An' there was me an' the hills an' there was the stars an' the black sky, an' we was all one thing. An' that one thing was holy. […] An' I got thinkin', on'y it wasn't thinking, it was deeper down than thinkin'. I got thinkin' how we was holy when we was one thing, an' mankin' was holy when it was one thing'" (83).

To provoke this kind of "deeper down than thinking" meditative state that is transformative, "recount[ing] the story of the Joads' conversions" is crucial but not enough. To affect the reader's consciousness and really effect change, Steinbeck resorts to an obsessive structural principle: the constant alternation between a restrictive viewpoint focusing on the Joads and an inclusive perspective on the historical human situation their story is part of.

Often studied as evidenced in the alternation between the Joad chapters and the interchapters, this technique may also be observed within the chapters. As Chris Kocela astutely observes, though for purposes that might need to be qualified, the narrative strategy works to "dismantle the barriers erected around the interchapters as interpretive commentaries on the more obviously fictional chapters."[24] In order to make this important point, the critic analyses the "conflation of historicity and timelessness" in interchapters,[25] the use of biblical allusions within the Joad narrative as well as the links constructed between the two types of chapters through the recurrence of a number of elements such as the land turtle in chapters 3 and 4. One could also point out the ambivalent character of some chapters such as chapter 15, both interchapter and fictive passage, which starts in a typically generic way to evolve into the narrative of a specific episode. Indeed, the usual Whitmanesque catalogue characteristic of Steinbeck's interchapters as well as anonymous characterization used to convey a sense of the emblematic function of the people mentioned precedes a perfectly individualized passage, as Mae and Al's hamburger stand gradually emerges from the mass of those "along 66 […] Al and Susy's Place – Carl's Lunch – Joe & Minnie – Will's Eats. Board-and-bat shacks. Two gasoline pumps in front," tended to by "Minnie or Suzy or Mae, middle-aging behind the counter" and "the cook [...] Joe or Carl or Al […] moody, rarely speaking" (154–5). And just as the crowds of anonymous customers, divided into reverenced truck drivers or "shitheels" by Mae, become individualized, through truck driver "Big Bill the Rat" and one poor family of migrants, so the action stops being expressed in the generic present tense or through dialogues involving unidentified speakers. As Mae's words start being framed in a narrative using the preterite, conversation is outlined more clearly through the use of inverted commas and explicit references to each speaker, paving the way for Mae's unexpected gesture of charity as a response to the migrants' humble request for bread and sweets.

An illustration of the novel's global narrative strategy, the seamless transition between generic situation and specific episode within the same chapter calls for a few comments. First, this individualizing process goes hand in hand with the evolution of Mae's vision concerning the migrants, from bothersome strangers to people in need. This is conveyed through her changing attitude, from one of annoyed distrust to one of silent charity as she sells the coveted sweets to the migrants' children for virtually nothing. In other words, the individualizing technique is seen to accompany what Warren French would call the education of Mae's heart to sympathy. Second, an interesting consequence of such a strategy is the effect produced on the reader. It is particularly apparent when the chapter concludes with the arrival of a second series of truck drivers after Big Bill and his companion have left. In stark contrast with the feeling of alienation conveyed by the description of the anonymous stands along 66 at the start of the chapter, Mae and Al's initially empty daily routine has acquired the meaningfulness of a ritual through the individuating process permitted by the opening of both Mae's and the reader's heart. Eventually, the truck drivers' apparently most ordinary order for a slice of pie, echoing Big Bill's own before the migrants' entrance, takes on the feeling of a ritualized moment of communion. Here Mae's mild flirtation and piece of cake are given just as much in exchange for the drivers' generous tips as for the love their gruff manners bring in when they leave the highway "where life whizzed by" (162). Selfless love and sympathy are thus evidenced in those most ordinary circumstances, though involving actors who are no saints. This is made clear through Al's final trickery with the slot machine – when he was the one who insisted that Mae undercharge the bread – or Big Bill's rude rejoinder to Mae's call for change when she discovers how much he has left:

> "So long," said Bill.
> Mae called, "Hey! Wait a minute. You got change."
> "You go to hell," said Bill, and the screen door slammed. (162)

When related to the rest of the novel, chapter 15 appears to offer an interesting metaliterary comment on the book's narration when one considers the gradual lengthening of fictional, individualized chapters and the consequent increasing textual space they take in the novel. In fact, the narrative appears to zoom in on the Joads in proportion as their "education of the heart" progresses and the constant opening up of the reader's awareness to the overall situation ceases to be rendered necessary by the Joads' exclusive focus on their own family. In other words, as sympathy progresses for the Joads, the reader's growing intimacy with them stops precluding a sense of their relatedness to others because the Joads, too, open up. In fact, chapter 15 and its metaliterary reflection of the whole narrative strategy as engineered by sympathy takes place after the key interchapter charting "the beginning – from 'I' to 'we'" (152). Just as the process has started for the migrants, so the opening powered by sympathy progressively breaks the structural frame cutting the fictive, individual story from that of "others," depicted in the general situation.

As can be seen, sympathy as this developing awareness of the interrelatedness of the individual and the collective is both a thematic and structural process in *The Grapes of Wrath*. This leads me to differ a little from a certain critical consensus according to which the thematic progression within the novel would be from Old to New Testament.[26] In fact, this conception of the novel as moving away from an ethos based on the conception of a tribal God of wrath to a universal one of love has also been seen as contradictory with Tom's murderous reaction to Casy's death near the end. Looking, however, at both conceptions of God as composing the Janus-faced visage of the novel's reconfiguration of divinity would solve the contradiction. In fact, if the Joads "slowly advance from a morality based on narrow tribal interests to a universal one of love and sharing,"[27] the importance of the theme of divine anger indicated by its inclusion in the title suggests less an evolution away from a religious symbolism of wrath to one of love than a commingling of the two. This again brings to mind Christ's famous wrath in the temple. Motivated by "the zeal of [His Father's] house,"[28] Jesus' driving the merchants out, with a "scourge of small cords,"[29] immediately precedes his answer to the Jews' question as to the authority allowing him such an act:

> Then answered the Jews and said unto him, What sign shewest thou unto us, seeing that thou doest these things?
>
> Jesus answered and said unto them, Destroy this temple, and in three days I will raise it up. [...]
>
> But he spake of the temple of his body.[30]

The passage thus relates Jesus' chastizing power of destruction to his resurrection. Converting the outer temple into an inner one manifests

His "zeal" for His Father's house and while expressed through wrath, is actually motivated by love. In this light, the wrath permeating Steinbeck's novel could also appear as deeply motivated by a radical love of humanity making the destruction of the outer temple necessary for a regenerated spirit of sympathy to be born. In the novel, the outer temple that must be emptied and even destroyed, if need be, takes the shape both of outer possessions and,[31] I would argue, of those fighting to retain exclusive hold on those possessions – both the "great owners" and all their defenders, those whom "the quality of owning freezes forever into 'I', and cuts [...] off forever from the 'we'" (153). This might help shed more light on the compatibility and even interrelatedness of Tom's murderous act and developing sympathy. Besides, this spirit of sympathetic wrath animating the novel, which is the very spirit of life activated in the migrants' cohesive fight for survival, also manifests mankind's unique transcending and transformative life force, called "Manself": "The last clear definite function of man – muscles aching to work, minds aching to create beyond the single need – this is man. [...] For man, unlike any other thing organic or inorganic in the universe, grows beyond his work, walks up the stairs of his concepts, emerges ahead of his accomplishments. [...] And this you can know – fear the time when Manself will not suffer and die for a concept, for this one quality is man, distinctive in the universe" (151).

In short, the overarching *mythos* in the novel, with its destructive/regenerative function rooted in sympathy and love, seems to be resurrection, which Tom's famous visionary speech attests to: "'I'll be all aroun' in the dark. I'll be ever'where – wherever you look. Wherever they's a fight so hungry people can eat, I'll be there. [...] An' when our folks eat the stuff they raise an' live in the houses they build – why, I'll be there'" (419).

Announcing the persistence of his Christlike spiritual presence, Tom's prophetic speech reads as the culmination of a secular Passion story, which is paradoxically, insistently, non-teleological.

II From Morality to Holiness: Steinbeck's Secular Re-enchantment of the World[32]

Biblical Mythos vs Biblical Telos: A Revised Pilgrim's Progress

The growing critical attention devoted to the inversion in *The Grapes of Wrath* of the exodus pattern, originally noted by Peter Lisca,[33] points to what might be felt as a structural contradiction in the novel between its overt biblical mythos and its refusal of a teleological vision. As Lester Jay Marks observes, Steinbeck himself was emphatically opposed to teleological thinking, which ran counter to his ethos of sympathetic understanding: "In their sometimes intolerant refusal to face facts as they are, teleological notions may substitute a fierce but ineffectual attempt to change conditions which are assumed to be undesirable, in place of the understanding-acceptance which would pave the way for a more sensible attempt at any change which might still be indicated."[34]

In the novel, this refusal of teleology is a recurring feature, as expressed in the dialogue between Tom and Casy when they first meet:

> The preacher nodded his head slowly. […] "Here I got the sperit sometimes an' nothin' to preach about. I got the call to lead the people, an' no place to lead 'em."
>
> "Lead 'em around and around," said Joad. "Sling 'em in the irrigation ditch. Tell 'em they'll burn in hell if they don't think like you. What the hell you want to lead 'em someplace for? Jus' lead 'em." (24)

An ironical piece of advice for someone who is soon to act as his family's guide to California, Tom's rejoinder still supports Elizabeth Napier's assertion that "in addition to recasting the Book of Exodus and the Passion and Resurrection of Christ, [Steinbeck] also structures *The Grapes of Wrath* explicitly as a revised *Pilgrim's Progress*. The Celestial City is exposed as a sham, divine guidance is absent, and there is active discouragement of the type of exegesis that gives Bunyan's work its weight and meaning."[35] On his return in the bosom of his family, Tom will, in fact, actively discourage Ma's hopeful vision of California as the Eden their western pilgrimage is to take them to:

> "I like to think how nice it's gonna be, maybe, in California. Never cold. An' fruit ever'place, an' people just bein' in the nicest places, little white houses in among the orange trees."
>
> Tom watched her working, and his eyes smiled. "It done you good jus' thinkin' about it. I knowed a fella from California. He didn't talk like us. […] An' he says the folks that pick the fruit live in dirty ol' camps an' don't hardly get enough to eat." (93)

Following the novel's structural logic, Tom's answer comes as a direct illustration of the obsolete character of Bunyan's book obliquely alluded to in the preceding interchapter. This lists belongings migrants had to part with before moving west, one of the "doomed things" being: "This book. My father had it. He liked a book. *Pilgrim's Progress.* Used to read it" (90). In direct contrast with Bunyan's teleological work and implicitly future-oriented mindset, Tom advocates the day-to-day philosophy he developed while in jail: "'Look, Ma, stop you worryin'. I'm a-gonna tell you somepin about bein' in the pen. You can't go thinkin' when you're gonna be out. You'd go nuts. You got to think about that day, an' then the nex' day. [...] Whyn't you do that? Jus' take ever' day'" (93).

Not only does Tom question the edenic goal of his family's travel, which will be confirmed in the novel's second half, "an excoriating exposé of the Celestial City, with shining angels and the Heavenly King replaced by vigilante mobs and corrupt overseers,"[36] Casy deconstructs its starting point, the belief in man's sinful nature: "'The hell with it! There ain't no sin and there ain't no virtue. There's just stuff people do. And some of the things folks do is nice, and some ain't nice, but that's as far as any man got a right to say'" (26).

Clearly deprived of a moral/spiritual point of departure and arrival as well as guide – Casy insistently refusing the role of preacher/teacher,[37] the Joads' journey is pointedly divested of all teleological character. Yet, this is not to say that the narrative loses all sense of purposiveness.

Darwinian Messianism

Arguably one of the most famous passages in the novel, chapter 3 provides a telltale instance of the kind of purposiveness at work in the novel:

> The concrete highway was edged with a mat of tangled, broken, dry grass, and the grass heads were heavy with oat beards *to* catch on a dog's coat, and foxtails *to* tangle in a horse's fetlocks, and clover burrs *to* fasten in sheep's wool; sleeping life waiting to be spread and dispersed, every seed armed with an appliance of dispersal, twisting darts and parachutes for the wind, little spears and balls of tiny thorns, and all waiting for animals and for the wind, for a man's trouser cuff or the hem of a woman's skirt, all passive but armed with appliances of activity, still, but each possessed of the anlage of movement. (18; emphasis added)

Extensively discussed in terms of the allegorical value of the land turtle whose description then follows, the significance of chapter 3 has been seen to lie in its metaliterary value. This metaliterary value, however, does not boil down to the allegorical dramatization of the Joads' story through the land turtle's stubborn efforts to proceed on its way. It also rests in the description of a purposive natural environment. Combining a sequence of resultative clauses and the personification of natural life "waiting to be spread," the introductory paragraph conveys the vision of a nature inhabited by a sense of purpose notably devoid of a transcendent character. In this respect, one could also note the sudden appearance of "a thick-furred yellow shepherd dog [...] trotting down the road [...] toward some definite destination" (24) immediately after Tom's remark to Casy regarding the uselessness of religious leadership aiming at a final destination. Steinbeck, then, directly illustrates the replacement of the traditional biblical teleological world view conducive to pilgrimage with the "telic mode of consideration" that Robert J. Richards sees as "permeating Darwin's early construction of his theory and [...] shap[ing] the expression of that theory in the *Origins of Species*."[38]

In an attempt to oppose the usual interpretation of Darwin's theory as "replacing a mind-graced nature with a universal mechanism bereft of moral value [and] render[ing] the modern world disenchanted,"[39] Richards insists that "the belief that Darwin's theory banished final causes or the application of purposes appears [...] rather exaggerated [but for] one use of 'final cause' that Darwin does repudiate: when a purposive trait is ascribed to the direct action of the Deity instead of to the operations of natural law."[40] In this sense, Steinbeck's world in *The Grapes of Wrath* is definitely Darwinian, which does not preclude its morality, as the critic also points out: "By the end of the 1860s, [Darwin] seems to have abandoned altogether the idea that God was a necessary foundation for his theory. But what he seems never to have abandoned is the ascription to natural selection itself of those properties of discrimination, power, and moral concern previously conferred on it by divine agency. These properties allowed the law of natural selection to lead to the end Darwin foresaw as the goal of the evolutionary process, [...] namely, the natural creation of man as a moral creature."[41]

Carrying this process to its ultimate conclusion, Tom Joad is seen to evolve into a Christlike character.[42] Yet, this is less the result of a preordained redemptive mission than of natural law defined as "causal interactions [forming] a network of radiating forces [...] govern[ing] all inorganic and organic formations."[43] In this sense, *The Grapes of Wrath* would dramatize a kind of Darwinian messianism illustrating the full flowering of Darwin's view of "moral impulses, ultimately, as acquired during the course of animal development – not implanted in a soul by God."[44]

As early as 1949, Woodburn O. Ross noted Steinbeck's "new religious attitude" as that of "the first significant novelist to begin to build a mystical religion upon a naturalistic base."[45] Forty years later, Railton called Steinbeck "a Darwinian prophet."[46] Building upon these critics' view of the interrelatedness of Steinbeck's naturalistic and religious views, one could also turn to Steinbeck's own claim in *Sea of Cortez*: "Most of the feelings we call religious [...] [are] really the understanding and the attempt to say that man is related to the whole thing, related inextricably to all reality, knowed and unknowable. This is a simple thing to say, but the profound feeling of it made a Jesus, a St Augustine, a St Francis, a Roger Bacon, a Charles Darwin, and an Einstein."[47] The juxtaposition of scientists and mystics, especially Darwin and Jesus, in Steinbeck's examples of religious people serves to make my point that there is no contradiction between the mythos of resurrection animating *The Grapes of Wrath* and the novel's non-teleological character. Contrary to Marks, who claims not to believe that "Steinbeck's conclusions are any more 'mystical' than [...] those reached by Darwin, Einstein, or Emerson,"[48] I would thus concur with Ross in observing a mystic sensitivity in *The Grapes of Wrath*. This, however, would imply a new definition of mysticism involving no divorce between the world of matter and that of spirit – thus invalidating Marks's objection to seeing mysticism in Steinbeck's art[49] – and would come close to George Levine's concept of "secular re-enchantment" as an unrecognized effect of Darwinian theory.[50]

III Kerygmatic Realism

Postmodern Modernism or Modernist Realism?

This vision of Steinbeck's novel as both challenging traditional biblical cosmology and offering the alternative, very secular picture of a re-enchanted world strikingly intersects with current discussions of re-enchantment or the return of the religious in postmodern literature.[51] This, in turn, recalls French's description of Steinbeck as "one of the significant prophets of Post-Modernism." Gloria Gaither takes this view in her essay "John Steinbeck: The Postmodern Mind in the Modern Age," while Chris Kocela discusses "*The Grapes of Wrath* as transitional between modernism and something 'other' – postmodernism."[52] Discussing their arguments is thus a prerequisite to try and grasp what may account for the critical consensus according to which *The Grapes of Wrath* "runs counter to one of the main developments in twentieth-century American literature – modernist fiction."[53]

A definite common point between Gaither and Kocela is their discussion of Steinbeck's "resistance to the whole concept of boundaries,"[54] which Kocela specifically explores in terms of postmodernist "frame-breaking":[55] "In Steinbeck's hands the relationship between fiction and history-as-it-happens may also be seen to express the central *postmodern* problem of a vanishing ontological divide between history and fiction. The more contemporary history is posited as the 'horizon' of the fictional adventures of the Joads, the more it is mythologized as a reenactment of biblical/symbolic, timeless, and hence *ahistorical* forms. And this in turn threatens the distinction between history and fiction on which the structure of the novel is based."[56] If such a collapse of boundaries is not to be denied as central to the narrative strategy in *The Grapes of Wrath,* Kocela's conclusion regarding the "purely textual" character of both fictional and textual worlds bears scrutiny. In fact, Kocela successively notes that "the more [...] history is made to appear timeless and symbolic, the more purely textual it becomes, and the less secure are its ties to a reality beyond the fictional story of the Joads," which "alerts the reader to the textuality of both fictional and historical worlds – an idea central to several definitions of postmodernist fiction."[57] To be sure, Steinbeck's narrative does "crack" "the framework in which fiction is grounded by history, and history by mythical reference."[58] Still, the matter is less one of degree – whereby Steinbeck would only "crack" the framework, not "irretrievably *break*" it – than one of nature.[59] As the critic notes:

> The distinction between modernism and postmodernism has been explored as "a shift of 'dominant' governing modes of critical interrogation." Modernist fiction, according to McHale, is characterized by an epistemological dominant, in that it foregrounds questions of how knowledge about a stable world can be established. Postmodernist fiction, on the other hand, backgrounds epistemological concerns to propose an ontological line of inquiry, asking which of many possible realities one inhabits at a given time.[60]

The postmodernist "ontological mode of questioning" rests, however, on a destabilizing sense of disorientation regarding such categories as reality and truth.[61] This, I would argue, is not what Steinbeck's fiction is ultimately trying to achieve. That narration in *The Grapes of Wrath* should *produce* destabilization is unquestionable and makes perfect sense in the light of Steinbeck's "restless search for a form to fit a new emerging consciousness":[62] "This postmodern mind in a Modern age experienced the despair that 'we're all, or most of us, the wards of the nineteenth-century sciences which denied existence of anything it could not reason or explain ... and [that] meanwhile a great part of the world was abandoned to children, insane people, fools and mystics, who were more interested in what is than in why it is.'"[63] Still, it does not follow that both fictional and historical worlds become purely textual. Rather, to take up Frye's expression, they seek to enter into a different kind of identity with the reader,[64] which would open up his awareness to the fluidity of borders,[65] rather than dematerialize (or "textualize") reality. Actually, the text's sound naturalistic basis would even seem to run counter to postmodernist interpretations of *The Grapes of Wrath* as "purely textual": concrete reality, whether animate or inanimate,[66] features too centrally ever for the reader to be lured into forgetting its actuality. In that sense, Steinbeck's novel sounds as a perfect expression of the "detraditionalized, post-religious imagination" Andrew Tate sees as characteristic of contemporary fiction,[67] and yet paradoxically allows for the resurfacing of a traditional narrative characteristic of scriptures. As Mark Knight and Thomas Woodman argue: "The biblical sacred is not so much the miraculous in the sense of extraordinary wonders as the natural seen in its ultimate depth. From this perspective realism may even prove the preferred option for the expression of biblical categories of the sacred in fiction, provided it is a realism conceived in sufficient depth and openness."[68] *The Grapes of Wrath*, I would argue, precisely offers this type of realism.

In their respective but congruent analyses of the novel, Barry Maine and Jean-François Côté both bring to light what Côté designates as the novel's "modernist realism":[69] "*The Grapes of Wrath*, [...] although it borrows from the tradition of modernism, especially in the interchapters, does not belong to it. It is not about language at all. *The Grapes of Wrath* is written in the realist tradition, and the language through which the Joad family is related to us is intended to be objective and transparent rather than expressionistic."[70] While the focus of Maine's essay is on Steinbeck's literary debt to Dos Passos, the critic comes to much the same conclusions as Côté in his study of the articulation between modernism and realism (also taking Dos Passos as reference) in *The Grapes of Wrath*: "Steinbeck borrowed conceptually from *U.S.A.* in planning the structure of his novel, borrowed technical procedures from *U.S.A.* in developing the interchapters, and benefitted from whatever stock of American speech Dos Passos had floated into literary currency. That is the full extent of the debt."[71] In other words, in contrast to *U.S.A.*, *The Grapes of Wrath* is no language experiment in the tradition of high modernism.[72] Contrasting Steinbeck's handling of his characters with Dos Passos's "mathematical formula [...] for defeat and futility [...], a blueprint for an ugly, nightmarish vision of American life and culture,"[73] Maine argues that *The Grapes of Wrath*'s "broader appeal" lies in the fact that we "believe in [Steinbeck's characters], because we can sense their presence beyond the text":[74] "In *U.S.A.*, [...] Man is defined strictly in terms of his material culture, which determines his features and values and character. By contrast, there is something in the Joads that does transcend history and the circumstances of time and place in *The Grapes of Wrath*, which may account for its broader appeal. Its message is more comforting and a more inspiring one."[75] That perception of "something" in the Joads transcending history and giving them life outside the novel is echoed in Côté's contention that the modernist dimension of Steinbeck's realism, particularly visible in his interchapters, consists in the text's opening up various levels of signification "just beneath the surface of realistic description."[76] Precluding an exclusively straightforward, realistic interpretation, those levels of signification convey a biblical symbolism that paradoxically "appears as a 'realistic pact,' by which we mean 're-actualized,' thanks to its modernist embedding."[77] This modernist "re-actualization" of biblical symbolism is what I now mean to explore.

Steinbeck's Multilayered Narrative: Polysemous Realism

Steinbeck's assertion, in a letter to his editor Pascal Covici, that there are five layers in *The Grapes of Wrath* is well known: "A reader will find as many as he can," and "what he takes from it will be scaled entirely on his own depth or hollowness."[78]

Obviously suggesting the traditional four levels of the *lectio divina*, the doctrine holding that sacred texts should be read on four different levels, Steinbeck's statement still offers a hermeneutic riddle with its description of five layers of meaning. The relatively few critics who have addressed this enigma turn to Dante's exposition of the "'levels of meaning' in literature, which comes from St Thomas Aquinas but is most usefully presented by Dante, who drew from Aquinas in *Convivio*."[79] In this theory, the four levels are called literal, allegorical, moral, and anagogical, which respectively, French proceeds to decipher in *The Grapes of Wrath* as "the history of the Joads' migration," "the illustration of an education of the heart," "the outrage [expressed] that such conditions exist and pleading for readers to play their part in alleviating and eliminating them," and, "on the anagogical level Tom Joad['s] sense of 'eternal glory' when he speaks lyrically of being 'all aroun' in the dark.'"[80]

In her illuminating discussion of the fourth level of meaning in *The Grapes of Wrath*, Clara Mallier convincingly demonstrates that the anagogical level of meaning in the novel is Emersonian.[81] Quoting Tom's speech, itself repeating Casy's teaching regarding the interrelatedness of men's souls with one another and the universe,[82] Mallier stresses the mystical character of this interrelatedness, which in turn supports the novel's moral (and political) message of solidarity. Contrary, however, to the moral character of solidarity, which rests on will, the mystical sense of relatedness evidenced in the novel "belongs to the spiritual arena for it is not related to will but is experienced as self-evident, which Ma again expresses":[83]

> "When you're young, Rosasharn, ever'thing that happens is a thing all by itself. It's a lonely thing. I know, I 'member, Rosasharn." Her mouth loved the name of her daughter. "You're gonna have a baby, Rosasharn, and that's somepin to you lonely and away. That's gonna hurt you, an' the hurt'll be lonely hurt, an' this here tent is alone in the worl', Rosasharn. [...] They's a time of change, an' when that comes, dyin' is a piece of all dyin', and bearin' is a piece of all bearin', an' bearin' and dyin' is two pieces of the same thing. An' then things ain't lonely any more. An' then a hurt don't hurt so bad, 'cause it ain't a lonely hurt no more, Rosasharn. I wisht I could tell you so you'd know, but I can't." And her voice was so soft, so full of love, that tears crowded into Rose of Sharon's eyes, and flowed over her eyes and blinded her. (209)

Mallier then emphasizes the fact that Emerson's "oversoul," which corresponds to the spiritual level of meaning in the novel, "may not be apprehended through intellect alone," so that the anagogical level of meaning in *The Grapes of Wrath* does not boil down to speeches expounding Emerson's philosophy but is rather "conveyed to the reader through devices closer to representation than abstract ideas. Though not 'ciphered' through enigmas as in sacred texts, the spiritual meaning of *The Grapes of Wrath* is encoded in the book's style."[84] Proceeding to list and closely analyse a number of these encoding techniques (such as Steinbeck's biblical style, the use of plurals and metonymic characterization to convey the sense of "organic unity" between people, or the numerous links constructed between cosmic and human time), Mallier concludes that "an important difference still separates the anagogical dimension of sacred texts from that of Steinbeck's novel, for the former is esoteric": "According to the *lectio divina*, the spiritual meaning of sacred texts is ciphered, encoded through symbols that only the exegete can decipher. Now, the spiritual meaning of *The Grapes of Wrath*, on the contrary, is exoteric: Casy gives the keys to it through his words, which make up a pedagogical palimpsest of Emerson's writings."[85]

Concluding that such an exoteric strategy is in keeping with the novel's political egalitarian ideal, which means to give equal access to its hermeneutic wealth, Mallier leaves still unsolved the issue of Steinbeck's fifth layer of meaning, tentatively addressed by French through a series of questions: "Steinbeck speaks of a fifth layer. May individuality be transcended altogether through the 'one big soul' Casy speaks about? [...] Is Steinbeck suggesting a layer of experience at which individual distinctions are obliterated in something like Emerson's 'oversoul'?"[86]

Returning to Northrop Frye's theory of verbal modes may help provide an answer. Comparing his own sequence of modes to the medieval theory of polysemous meaning, Frye states:

> In the medieval theory of polysemous meaning, or at least in Dante's exposition of it, there is nothing that directly corresponds to our conceptual mode, but there are two levels of what I am calling the rhetorical one. The first is "allegorical" (better called analogical or typological); answering the question *quid credas*, what you should believe; the other moral or tropological, answering the question *quid agas*, what you should do. We can call these the theory and practice respectively of Christian ideology. (*WP*, 16)

If Frye's descriptive mode corresponds to the literal level of medieval theory, this statement appears to settle the matter of the equivalence between his first three verbal modes (descriptive, conceptual, and rhetorical) and those of medieval theory. The next step, though a tricky one, would be to try and assess the relationship between the medieval fourth – anagogical – level of meaning and Frye's fourth and fifth modes: respectively, the "literary" and "kerygmatic" modes.

This is where we come to the whole point of Frye's theoretical analysis of the Bible and literature, which, as he pointed out, is not to consider the Bible as literature. Rather, in his sequence of verbal modes, the critic aims at coming to grips with "a mode of language on the *other side* of the poetic" that would "describe a verbal aspect of the Bible that has affinities with the two figured languages of rhetoric and poetry, and yet is not quite either" (*WP*, 100–1). As Frye explains, however, while this focus on the Bible was a preliminary step developed in *The Great Code*, his interest in linking the Bible to Western literature has always been "the common language in which they were written" (*WP*, xiv). Accordingly, *Words with Power* pays more explicit attention to "[literature's] communicating power across the centuries through all ideological changes" (*WP*, xiii).

As Frye repeatedly asserts, in the face of religious fundamentalism as well as deep-rooted prejudice regarding the fictive character of literature as opposed to religion's quest for truth, "the Bible is, with unimportant exceptions, written in the literary language of myth and metaphor; it is, in short, a work of literature plus" (*WP*, xiv–xv): "The present book attempts to explain once more what that 'plus' is, why the beginning of the response to the Bible must be a literary response, and why, within the Bible itself, all the values connected with the term 'truth' can be reached only by passing through myth and metaphor" (*WP*, xv).

Frye's examination of the literary and kerygmatic modes thus appears as a comparative effort to differentiate between literary language and the language of revelation on the basis of their common use of myth and metaphor. Both of these, Frye argues, tend to produce in the reader/hearer's mind an identification process pointing in the direction of what the critic seeks to establish: "an order of words that is neither subjective nor objective, though it interpenetrates with both" (*WP*, xxiii). Indeed, while Frye formerly demonstrated that the goal of myth as a literary structure was to produce the sense of "discovery" or "recognition" expressed in the word *anagnorisis*,[87] metaphor, for all the ornamental – purely literary – uses often made of it, remains for Frye "a primitive form of awareness, established long before the distinction of subject and object became normal" (*WP*, xxiii). The question then arises about the distinction between two verbal modes resorting to both myth and metaphor as conducive to the identification process Frye is interested in.

This is where Frye brings in the notion of "reality" to contrast the arbitrary kind of identification created by the literary mode with the kind of intrinsic, "real" identity operating in the kerygmatic mode in the moment of revelation: "In poetry anything can be juxtaposed, or implicitly identified with, anything else. Kerygma takes this a step further and says: 'You are what you identify with.' We are close to the kerygmatic whenever we meet the statement, as we do surprisingly often in contemporary writing, that it seems to be language that uses man rather than man that uses language" (*WP*, 116). In that sense, Frye maintains, the literal meaning of the Bible or of any text eliciting this kind of response is not the usual literal meaning understood to produce a verbal imitation of external reality but rather the mythical and metaphorical meaning causing this experience of an inner identity: "The initiative excluded [...] from the imaginative and the poetic, the principle that opens the way into the kerygmatic, is the principle of the reality of what is created in the production and response to literature" (*WP*, 129). Such a type of response is not reserved to religious texts, even if the revelatory power associated with the Bible and particularly Jesus' Word is the model for it. Frye actually refers to the Pauline concept of *soma pneumatikon* to describe the encompassing aspect of human awareness that such an identity process affects: "Paul distinguishes the *soma psychikon*, which is mortal, from the *soma pneumatikon*, the spiritual body (I Corinthians 15:44). This is also a body (Paul means that it *is* a body, not that it *has* one). We possess it in this life also, and it is the element in us that enables us to understand the scripture and other aspects of revelation (2:14)" (*WP*, 124). This "spiritual body," which "seems to have some genuine independence of the single permanently anchored identity to which the *soma psychikon* is confined" and that is "the spiritual body of the risen Christ that is everywhere and in everyone, and [...] may be a part of us or we may be a part of it" (*WP*, 125–6) clearly recalls Tom's final visionary speech in *The Grapes of Wrath*. This, in turn, alerts us to one level of signification in the novel that may not be reduced to an exoteric encoding of Emersonian philosophy but rather, ultimately, seeks to address the reader's soma pneumatikon as the locus of a subtle, transformative exchange:

> The *soma pneumatikon*, then, suggests a certain fluidity of personality, in which such metaphors as the "one flesh" erotic metaphor, or metaphors of being influenced by another personality or the work of a creative artist, begin to take on more reality.
>
> In *The Great Code* I used the word interpenetration to describe this fluidity of personality in its complete form. (*WP*, 126)

Such an inner transformation, I would argue, is the ultimate aim of Steinbeck's poetics of sympathy in the novel. One may wonder, however, where to locate the manifestation of such mystical aesthetics that are both conveyed through words and transcend them. Jean-François Côté's suggestion of a re-actualization of biblical symbolism then comes to mind, for it perfectly corresponds to Frye's analysis of the spiritual function and power of the symbol:

> Originally, a symbol was a token or counter, like the stub of a theater ticket which is not the performance, but will take us to where the performance is. It still retains the sense of something that may be of limited interest or value in itself, but points in the direction of something that can be approached directly only with its help. A symbol may be purely arbitrary ("extrinsic," as Carlyle calls it), but as a rule it has or develops some analogous or other connection with what it points to, so that it can expand in that direction, taking us with it. Practically all techniques of meditation, for example, work with symbols, verbal or pictorial, that expand toward an identity, however defined, with what they symbolize. (*WP*, 109)

Looking at Steinbeck's manipulation of biblical symbolism does reveal such an expansion in the direction of what "can be approached directly only with its help," when one bears in mind that the writer's fundamental aim is to awaken Christian sympathy in the reader's heart. Love, Frye notes, when it ceases to be taken in its sentimental sense, "seems impossible to dissociate [from] the conceptions of spiritual personality" (*WP*, 126): "The capacity to merge with another person's being without violating it seems to be at the center of love [...]. John Donne uses a beautiful figure in this connection based on the metaphor of an individual life as a book. The spiritual world, he says, is a library 'where all books lie open to one another'" (*WP*, 126).

This spiritual merging may not happen all at once, however, and like all initiations, occurs in steps in the novel. Reflected in the main characters' own progressive expansion outside the confining limits of their individualistic needs and wishes, the readers' initiation opens them up to a greater awareness of the actual bond existing between themselves and others. This is achieved through a number of narrative devices, the most visible of which being the modernist shape of the novel, alternating a realistic and empathetic focus on the Joads' individual plight and a depiction of the collective situation in the interchapters. The aim of the narrative *telos*, then, is to have the reader pass from a sequential reading of the link between the individual and the collective to a metonymic (Emersonian) and ultimately metaphoric (Christian) spiritual experience of their interrelatedness. Now, biblical symbolism is the key to such a reading experience, notably as it conflates a superficially realistic characterization with an awareness of the characters' spiritual potential, which is then gradually made actual. This is particularly striking in the case of Rose of Sharon, who is described from the start with all the attributes of saintly maternity: "Rose of Sharon was pregnant and careful. Her hair, braided and wrapped around her head, made *an ash-blond crown*. Her round soft face, which had been voluptuous and inviting a few months ago, had already put on the barrier of pregnancy, the *self-sufficient smile, the knowing-perfection look*" (97; emphasis added). For this potential of saintly maternity to become actualized will take the whole novel and the young girl's actual losing of her baby, coupled with her husband's desertion, will be the necessary trials in her pilgrimage from potential to actualization. In this light, the final scene in the barn reads as Rose of Sharon's apotheosis, conflating realism and symbolism in the factual description of her suckling the dying man, while her concluding mysterious smile completes her spiritual identity as saintly mother. In Ditsky's words: "The need for intellectualization has been obviated by direct experience. Rose of Sharon's action communicates an immediate redemption of a 'chosen people.'"[88]

Beyond the anagogical level of meaning, there seems to exist a fifth layer of signification, essentially operating through style, structure, and symbolism to create an inner conversion in the reader to the actual experience of Charity. Though Steinbeck's aim is primarily political, I would not conclude with Clara Mallier that spiritual meaning in Steinbeck's novel remains simply exoteric. Indeed, even if the narrative provides clues as to its spiritual import in the shape of the characters' own conversions, it still operates on "the mysterious borderland between the poetic and the kerygmatic" (*WP*, 111), drawing us towards an "intermediate verbal world, where a Word not our own, though also our own, proclaims and a Spirit not our own, though also our own, responds" (*WP*, 118). In that sense, the arguably artistic character of the final tableau in the barn, which, Ditsky notes, "is a Louvre of mixed subjects: a Nativity, a *Mona Lisa*, an immense and heroic Delacroix,"[89] produces less aesthetic distance than a mood of contemplation referring the reader back to his or her own inner world.[90] The meditative state thus portrayed and achieved is no ecstatic rapture towards immortal realms but such an immanent, bodily experience as to have initially shocked some readers. Its conjunction of the traditionally opposed realms of spirit and flesh, in a still explicitly Christian frame,[91] curiously gestures towards what critics currently analyse as the postmodern form of contemporary theology, which moves away from modern atheologies or death of God theologies to a re-enchantment of the world premised on a re-examination of Christian tradition: "This would appear to be the direction postmodern theology is moving in – away from the atheologies of Mark C. Taylor and Don Cupitt, away from the 'death of God' theologies of Thomas Altizer and Charles Winquist, and towards a reappraisal and re-examination of the tradition (Augustine, Gregory of Nyssa, Pseudo-Dionysus, Meister Eckhart and Karl Barth, for example) in the light of critical theory."[92]

One then comes circling back to French's suggestion that Steinbeck may be "one of the significant prophets of Post-Modernism." So he appears to be, provided critical focus should not remain restricted to the writer's undeniable deconstruction of traditional Christian theology but open up to the deeper level of spiritual re-connection such a deconstruction strives to produce. Jesus' anger urged that the external stone temple be replaced by the temple of the body: *The Grapes of Wrath*, I would argue, does just that.

5 "In the Name of the Lost Father": Postsecular Mysticism in *On the Road*

In his comparative study of *The Grapes of Wrath* and *On the Road*, Jason Spangler stresses the similarity of the narrative strategies, arguing that both novels rely on modernist aesthetics while at the same time being animated by an antimodern critique: "Kerouac and Steinbeck champion their characters who challenge authority and the status quo just as they themselves accept that a main function of literary modernism is to challenge, through experiment, authoritative ways of writing. In this way, both authors engage in the aesthetics of modernism while simultaneously working against the cultural authority of modern progress."[1]

On the other hand, such a critique, Spangler argues, leads them both towards "attempts to recover some of the spirituality jettisoned by modernist aesthetics, [which] can be considered a neo-Romantic gesture."[2] Some category other than "modernism" thus seems called for to describe the novelists' achievements. This category is suggested by the convergence between Spangler's remark that "*The Grapes of Wrath* and *On the Road* attack the cold logic of modernity by creating characters who refuse to accept the particular world view promulgated by the forces of control and who instead seek to recuperate a sense of enchantment or spirituality in the midst of an ideological lockdown"[3] and John McClure's analysis of postsecular culture and fiction: "Before turning to the fiction itself, I want to sketch out a map of the broader postsecular movements with which it is engaged. These movements [...] all reflect a strong but selective disenchantment with secular values and modes of being and a determination to invent alternatives. The novelists whose work I explore share this disenchantment and determination."[4]

When one examines this "sense of enchantment or spirituality" that both Steinbeck and Kerouac would be trying to retrieve in the light of the categories of myth, metaphor, and verbal mode as envisioned by Frye, Kerouac's *On the Road* does appear curiously consonant with Steinbeck's *Grapes of Wrath*, though in an ironical and probably unconsciously parodic way. Indeed, Steinbeck's underlying *mythos* of Resurrection appears superseded by that of Crucifixion.

I A(nta)gonistic Redemption: Kerouac's Paradoxical Psalm of Plaint

"My God, Why Hast Thou Forsaken Me?" Crucifixion as Secular Experience in On the Road

In his extensive study of the spiritual import of Kerouac's life and fiction, Ben Giamo stresses that "throughout his life, [Kerouac was] preoccupied with the crucifixion of Christ," particularly in his later years: "'As Jack grew older,' Ginsberg observed, 'in despair and lacking the means to calm his mind and let go of the suffering, he tended more and more to grasp at the Cross. And so, in his later years, he made many paintings of the Cross, [...] of Christ crucified [...]; seeing himself on the Cross, and finally conceiving of himself as being crucified. He was undergoing crucifixion in the mortification of his body as he drank.'"[5]

I would contend that this obsession with the Cross is already reflected in *On the Road* in the combination of the figure of the absent father and "the oscillation between ecstasy and suffering [that] appears to be the maxim of the novel."[6] This fundamental "movement between opposite emotive forces,"[7] interestingly, parallels the plaint-and-praise contrast often analysed as a structuring device in Psalm 22,[8] which starts with Jesus' famous cry of despair and develops into prophetic praise. The similarity established, however, at once signals the distance between the two texts, as the elegiac mood of Kerouac's final one-sentence paragraph hardly qualifies as prophetic praise. In fact, the promised conversion of nations to the reaffirmed kingdom of the redeeming Lord that concludes the psalm appears negated by the interrogative and iconoclastic image of God as "Pooh Bear?" while the sentence ends with the image of Dean Moriarty, whose "father we never found" (281). In other words, Kerouac's story appears wedged between the death of Sal's father, which was the original beginning Kerouac had envisioned for the novel,[9] and the failed quest for Dean Moriarty's. Between Sal's consequent "feeling that everything was dead" (3) at the beginning and his final nostalgic memory of fatherless Dean, the text appears to circle back to a fundamental experience of suffering orphanhood. In that sense, the biblical mythos animating *On the Road* reads like a secular version of Jesus' cry of despair, which remains unanswered. As Ben Giamo notes, *On the Road* was written before Kerouac's Buddhist phase of the mid-1950s and was explicitly referred to by its author as "Pre-enlightenment work" (185). This accounts for the absence of the figure of transcendence in the novel, but takes nothing away from the spiritual nature of the erratic trips making up the plot. However, "the spiritual quest [remains embedded] in the phenomenal world of sensation and, at times, in sensory indulgence."[10] Rather than opening out onto a transcendent experience of Redemption through suffering, the text thus remains mired in a feeling of alienation from the father figure. Besides, the only way out of the ecstasy/despair pattern is achieved in the final fundamentally unsatisfactory sense of equilibrium derived from Sal's decision to give up his questing life on the road with Dean. To this extent, the sense of balance achieved is at best a dubious one. Turning away from Dean, Sal also withdraws from the redemptive promise of his "life on the road," which had originally been his response to his feeling that everything was dead. In a way, to achieve inner balance, Sal settles for a kind of deathlike life, as confirmed by his final statement regarding the unenlightened knowledge derived from his trips: "nobody, nobody knows what's going to happen to anybody besides the forlorn rags of growing old" (281).

In this sense, if *On the Road* and *The Grapes of Wrath* arguably both "seek to recuperate a sense of enchantment or spirituality,"[11] they go about it in diametrically opposed ways. For Steinbeck, the very secular, sociopolitical nature of his oppressed characters' anger and suffering eventually turns into an individual and symbolic experience of redemption akin to the conversion process taking place in the psalm. In Kerouac's novel, on the contrary, the characters would seem to follow a reverse route, whereby their essentially spiritual malaise fails to develop into an experience of redemption because it remains trapped in the quagmire of unrestrained sensual indulgence. Failing to provide an avenue towards transcendence, Dean's "wild yea-saying overburst of American joy" (9) turns into madness and the ecstatic/exhausted pattern structuring the plot increasingly seems symptomatic of his and Sal's manic-depressive disorder allayed by regular drinking bouts (also alternately causing exaltation and depression once the effects of alcohol wear down).[12]

So, on the one hand, it is true that Sal and Dean's "altered morality" might be seen as descending from what D.H. Lawrence considered to be Whitman's achievement: the "smash[ing] of the old moral conception, that the soul of man is something 'superior' and 'above' the flesh,"[13] a view that is given sublime expression in Steinbeck's flesh-and-blood portrait of Charity at the end of *The Grapes of Wrath*. Though definitely striking a final blow at Puritan morality, the deliberate marginality expressed in *On the Road* is also heir to another, more radical strand in American fiction: spiritual rebellion.

Beat Life as Spiritual Warfare and Mystic Experimentation

This is where one may locate the major difference between Steinbeck and Kerouac. Whereas the former's moral anger regarding the historical situation of the "Okies" subordinates the spiritual power of his novel's symbolism to political denunciation, Kerouac's apparently hedonistic rebellion against the 1950s complacent mores is at heart of a spiritual nature. In this respect, the literary line of descent would rather seem to relate him both to Melville's romantic hubris and Fitzgerald's modernist despair.

Regarding Kerouac's spiritual kinship with Melville, Mario D'Avanzo's intertextual reading of *Bartleby* and Thomas Carlyle's *Sartor Resartus* provides a most interesting point of entry. Reading Melville's novella as an ironic rewriting of Carlyle's redemptive philosophy, D'Avanzo enables us to see Melville's story as a direct literary forerunner of Kerouac's. According to the critic, Bartleby is a rebellious son of man ready to confront the necessitarian and utilitarian doxa of his age, even at the cost of his own life:

> Bartleby's "storming" of the citadel that is Wall Street takes its source and meaning in Carlyle's account of the embattled soul asserting itself. [...]
>
> Beneath the surface of "Bartleby" (a surface of astonishing camouflage for Melville's underlying meaning), there is grimmest battle, though Melville's hero ironically carries it on so mildly and apparently passively; it ends in defeat for Bartleby, but in his dissent he remains heroic, a kind of Ahab without tragic vitality or aggressive authority. [...] The paradox of Bartleby's character is this: he cannot change or subdue the Citadel (Wall Street) – as Carlyle asserts he can – but he can reject it and in this choice of action lies his freedom. Bartleby practices what Teufelsdröckh preaches: the man of spirit must confront, rebel and resist Tophet – i.e., all that Wall Street represents – even though it destroys him.

> Bartleby has his mandate in Teufelsdröckh. Tophet, Wall Street, the Citadel, the lawyer (they are all the same) must be confronted by the son of Man.[14]

Likewise, Sal's restlessness and constant association with marginals is a clear indictment of the smug materialism and bourgeois lifestyle of his time. Besides, if Bartleby's stance to his work is one of passive resistance for spiritual sake, Sal's reluctance to hold a job also stems from a profound sense of its utter meaninglessness: "I [...] worked awhile in the wholesale fruit market where I almost got hired in 1947 – the hardest job of my life. [...] I lugged watermelon crates over the ice floor of reefers into the blazing sun, sneezing. In God's name and under the stars, what for?" (163). In fact, the very few times he does get hired, Sal proves totally unequal to his task, both as a cop in San Francisco with Remi Boncoeur and later as a grape picker with his Mexican girlfriend, Terry, and her little boy. In the latter instance, he even uncharacteristically resorts to prayer when faced with his own incapacity: "What kind of old man was I that couldn't support his own ass, let alone theirs? [...] I looked up at the dark sky and prayed to God for a better break in life and a better chance to do something for the little people I loved. Nobody was paying any attention to me up there. I should have known better" (87–8). Sal's simultaneous rejection of God and work perfectly illustrates his spiritual kinship with Bartleby. As D'Avanzo suggests: "Duty has no meaning for Bartleby as it had for Carlyle, who claims that it is a 'divine Messenger and Guide' [...]. And duty involves not only work, but faith in God."[15] In this sense, the critic's analysis of Bartleby's malaise as "an ironic inversion of the spiritual development of Professor Diogenes Teufelsdröckh, and the Carlylean hero as a man of letters,"[16] would seem to apply to Sal. Like his romantic predecessor, Sal's attitude suggests that, contrary to Carlyle's admonition to follow the "God-given mandate 'Work thou in Welldoing' [...] mysteriously written in our hearts," "negating work and refusing good works is at least to be free."[17] Besides, the refusal of the outward respectability granted by work and expressed through clothes is another theme linking Sal's spiritual rebellion to Bartleby's. As D'Avanzo remarks:

> Melville does battle not only against necessitarian theology and the "divine injunction" of charity, but also against the vested authority and well-buttoned respectability of the lawyer. The lawyer-narrator, as we have

> seen, would base all distinctions and judgments on external appearances, never getting beneath the surface of Bartleby's actions to understand his soul. Melville carries these themes by using Carlyle's organizing metaphor of clothes. [...]
>
> Conventional morality, polity and class distinctions, in fact all "earthly interest" – that which Bartleby is rebelling against – are all linked with the philosophy of clothes.[18]

In this respect, it is significant that, having to initially borrow his friend Remi's much too big trousers to make his round, Sal ends up "flapping around like Charlie Chaplin to [his] first night of work" (57). The suit of law and order just does not fit. Given a choice, Sal much prefers Dean's "dirty clothes [that] clung to him so gracefully, as though you couldn't buy a better fit from a custom tailor but only earn it from the Natural Tailor of Natural Joy, as Dean had, in his stresses" (9).

This is where Sal's rebellion against his society's contented materialism parts from Bartleby's refusal of the utilitarianism of his time. For if Kerouac's novel does conclude on the melancholy admission of death's inescapability, Sal's frantic trips do not seem to imply the nihilism of Bartleby's "spiritual paralysis": "As an ironic spiritual wanderer, Bartleby ends his quest not in affirmation, as Teufelsdröckh does, but in willed death, the ultimate negation. Bartleby's fate can be considered as Melville's answer to the Carlylean view of spiritual redemption. [...] Bartleby's prison house of the soul, taking its source in *Sartor Resartus*, provides the access not to a transcendental world but to death and, apparently, nothingness."[19] Conversely, the death wish that Sal occasionally recognizes as also animating his quest expresses a paradoxical urge to experience a primeval, mystic kind of bliss: "The one thing that we yearn for in our living days, that makes us sigh and groan and undergo sweet nauseas of all kinds, is the remembrance of some lost bliss that was probably experienced in the womb and can only be reproduced (though we hate to admit it) in death. [...] I told it to Dean and he instantly recognized it as the mere simple longing for pure death; and because we're all of us never in life again, he, rightly, would have nothing to do with it, and I agreed with him then" (112).

In a way complementary to Sal's, Dean's destructive lifestyle is also a life-affirming gesture and his characteristic "wild yea-saying overburst of American joy" (9) echoes Teufelsdröckh's "Everlasting Yea," the final stage in the Carlylean hero's spiritual growth:

> Teufelsdröckh's progress of the soul moves from negation ("The Everlasting No") to apathy ("The Centre of Indifference"). By a leap of faith he arrives at affirmation in God ("The Everlasting Yea")."Integration, harmony, and order are shaped out of the chaos around him. Man fulfils himself spiritually in work, or as Carlyle states:
>
> "Our works are the mirror wherein the spirit first sees its natural lineaments. ... Know what thou canst work at. ... Doubt of any sort cannot be removed except by Action. ... Whoso walks and works, it is well with him. ... Yes here in this poor, miserable, hampered despicable Actual, wherein thou even now standest, here or nowhere is thy Ideal: work it out therefrom; and working, believe, live, be free. Fool! the Ideal is in thyself, the impediment too is in thyself. ... Produce! Produce! were it but the pitifulest infinitesimal fraction of a product, produce it, in God's name!"[20]

D'Avanzo's analysis provides an interesting viewpoint on the way Dean's attitude is an obvious counterpart of Teufelsdröckh's. Although Dean might seem a strange disciple of Carlyle's, he does obey his injunction to "walk, work, believe, live and be free," for "Doubt of any sort cannot be removed except by Action." In fact, as the living embodiment of frenzied action, he pushes it to its logical extreme. Whether working or walking/travelling (or loving), for him life is a constant race. Leaving literally no room for doubt, he does not hesitate to claim God's existence: "'God exists without qualms. As we roll along this way I am positive beyond doubt that everything will be taken care of for us [...].' I had never dreamed Dean would become a mystic" (109). In fact, Dean's various trips with Sal are attempts to overcome the limitations of what Carlyle names "our terrestrial being":

> "It continues ever true," says [Teufelsdröckh], "that Saturn, or Chronos, or what we call TIME, devours all his Children: only by incessant Running, by incessant Working, may you (for some threescore-and-ten years) escape him; and you too he devours at last. Can any Sovereign, or Holy Alliance of Sovereigns, bid Time stand still; even in thought, shake themselves free of Time? Our whole terrestrial being is based on Time, and built of Time; it is wholly a Movement, a Time-impulse; Time is the author of it, the material of it. Hence also our Whole Duty, which is to move, to work, – in the right direction."[21]

So, indeed, in his constant rush, Dean's recurring obsession is "to know time." In Giamo's terms:

> The only reprieve from the terminus of chronological time is a high-octane mixture of speed and desire embodied in IT. IT, a transcendent state of pure excitement, stops the felt experience of linear time screeching in its tracks. It is first evoked by Dean when in the company of Rollo Greb, whose tense excitement with life "blew out of eyes in stabs of fiendish light." Dean tries to explain this strange suspension of being and time to Sal in a rush of bop-isms: "That's what I was trying to tell you – that's what I want to be. I want to be like him. He's never hung up, he goes every direction, he lets it all out, he knows time, he has nothing to do but rock back and forth. [...] You see, if you go like him all the time you'll finally get it."[22]

The paradoxical nature of Dean's quest is that he aims at a kind of mystic ecstasy that would take him beyond the limits of ordinary experience (notably chronological time) through a surfeit of sensations. So he races across America as if to defeat the limitations of time and space, just as he challenges physical limitations by indulging in fits of non-stop reckless driving or, at one stage, uninterrupted sequences of sex with Camille and Marylou alternately, immediately followed by all-night discussions with Carlo Marx, taking Benzedrine in an attempt "to communicate with absolute honesty and absolute completeness everything on our minds" (38). Frenzied travelling, drinking, drugs, sex, talk, and music are thus all means for Dean to immerse himself in the raw power of sensual life in order to attain "It," the experience beyond ordinary physical and mental limitations. In other words, Dean (and Sal after him) is engaged in a paradoxical hedonistic quest for transcendence, apparently not so far removed from the famous mystic *coincidentia oppositorum*. The quest is doomed, however, precisely because of its medium. As Giamo, quoting F.S.C. Northrop, suggests: "'Hedonism as a complete philosophy of life is inadequate – not because it is naughty or because sensed things are not real, but merely because determinate things are transitory; and a philosophy which treats determinate pleasures as if they were the basis for living under all circumstances treats pleasure as an immortal law rather than the actual transitory thing which it is.'"[23] I would suggest that more than a mere "philosophy," sensual indulgence is a spiritual (admittedly fated) practice which may be understood as a deliberate experimentation of what, with Steinbeck, remained mainly symbolic: immanent transcendence. When the focus of Steinbeck's observation was nature and collective history, Kerouac's is the human individual, body and mind. Still, though fated, the paradoxical and hyperbolic character of

Dean and Sal's quest might also be read as a creative response to Paul Ricoeur's later call for a re-actualization of Christ's plaint as contemporary, secular mankind's prayer for compassion.

"Go Moan for Man": On the Road *as Re-actualized Psalm of Plaint*

Ricoeur concludes his analysis of Psalm 22 by raising a question:[24] in our post-Nietzschean, Godless times, how could plaint as prayer or invocation be rehabilitated? Trying to outline a number of avenues towards an answer, Ricoeur is emphatic about the necessity not to tone down the radical character of the spiritual feeling of loss articulated through the question of God's desertion. Arguing against its traditional authoritative interpretation as a manifestation of divine retribution, the philosopher suggests that the plaint is a prayer for God's compassion coming from a conscience at a loss to see how such compassion might be reconciled with divine justice. For Ricoeur, the plaint as prayer should cease to be uniquely read in punitive terms and its interpretation renounce the justifying claims of traditional theodicy if its call for compassion is ever to be heard.[25]

When brought to bear on Kerouac's novel, Ricoeur's admonition helps cast a new light on Sal's refusal of "responsibility and his resultant, overwhelming emptiness,"[26] best expressed during his third trip with Dean:

> "Ah, man, Dean, I'm sorry, I never acted this way before with you. Well, now you know me. You know I don't have close relationships with anybody any more – I don't know what to do with these things. [...]"
>
> "It's not my fault! It's not my fault !" I told him. "Nothing in this lousy world is my fault, don't you see that? I don't want it to be and it can't be and it *won't* be."
>
> "Yes, man, yes, man. But please harken back and believe me."
>
> "I do believe you, I do." This was the sad story of that afternoon. (194)

Occurring in one of the rare (if not unique) instances of an overt quarrel initiated by Sal with his iconic role model, Dean – elsewhere explicitly said to "look like God" (259) – this strange outburst makes better sense when read in the context of Psalm 22. Following his admission that he will have no close relationship with anyone, Sal's exclamation may be heard as his refusal to take on responsibility in general and for others in particular on account of the attendant burden of guilt such responsibility brings – a burden of vicarious guilt best symbolized by the Crucifixion (and painfully carried by many a Christian conscience). In turn, his Christlike rebellion precedes his final redemptive conversion to faithful friendship: "I do believe you, I do."

And so, from then on, Sal will in fact take responsibility for Dean as his "brother" (206). Having shed his personal burden of inherited guilt through his outraged outcry, he is then free to open up to a more mature sense of brotherly responsibility. In this perspective, not just this one passage but the various trips may be apprehended as resulting from more than an adolescent urge to flee responsibility. They express a paradigmatic spiritual rebellion against the weight of guilt accompanying the feeling of responsibility for one's brethren. However, through his narrative, which progressively leads Sal to not only endorse responsibility for Dean's mad actions but forgive his God-like friend's desertion in Mexico out of sympathy for "the impossible complexity of his life" (276), Kerouac in a way fulfils Ricoeur's call for new verbal forms to re-actualize the prayer of plaint as a call for and practice of compassion.[27] Through Sal's unfailing sympathetic look at Dean, whose crazed attitudes increasingly estrange him from others, Kerouac ends up producing a beat eulogy for the "holy con-man" (194), whose madness he shows to be the paradoxical manifestation of a spiritual craving for communion: "Dean just raced in society, eager for bread and love" (10).

In fact, Dean is the paradigmatic "beat." As Giamo reminds us, the very definition of "the consciousness of being beat" is "of sharing in the plight of others":[28] "If Kerouac taught us anything, even in his darkest hour, it was this: the notion of sympathy engenders compassion. This is how we should take the road – 'with sympathy, says Whitman. Sympathy … Feeling with. Feeling with them as they feel with themselves. Catching the vibration of their soul and flesh as we pass.'"[29]

On the Road is a re-actualized cry for compassion on behalf of the "holy-eyed lost soul" (201), the paradigmatic portrayal of beat humanity. As a beat prayer of plaint, it appears to rely on a secularized version of Ricoeur's advocated "theology of paradox," where salvation is expected from the very pit of despair. For Ricoeur, this agonistic character of the redemption expressed in the conversion from plaint to praise is fundamental to the understanding of Psalm 22. In the novel, the paradoxical (even oxymoronic) character of this spiritual struggle is most apparent in the parodic treatment of Sal's peregrinations as Pilgrim's progress.

II *On the Road* as Revised *Pilgrim's Progress*: Postsecular Mysticism as Religious Parody

On the Road *as* Pilgrim's Progress

> After finishing the Wolfe essay, Kerouac outlined ambitious new plans for the book he was still calling "On the Road." At this stage he envisioned it as a quest novel like Cervantes's *Don Quixote* or John Bunyan's *Pilgrim's Progress*.[30]

The above-quoted sources of inspiration for Kerouac's novel are clear indications of the simultaneously parodic and spiritual character of its orientation. And so the clues to the spiritual (and even specifically Christian) nature of Sal's experiences on the road do abound in the novel, starting with the narrator's own name, "Salvatore Paradise," down to the many images explicitly likening his trips to a pilgrimage. The first time Sal catches sight of Denver, for instance, it "loom[s] ahead of [him] like the Promised Land" (15) while, at the start of his third trip, he fancies seeing "God in the sky in the form of huge gold sunburning clouds above the desert that seemed to point a finger at me and say, 'Pass here and go on, you're on the road to heaven.' Ah well, alackaday," as Sal confesses, "I was more interested in some old rotted covered wagons and pool tables sitting in the Nevada desert near a Coca-Cola stand and where there were huts with the weatherbeaten signs still flapping in the haunted shrouded desert wind, saying, 'Rattlesnake Bill lived here'" (165).

In no ambiguous terms, Sal thus describes himself as a lost soul on the road to redemption. Indeed, there are whole stretches of narrative explicitly allowing a reading of his trips with Dean as metaphorical journeys of spiritual ascent. One clear instance of this is their first common drive to California. On leaving Old Bull Lee's house in Louisiana, they first "cross eternity again" (141) in the shape of the Mississippi River, then, with a radio "mystery program" on, find themselves "in the swamps […], pass[ing] an apparition; it was a Negro man in a white shirt walking along with his arms up-spread to the inky firmament. He must have been praying or calling down a curse" (142). Finally able to "get out of this mansion of the snake, this mireful drooping dark" and "cross the evil old Sabine River that is responsible for all these swamps, [they] zoom through Beaumont, over the Trinity River at Liberty" (143), before once again being "stuck in the mud" of the "rainy Texas wilderness" (145). This familiar pattern of cyclical spiritual obstruction and higher level of liberation then leads them to follow Dean's injunction to "disemburden [themselves] of all [their] clothes" (146), thus putting into practice "Teufelsdröckh['s remark] in a chapter entitled 'The World out of Clothes' that to the degree that man strips off his rags or 'adventitious wrappings' [...] he may see and examine his soul. And what he sees, according to Carlyle, may be 'an unutterable mystery of Mysteries.'"[31] As it happens, in an ironical narrative twist, the mystery rather turns out to be one for others, when they come upon the happy trio – Dean's girlfriend Marylou being one member of the party – and find them stark naked. Still, the symbolic trail is not abandoned, as the three friends then proceed to El Paso and Juaréz, "sown in a tremendous valley so big you could see several railroads puffing at the same time in every direction, as though it was the Valley of the World" (147), into which they descend before the final ascent: after they take on a hitchhiker who symbolically claims to be "coming back home" (149), they wake up in the Arizona mountains to "a heaven of sunrise" (149), before "Dean t[akes] the wheel and carrie[s them] clear to the top of the world" (152). Once they get to their destination, however, "the fabulous white city of San Francisco on her eleven mystic hills" (154), their spiritual guide drops them on a street, moneyless, to join his wife Camille. This initiates Sal's final ordeal, as he alternately "loses faith" in Dean (155) and is deserted by Marylou. Then, in the middle of this "beatest time of [his] life" (155), Sal suddenly experiences a moment of mystic rapture:

> For just a moment I had reached the point of ecstasy that I always wanted to reach, which was the complete step across chronological time into timeless shadows, and wonderment in the bleakness of the mortal realm, and the sensation of death kicking at my heels to move on, with a phantom dogging its own heels, and myself hurrying to a plank where all angels dove off and flew into the holy void of uncreated emptiness, the potent and inconceivable radiancies shining in bright Mind Essence, innumerable lotus-lands falling open in the magic mothswarm of heaven. [...] I felt sweet, swinging bliss [...]. I thought I was going to die the very next moment. But I didn't die [...]. That was the way Dean found me when he finally decided I was worth saving. (157–8)

Despite the mixture of Christian and Buddhist images in the narrative of the mystic experience itself,[32] Sal's overall experience remains told as the paradigmatic Christian conversion from utter spiritual desolation to mystic ecstasy and final salvation. Still, the trip does not end with

Dean's redemptive return. Eventually, as always, Sal and Dean separate and Sal goes back East, to the safety of his aunt's home in New York. The pattern of the pilgrim's quest, though recognizable, is thus inverted since, starting from the river of eternity – the Mississippi River acting as an obvious counterpoint to the classic River of Death, the last obstacle in Christian's pilgrimage to the Celestial City – Sal ends up going back to his family home. Overall, his second trip (like all others), is a regressive one back to maternal protection, in keeping with his regressive dream of the Shrouded Traveller: "I told [Carlo Marx] a dream I had about a strange Arabian figure that was pursuing me across the desert; that I tried to avoid; that finally overtook me just before I reached the Protective City. […] Naturally, now that I look back on it, this is only death: death will overtake us before heaven. The one thing that we yearn for in our living days […] is the remembrance of *some lost bliss that was probably experienced in the womb* and can only be reproduced […] in death" (112; emphasis added). Contrary to the pilgrim's dedicated orientation towards the eternity of the Celestial City, Sal's quest thus seems animated by a profound, regressive death wish, which Dean initially convinces him to renounce; however, as Sal states, he only agreed with Dean "then" (112). Fundamentally, Sal's quest remains regressive, a parody of the classic pilgrim's progress.

The Beat Trip as Christian Spiritual Quest: Paradox and Parodic Inversion

Arguably, the fundamental inversion from which all others result in the novel is that of the father figure. Not only is the transcendent Father of the Christian quest replaced by the beat pilgrim's flesh-and-blood one, this hidden God that Dean – and Sal with him – keeps looking for is the very reverse of the spiritual seeker's protective redeemer: "'But hey, look down there in the night thar, hup, hup, a buncha old bums by a fire by the rail, damn me.' [Dean] almost slowed down. 'You see, I never know whether my father's there or not.' […] We drove on. Somewhere behind us or in front of us in the huge night his father lay drunk under a bush, and no doubt about it – spittle on his chin, water on his pants, molasses in his ears, scabs on his nose, maybe blood in his hair and the moon shining down on him" (211). Both Dean's meaningless stutter and Sal's confident description, respectively, are parodic comments on the gift of tongues and unshakable faith felt in the vicinity of the Lord, while the "huge night" in which Dean's father is envisioned contrasts with the usual blinding light associated with the divine. In keeping with this carnivalesque inversion, all the elements of the religious quest are there, in revised form.

The spiritual guides, the new evangelists, are all beats, that is, mad marginals behaving like parodic versions of ecstatic mystics. Old Bull Lee, first: "a teacher [who] had every right to teach because he spent all his time learning" (129), is an avid experimenter who has been round the world and become involved in all kinds of situations "merely for the experience" (130):

> Now the final study was the drug habit. He was now in New Orleans, slipping along the streets with shady characters and haunting connection bars. [...]
>
> He spent all his time talking and teaching others. Jane sat at his feet; so did I; so did Dean; and so had Carlo Marx. (130–1)

A drug addict engaged in "experimenting with narcoanalysis," who found that he "had seven separate personalities, each growing worse and worse on the way down, till finally he was a raving idiot and had to be restrained with chains" (131), he is a characteristic beat guide, both ideally and ironically well placed to warn Sal against his main mentor, Dean: "Dean had gotten worse, he confided in me. 'He seems to me to be headed for his ideal fate, which is compulsive psychosis dashed with a jigger of psychopathic irresponsibility and violence'" (133). Dean, for one, is explicitly referred to as "chief prophet" (175), while all other major characters stand as his "disciples" (177). He is even explicitly cast in the role of Christ, albeit a parodic one, the "Holy Goof" (176), who is put on a parodic trial at the start of part III:

> I suddenly realized that Dean, by virtue of his enormous series of sins, was becoming the Idiot, the Imbecile, the Saint of the lot. [...]
>
> That's what Dean was, the HOLY GOOF. [...]
>
> Now his disciples were married and the wives of his disciples had him on the carpet for the sexuality and the life he had helped bring into being. [...]
>
> He was BEAT – the root, the soul of Beatific. What was he knowing? He tried all in his power to tell me what he was knowing, and they envied that about me, my position at his side, defending him and drinking him in as they once tried to do. (176–7)

Not only is Dean presented as a carnivalesque inversion of the Redeemer "by virtue of his enormous series of sins," through an expert narrative sleight of hand, he regains saintliness precisely on account of the inversion he stands for. His characteristic maniacal goofing is turned into a form of supreme, secret knowledge, which, as spiritual master, he allows Sal to "drink in." This, in turn, points not only to the parodic but also paradoxical – even oxymoronic – character of the beat spiritual quest, not so far removed from the "theology of paradox" called for by Ricoeur in his reading of the plaint as prayer for compassion. For, through his parodic embodiment of Christ's selfless suffering, Dean is made to appear as a new, saintly kind of martyr, "ragged and broken and idiotic [...], his bony mad face covered with sweat and throbbing veins, saying, 'Yes, yes, yes,' as though tremendous revelations were pouring into him all the time now, and I am convinced they were" (177).

As always, Sal's sympathetic stance is instrumental in the oxymoronic construction of Dean as sinful idiot and saint, a central element in an overall systematic narrative strategy of carnivalesque inversion. Such a technique can also be seen in the very character of the beat quest as hedonistic progress, where renunciation gives way to full self-indulgence, as the characters' "kicks" are, paradoxically, supposed to lead them to the IT of transcendence. Besides, what sense of teleological orientation such a statement might still appear to suggest is constantly negated through the repeated purposelessness and meaninglessness of the characters' wild peregrinations: "It was a completely meaningless set of circumstances that made Dean come, and similarly I went off with him for no reason" (105). Each time they are being questioned about the aim of their trip, both Sal and Dean find it impossible to answer. Either they respond by leaving yet again, or through giggles (Dean's favourite reaction), one most significant rejoinder being Sal's to Old Bull Lee's enquiry as to the purpose of his trip west:

> "Sal, what are you going to the Coast for?"
> "Only for a few days. I'm coming back to school." (131)

Significantly shunning the issue of purpose by making it a matter of duration, Sal himself will eventually question the meaning of his going west: "What I accomplished by coming to Frisco I don't know. Camille wanted me to leave; Dean didn't care one way or the other" (161).

In this purposeless quest seemingly totally devoid of any teleological agenda, compulsion makes for the necessitarian theology of the classic quest. Throughout the novel, instinctual urges prompt the characters to action. Just as Sal simply "ha[s] to go" West (52), so Dean compulsively goes off with him, despite his wife Camille's utter despair:

> "But what is the purpose of all this? Why are you doing this to me?"
> "It's nothing, it's nothing, darling – ah – hem – Sal has pleaded and begged with me to come and get him, *it is absolutely necessary* for me to – but we won't go into all these explanations – and I'll tell you why [...]." And he told her why, and of course it made no sense. (100; emphasis added)

A Dionysian impulse thus seems to be prodding Sal and Dean on a kind of Nietzschean quest, paradoxically not premised on the death of God, as Dean is characteristically portrayed as "mad with belief": "He was out of his mind with real belief. 'And of course now no one can tell us that there is no God. We've passed through all forms. You remember, Sal, when I first came to New York and I wanted Chad King to teach me about Nietzsche. You see how long ago? Everything is fine, God exists, we know time'" (108). Later in San Francisco, during the ecstatic moment crowning his "beatest time" of solitude and hunger, once again a parodic revision of mystic asceticism and rapture, Sal will experience Dean's teaching, as he realizes that "[he has] died and been reborn numberless times" (157). Actual revelation thus seems to attend the beat seeker, parodic as his suffering is of Christic humiliation. Would there be a "beat way" to Redemption?

Problematic Redemption: Progression or Regression?

For all the vagaries of their quests – for each part is about a new trip – Sal and Dean do go through an overall evolution, both personal and relational. While Dean's psychological state seems to deteriorate to the point where "he couldn't talk any more. He hopped and laughed, he stuttered and fluttered his hands and said, 'Ah – ah – you must listen to hear.' We listened, all ears. But he forgot what he wanted to say" (278), Sal's growth seems to take him in the direction of a more mature sense of responsibility. The "pivotal point of [his] friendship" with Dean occurs at the start of part III and coincides with a symbolic reversal in their journey: rather than taking them away from Sal's East to Dean's supposedly Wild West, the trip they embark on takes them back east – with Sal even initially planning to go as far as Italy – to Sal's family roots.

Still, despite Sal's undeniable developing sense of commitment, as he feels "concern for [Dean as] a man who was years younger than I, five years, and whose fate was wound with mine across the passage of the recent years" (172), this quest for roots, a substitute for the former western call of the wild, is no unambiguous progress. Indeed, what mars Sal's progress is its underlying regressive urge. As epitomized by his dream of the Shrouded Traveller, his craving is a back-to-the-womb movement, most aptly represented by his nightmarish, osmotic experience in a Detroit all-night movie. In company with a beat crowd of individuals "with nothing to do, nowhere to go, nobody to believe in," Dean and Sal spend the night in front of the same two films, symbolically, respectively, about the Far West and Far East, and end up "permeated completely with the strange Gray Myth of the West and the weird dark Myth of the East when morning came" (222):

> All my actions since then have been dictated automatically to my subconscious by this horrible osmotic experience. [...] In the gray dawn [...] I was sleeping [...] as six attendants of the theatre converged with their night's total of swept-up rubbish and created a huge dusty pile [...] – till they almost swept me away too. [...] Had they taken me with it, Dean would never have seen me again. He would have had to roam the entire United States and look in every garbage pail from coast to coast before he found me embryonically convoluted among the rubbishes of my life, his life, and the life of everybody concerned and not concerned. What would I have said to him from my rubbish womb? "Don't bother me, man, I'm happy where I am." (222–3)

After the symbolic regression apparent in this "roaming from coast to coast," the two friends' next and final trip to the Mexican "magic *south*" (241) would seem to herald the end of this regressive process. Actually, Sal does describe Mexico as "the magic land at the end of the road" (251). Once more, however, the miraculous "heaven" (253) is a regressive one, a "Fellahin" paradise, "where it all began and where Adam was suckled and taught to know" (256): "I was alone in my eternity at the wheel, and the road ran straight as an arrow. Not like driving across Carolina, or Texas, or Arizona, or Illinois; but like driving across the world and into places where we would finally learn ourselves among the Fellahin Indians of the world, the essential strain of the basic primitive, wailing humanity that stretches in a belt around the equatorial belly of the world" (255).

Mexico itself appears to Sal as "the great and final wild uninhibited Fellahin-childlike city that we knew we would find at the end of the road" (275), synthesizing his view of paradise – incidentally his own family name – as the blissful, infantile realm of unrepressed instinct. This time, this last regressive quest, involving sex, drugs, and a whole night's osmotic experience in the dark jungle, nearly costs Sal his life: "Then I got fever and became delirious and unconscious. Dysentry" (275).

A carnivalesque rewriting of the recognizably Christian spiritual quest, Sal's beat trip takes him in the opposite direction: rather than being "born anew in the Spirit (Jn 3,5) into eternal life – that is life not subject to death-as-final-destiny,"[33] his regressive urge makes death the inevitable destination, while Dean's uncontrolled zest for life leads him increasingly to stray away from the road of sanity. In the end, the beat quest for transcendence is doomed, though not primarily on account of its paradoxical character. Indeed, the latter could be interpreted as a postsecular variation on the Gospels, where the cross is regarded as "the power of God [paradoxically revealed] in weakness," while, according to Luke, true Christian disciples are most likely to be "'the poor' – that is those who are in some way marginal, physically, socially, or spiritually" (Lk 6, 20–6).[34] In the end, the beat quest is fated because of its underlying regressive denial of redemption.

III The Demise of the Word

> As Fredrick Jameson argues, "perhaps the supreme formal feature of all the postmodernisms" is "a new kind of … depthlessness" (9). Rather than the careful construction of nuanced levels of symbolic resonance which give a multilayered sense of depth to modernist art, Kerouac experimented with what he called the "spontaneous prose method," an attempt to record both the mind's surfaces and America's surfaces on paper as directly and immediately (literally without mediation) as possible.[35]

While such an analysis would unmistakably relate Steinbeck's multilayered aesthetics to modernism, by the same account, Kerouac would then become the new apostle for postmodernism. As Alex Albright rightly notes, however: "Despite Kerouac's blustery claims to the contrary, spontaneous writing did not originate with him. […] André Breton and the surrealists had experimented with automatic writing and free association. John Tytell notes the automatic writing experiments of William James and Gertrude Stein at Harvard."[36]

As for Douglas Malcom, "the run-on sentence that ends [Kerouac's] novel owes [much] to the modernist notion of stream of consciousness developed by writers like Joyce and Woolf" while "the Romanticism through which he views his own life and those of his friends prevents him from achieving a postmodernist vision even though many of his materials [...] point in this direction."[37] Is Kerouac's aesthetics, then, to be related to modernism or postmodernism?

As my whole critical endeavour has tried to show, "modernist" and "postmodernist" labels might be more adequately granted when a writer's aesthetics is related to his stance to the spiritual. In fact, aesthetics would seem to accrue from such a fundamental attitude. Just as Steinbeck's symbolic realism appears to derive from his simultaneously scientific and visionary grasp of nature and reality, Kerouac's fundamental spiritual despair accounts for a deliberately "flat" – though exuberant – realism, best represented by the image of the road and conveyed by his famous original roll of a manuscript. In this perspective, and following a typically esoteric cyclical evolution, Kerouac's aesthetics would rather seem to renew a bond with modernist despair (and its consequent inflated rhetoric, as has been observed with Fitzgerald), after Steinbeck's kerygmatic prose had departed from it. This still leaves open the question of the definition of postmodernism in fiction, some viewing it as a radicalization of modernist spiritual angst, while others contend that aspects of its undisputed formal innovations seek to re-enchant the world. If radicalization there be, the present study would tend to observe it as affecting the rift between these two opposed tendencies in postmodernist fiction. In this sense, *On the Road* would stand at a spiritual crossroads between these two conflicting impulses, torn between a genuine search for transcendence and radical despair. This accounts for what might best be called Kerouac's aesthetics of osmotic confusion.

"An Undifferentiated Aesthetic Continuum": Kerouac's Poetics of Ecstatic Oneness

Analysing Ginsberg's efforts to "make language into mantra [...] through compositional method," Amy Hungerford explains that the poet's "long-standing effort to make poetic composition spontaneous" came from his conviction that "in achieving this degree of spontaneity in the written record, he could reproduce in the reader the exact state of consciousness in which the poem was composed."[38] Indeed, Ginsberg's aim was to effect change in his reader/listener through the sheer power of poetic words, just as "in the yogic tradition, [...] vibrations produced in the body can transform the consciousness directly, bypassing the intellect."[39] Likewise, Kerouac's spontaneous prose in *On the Road* seems to aim at re-creating Sal's longed-for ecstatic state, finally achieved in San Francisco as he finds himself moneyless and deserted by both Dean and Marylou. In his analysis of the passage, Ben Giamo comments: "The Buddhist terms, concepts, and images that flash through the passage deliver Sal into a briefly felt state of nirvana or the All-At-One-Ment, as the Buddha puts it in the *Diamond Sutra*, and what F.S.C. Northrop refers to as the undifferentiated, all-embracing, indeterminate aesthetic continuum. Other arbitrary conceptions for this state of nonbeing include emptiness – void – ultimate escape; by any other name, it would feel like 'sweet, swinging bliss.'"[40] The image of an "indeterminate aesthetic continuum" used to qualify Sal's "complete step across chronological time into timeless shadows" (156) also perfectly describes Kerouac's effort to create an uninterrupted sequential prose mirroring the frenzy of his trips.[41] His spontaneous prose thus seems aimed at creating the same kind of entrancing effect that speed causes the characters on the road: an experience that is both in time and seeks to transcend it, a timelessness defining Dean's famous "IT."

Music also produces this timeless, ecstatic feeling, as noted by Douglas Malcom:

> "IT" then appears to be some enigmatic aspect of the music that unites the musicians and listeners in a common purpose and apparently raises the moment to transcendent heights.
>
> Stephen Nachmanovitch remarks that such a union is characteristic of all improvisation: "The time of inspiration, the time of technically structuring and realizing the music, the time of playing it, and the time of Memory and intention (which postulate past and future) and intuition (which indicates the eternal present) are fused."[42]

As Malcom's analysis suggests, such a timeless experience relies on both an individual and collective feeling of "union," recalling Sal's essential motivation for getting on the road – a craving for brotherhood:

> Yes, and it wasn't only because I was a writer and needed new experiences that I wanted to know Dean more, [...] but because, somehow, in spite of our difference in character, he reminded me of some long-lost brother. [...] And in his excited way of speaking I heard again the voices of old companions and brothers under the bridge, among the motorcycles, along the wash-lined neighbourhood and drowsy doorsteps of afternoon where boys played guitars while their older brothers worked in the mills. (9)

In one of their most hectic moments on the road, as they are travelling east, Sal makes a significant remark regarding humankind's essential oneness: "I told Dean that the thing that bound us all together in this world was invisible, and to prove it pointed to long lines of telephone poles that curved off out of sight over the bend of a hundred miles of salt" (191). Besides, such a feeling of universal oneness also causes Sal's other main ecstatic experience, as he crosses the Mississippi River to New Orleans: "The ferry fires glowed in the night; the same Negroes plied the shovel and sang. Old Big Slim Hazard once worked on the Algiers ferry as a deckhand; this made me think of Mississippi Gene too; and as the river poured down from mid-America by starlight I knew, I knew like mad that everything I had ever known and would ever know was One" (134).

The extract makes the link between Sal's association of ideas and mystic revelation directly explicit, a clear indication of the narrative aim of his continuous prose: producing a feeling of ecstatic oneness.

Transcending one's sense of alienation by transgressing the limits of the ordinary experience of time, space, and otherness, such seems to be the redemptive aim of Kerouac's spontaneous, entrancing prose. Ecstatic moments, however, remain sparse, and the other side of the osmotic coin is meaninglessness and confusion.

Words without Word: Kerouac's Literal Realism

Commenting upon Ginsberg's "Wichita Vortex Sutra," Hungerford notes how "in that poem, language is emptied of content in order to display the occult power of the word itself."[43] While, contrary to Ginsberg, Kerouac's goal was not essentially political, one finds in his novel the same effort to produce what Ginsberg, speaking of his early poetry, called "literal realism."[44] With Kerouac, however, such "literal realism" – which, for Ginsberg, rests on the same romantic understanding of the power of the letter that Northrop Frye develops regarding "literal" biblical meaning – rather empties his transparently Christian frame of all symbolic import.

One significant example of this can be seen in the way God's Word is represented in the novel: as critics have noted, Sal meets a number of mad, beat prophets in *On the Road*, which is to be related to his and Dean's quest for direction from a father figure. While this subversive secularization of the Father, who is the usual source and object of the spiritual quest, already divests Him of all symbolic transcendence, there is even one instance when Sal projects himself into the Prophet's role: "I pictured myself in a Denver bar that night, with all the gang, and in their eyes I would be strange and ragged and like the Prophet who has walked across the land to bring the dark Word, and the only Word I had was 'Wow!'" (33). In Sal's representation, God's infinite power of creation symbolized by His Word thus boils down to an exclamation void of content. This appears as one instance in Kerouac's systematic subversive suppression of religious symbolism, its most consistent expression probably being the way his oxymoronic narration consistently conflates madness and mysticism. Throughout the novel, Sal characteristically turns Dean's madness into saintliness, calling his increasing confusion mystic purity (109), describing his agitation as "pious frenzy" (223), and generally making his manic depression into a secularized and paradigmatic expression of the Cross: "We made hasty preparations for Dean. [...] Preparations had to be made [...] to fit his suffering bulk and bursting ecstasies" (236). Should the reader naïvely believe Sal, Dean could be seen as embodying the well-known madness of some mystics, the mystic experience itself being traditionally described as *coincidentia oppositorum*, the meeting of opposites. However, the slight narrative distance still preserved between Sal's younger self and his more mature, narrative persona prevents the (con)fusion between bipolarity and mysticism from being complete and the literal character of Dean's madness from being totally taken for symbolic sainthood. Eventually, the end of the road produces much the same disappointed anticlimax as can be found at the end of *The Great Gatsby*: though Dean's death is not actual, his departure signals the end of Sal's romantic dream, which, in the context of a reality divested of all symbolic transcendence, cannot but result in nostalgic disenchantment.

If we take Amy Hungerford's cue regarding what she names "postmodern belief" as belief in meaninglessness, we could say that Kerouac took it to its literal, logical extreme: spiritual despair. However, as Hungerford shows, such "belief without content" has its creative side:

> In American culture, belief that does not emphasize the content of doctrine has roots in the transcendentalist thinkers of the early nineteenth century, and among the Romantics more generally. Belief without content for Emerson [...] makes way for a critique of institutional religion and its discourses of doctrine and theology. This book will argue that a century

> and a half later, with religious critique so firmly a part of our secular condition, belief without meaning becomes both a way to maintain religious belief rather than critique its institutions and a way to buttress the authority of the literature that seeks to imagine such belief.[45]

This spiritually creative side of postsecular postmodernity is what I would now like to address with Morrison's *Beloved*.

6 "I Will Call Them My People": Toni Morrison's Postsecular Gospel of Self and Community

Essentially transgressive and even regressive, Kerouac's beat urge for transcendence ultimately caused his own downfall. In Ben Giamo's words: "Kerouac lived and died by the Dionysian double-edged sword (having lost sight of that very fine line between ecstasy and destruction). [...] We must keep in mind that Kerouac would never have hit rock bottom had he not aspired to the high heavens."[1] As Giamo suggests, beat philosophy is one of excess and transgression. "Having lost sight of that very fine line between ecstasy and destruction," Kerouac falls prey to "the great exciter of the *Yes* function in man" – alcohol:

> William James's understanding of the uses of alcohol to further religious ecstasy and spiritual insight applies directly to Kerouac's temperament and to the purity of his aim to transcend the "sober hour":
>
> The sway of alcohol over mankind is unquestionably due to its power to stimulate the mystical faculties of human nature, usually crushed to earth by the cold facts and dry criticisms of the sober hour. Sobriety diminishes, discriminates and says no; drunkenness expands, unites, and says yes. It is in fact the great exciter of the *Yes* function in man.[2]

While shedding light on one reason for Dean's characteristic "wild yea-saying overburst of American joy" (9), James's analysis of the effects of alcohol also, interestingly, intersects with John McClure's analysis of the dangers of spiritual enchantment:

> "Enchantment," [Jane Bennett] writes, involves "a feeling of being connected in an affirmative way to existence; it is to be under the momentary impression that the natural and cultural worlds offer gifts." [...] Bennett's

> cogent definition highlights at once the power of enchantment and its characteristic ephemerality. But just as certain religious systems seem to be the expression of a profound sense of guilt and unworthiness [...], so others (transcendentalism, for instance, or some New Age philosophies that draw on it) seem to be enchanted by enchantment and to represent the cosmos in its light, as a domain of pure affirmation and abundance, all gift, no grind.[3]

Kerouac, it seems, wavered between these two religious attitudes,[4] both of which can be felt in *On the Road*. However, as McClure argues, "in each case, [...] a certain reduction of the real has been effected and a necessary balance has been lost."[5] This is a pitfall Toni Morrison strives to circumvent as she "fully delineates" the "perils of enchanted enclosure" in *Beloved*.[6]

I Transgression and Redemption in *Beloved*: The Art of Diakrisis

One major and obvious difference between Kerouac and Morrison is their opposing stance to marginality. A matter of choice for the icon of the beat generation, this is certainly not so with African-American writer Toni Morrison. Nevertheless, for both, marginality leads to a rebellious revision of mainstream irreligious ideology. For Kerouac, whose personal agenda, contrary to other beat writers, was insistently non-political,[7] the motivating force was the materialism of American society, whose closure to transcendence fed his romantic urge to transgress the ordinary physical and mental limits of daily experience. In the case of Morrison, whose agenda has inevitably been political, the aim is to topple the ideological edifice supporting her country's history of racial oppression – one of its structuring principles being transgression.

From Slavery to Infanticide: Transgression as Sin

Etymologically, transgression is a trespassing of limits, which may be taken in a literal or figurative sense. As *Beloved* shows, in the case of African-American history, both levels of meaning apply. The physical and psychological dead end the plot starts with progressively appears as the result of a series of transgressions that trap the characters in a vicious circle.

The original transgression, of course, is literal, slavery being a physical encroachment upon somebody else's territory. As the novel's dedication surmises, "sixty million and more" were taken away from their homeland across the Atlantic to foreign territory. As the novel goes on to show, however, the geographical intrusion and displacement is only the surface level of a deeper, double ontological transgression wrought by slavery, consisting in the simultaneous elevation of the white enslaver to the rank of Godlike master, while the black slave was denied humanity.

The first aspect of this ontological transgression, the deification of the white man as omnipotent lord, is exposed in a number of ways in *Beloved*. It is quite explicit in the most brutal forms of slavery such as the one embodied by schoolteacher. It is more devious – though no less powerful – in the case of the patriarchal stance adopted by Garner, his predecessor and initial owner of the novel's black protagonists. An obvious pun on the original biblical gardener, Garner's name signals his hubris. As Paul D eventually ponders:

> For years Paul D believed schoolteacher broke into children what Garner had raised into men. [...] Now, [...] he wondered how much difference there really was between before schoolteacher and after. Garner called and announced them men – but only on Sweet Home, and by his leave. Was he naming what he saw or creating what he did not? [...] What would he have been anyway – before Sweet Home – without Garner? In Sixo's country, or his mother's? Or, God help him, on the boat? Did a whiteman saying it make it so? Suppose Garner woke up one morning and changed his mind? Took the word away. (220)

In a way, the death of this sham God does take the humanizing word away, as schoolteacher undertakes to "re-educate" the slaves and teach them their true status in the chain of beings: a cross between humans and animals, whose respective characteristics he will carefully list. In schoolteacher's perverted social order, Garner's benevolent slavery is a legal transgression: "'There's laws against what he done: letting niggers hire out their own time to buy themselves. He even let em have guns! And you think he mated them niggers to get him some more? Hell no! He planned for them to marry!'" (226). Proceeding to set things "aright," schoolteacher has Sethe milked like a cow and then beaten for complaining about it, while Paul D is collared, has to wear a bit in his mouth, and ends up feeling inferior to the evil plantation rooster ironically named Mister (72). Responding to schoolteacher's cruelty with yet another transgression, both literal and legal, the slaves attempt to flee. Recalling her heroic determination to go, against all odds, and join her children, Sethe's rebellion even takes Promethean proportions: "What I had to get through later I got through because of you. Passed right by those boys hanging in the trees. [...] I walked right on by because only me had your milk, and God do what He would, I was going to get it to you" (198).

So the original ontological transgression of slavery leads to Sethe's own sinful determination, which, in turn, will cause schoolteacher's encroachment upon her new territory: her mother-in-law Baby Suggs's yard. Legal if not right, schoolteacher's claim to his property, in accordance with the Fugitive Slave Law, provokes Sethe's ultimate act of rebellion: infanticide. On a par with the white enslaver's own outrageous claim to his power of life and death over his slaves, Sethe's act recapitulates all the dimensions of transgression seen so far. An obvious case of transgression in ontological, moral, and legal terms, her infanticide is metaphorically described as a literal passage "through the veil, out, away, over there where no one could hurt them. [...] Outside this place" (163). In this respect, it is also a transgression in a literal sense and earns her the traditional animalistic charge levelled at black people by whites, but this time coming from Paul D: "you got two feet, Sethe, not four" (165).

The Return of the Dead: Transgression as Regression

Such is the unstated background – which the reader gradually pieces together – at the start of the story. "Unspeakable thoughts," Sethe's memories would have remained "unspoken" (199) but for Morrison's creative transgression in the shape of the character called Beloved, Sethe's murdered baby daughter returned from the dead as a grown girl, nearly two decades after her mother's infanticide.

By the writer's own admission, her aim was to "have the past sit at the table and demand to be heard." So, Beloved effects yet another spatial and ontological transgression, as she crosses the frontier between the world of the living and the dead. Although her supernatural status is never explicitly stated, a number of clues are interspersed throughout the passage describing her sudden appearance: the focus on her baby's "soft and new" hands and feet, Sethe's association of her unaccountable emergency on seeing the young woman's face with breaking waters (51) and the absence of the dog, Here Boy, known never to be around when the baby's spirit is present (12). Besides, Beloved's own difficulty to breathe, keep her eyes open, and hold her head straight, together with her unquenchable thirst and extreme tiredness, all coalesce as infant's behaviour. Last of all, her name evokes the only word Sethe was able to have carved on her dead baby's grave in exchange for sex with the engraver, "the remembrance of glittering headstone" causing Sethe to feel "especially kindly toward her" (53).

The clearest sign of Beloved's supernatural embodiment of the past is her effect on the characters. In her company, both Sethe and Paul D are made to confront repressed memories: while inexplicably moved to grant Beloved's repeated wish that she speak about her past, Sethe suddenly "remembers something she had forgotten she knew. Something privately shameful that had seeped into a slit in her mind" (61). As for Paul D, under Beloved's spell, the "tobacco tin [of his repressed past] lodged in his chest" gives way, though "nothing *in this world* could pry it open" (113; emphasis added).

At first sight, Beloved's transgressive return would thus seem cathartic and even redemptive, ending as it does the characters' alienating relationship with their past as slaves. Indeed, for Sethe, with each day, there starts anew the "serious work of beating back the past" (73): "Her brain was not interested in the future. Loaded with the past and hungry for more, it left her no room to imagine, let alone plan for, the next day" (70).

"Work[ing] hard to remember as close to nothing as was safe" (6) proves of little avail though, and the gradual confrontation with the past that Beloved causes should come as a relief. However, rather than healing the characters' regressive absorption in their pasts, Beloved activates it. For not only does she force a physical communion with Paul D that opens up his chest of memories (117), her fusional relationship with Sethe – that of the suckling she was when murdered – progressively threatens to engulf and kill her mother.

The manifestation of a "bottomless longing," "some plea barely in control" (58) to be loved, Beloved's fusional demand for reparation meets Sethe's wish for forgiveness but will never fulfil it: "Denver thought she understood the connection between her mother and Beloved: Sethe was trying to make up for the handsaw; Beloved was making her pay for it. But there would never be an end to that. [...] It was as though Sethe didn't really want forgiveness given; she wanted it refused. And Beloved helped her out" (252). Being herself the embodiment of transgression (in Beloved's own words: "there is no place where I stop," 210), the beloved child, who is "not separate from her" (210), turns into an incubus threatening Sethe's life: "Then it seemed to Denver the thing was done: Beloved bending over Sethe looked the mother, Sethe the teething child. [...] The bigger Beloved got, the smaller Sethe became; [...] She sat in the chair licking her lips like a chastised child while Beloved ate up her life, took it, swelled up with it, grew taller on it. And the older woman yielded it up without a murmur" (250).

The last step in the chain of transgression set off by physical slavery, Sethe's death is eventually prevented by Denver, who turns transgression into a redemptive act.

"Know It, and Go on Out the Yard": Redemptive Transgression and the Power of the Collective Word

> So it was she who had to step off the edge of the world and die because if she didn't, they all would. (239)

Thus, in no uncertain terms, Denver's exit from her mother's house is presented as a fall. Quite a feat since she has not left the house in years, Denver's literal transgression (she goes beyond the limits of her mother's property) is prompted by yet another manifestation from the beyond: that of her dead grandmother, Baby Suggs. Prodded on by Baby Suggs's admonition to "know" the dangers of the outside world and still "go on out the yard" (244), Denver does "step off the edge of the world [to] go ask [...] for help" (243). Only, this time, rather than severing her bond with the rest of humanity, as Beloved's return had done for Sethe, Denver's courageous trespassing of limits restores her link with the neighbouring black community. Starting with her former schoolmistress, Lady Jones, Denver's venture into the outside world leads to the emergence of her adult self:

> "Food. My ma'am, she doesn't feel good."
> "Oh, baby," said Mrs Jones. "Oh, baby."
> Denver looked up at her. She did not know it then, but it was the word "baby," said softly and with such kindness, that inaugurated her life in the world as a woman. (248)

The community of black women will respond, in their turn, by helping Denver sever the destructive fusional bond between Sethe and her daughter returned from the dead. Echoing Baby Suggs's assertion that "Good is knowing when to stop" (87), Ella manages to "convince the others that rescue [is] in order" (256): "As long as the ghost showed out from its ghostly place – shaking stuff, crying, smashing and such – Ella respected it. But if it took flesh and came in her world, well, the shoe was on the other foot. She didn't mind a little communication between the two worlds, but this was an invasion" (257).

Under Ella's leadership, the community of black women assembles outside the limits of Sethe's property, in a gesture symbolizing the necessary respect for boundaries. Through their Wordlike chant, they drive Beloved away and restore the natural distance between mother and daughter, the living and the dead, putting an end to the vicious circle of transgression initiated by slavery:

> When the women assembled outside 124, Sethe was breaking a lump of ice into chinks. [...] When the music entered the window [...] it was as though the Clearing had come to her with all its heat and simmering leaves, where the voices of women searched for the right combination, the key, the code, the sound that broke the back of words. Building voice upon voice until they found it, and when they did it was a wave of sound wide enough to sound deep water and knock the pods off chestnut trees. It broke over Sethe and she trembled like the baptized in its wash. (261)

Such a restoration of ontological order, then, makes it possible for Paul D to come back and offer to "put his story next to [Sethe's]":

> Suddenly [Paul D] remembers Sixo trying to describe what he felt about the Thirty-Mile Woman. "She is a friend of my mind. She gather me, man. The pieces I am, she gather them and give them back to me in *all the right order*. It's good, you know, when you got a woman who is a friend of your mind." [...]
>
> Only this woman Sethe could have left him his manhood like that. He wants to put his story next to hers.
>
> "Sethe," he says, "me and you, we got more yesterday than anybody. We need some kind of tomorrow."
>
> He leans over and takes her hand. With the other he touches her face. "You your best thing, Sethe. You are." His holding fingers are holding hers.
>
> "Me? Me?" (272–3; emphasis added)

Sethe's final words indicate the redemptive character of Paul D's offer of a loving partnership in place of Beloved's demand for fusion. Rather than threatening Sethe with extinction, Paul D's assertion of self-worth resurrects Sethe's sense of self from the clutches of a past of slavery that "could take your whole self for anything that came to mind" and "dirty you so bad you forgot who you were and couldn't think it up" (251): "The best thing she was, was her children. Whites might dirty *her* all right, but not her best thing, her beautiful, magical best thing – the part of her that was clean" (251). Breaking the vicious circle of transgression that culminated in Sethe's paradoxical reach for redemption – saving the part of her that was "clean" – through infanticide, Paul D's "blessedness" (272) effects what even Baby Suggs's powerful sermons in the Clearing were eventually unable to achieve: the resurrection and redemption of self through love. In fact, as McClure convincingly demonstrates, Baby Suggs's spontaneous preaching is part of a logic of "enchanted enclosure," resting on "a well-intentioned and necessary project of opening," whose perils are "fully delineated in [...] *Beloved*."[8] Producing "false clarity,"[9] the rapturous enchantment of the kind created by Baby Suggs's ecstatic services in open nature rests on a dangerous erasure of limits between humanity and divinity, causing Baby Suggs's own downfall. "Dreaming of a black community linked – the living and the dead – by love, [...] Baby Suggs overestimates both the moral maturity of her community and the protection granted by the spirits":[10] "Baby Suggs' three (maybe four) pies grew to ten (maybe twelve). [...] Too much, they thought. [...] Loaves and fishes were His powers – they did not belong to an ex-slave who had probably never carried one hundred pounds to the scale, or picked okra with a baby on her back. [...] It made them furious" (137). In a way, Morrison thus responds to Kerouac's regressive quest for beatific fusion with her own Pauline call for redemptive (self-) love based on discrimination. As McClure points out, "the biblical art designed to protect people" from the simplistic "abolition of obscurities and complexities" produced by enchantment is "the art of discernment (*'diakrisis'*)":

> Discernment, as Paul and other biblical authors describe it, is a faculty made necessary by the abstract nature of divine law, which must always be interpreted when applied, and the fallen nature of the creation, which condemns humans to grope for the truth in a domain dense with deception. [...]
>
> The Pauline letters caution that the art of discernment is a difficult one, slowly learned. Spiritual beginners are "babes" or "infants," and it is only by "reason of use" that humans "have their senses exercised to discern both good and evil" (Hebrews 5:12–14).[11]

In this sense, the novel's lesson in *diakrisis* could be summed up by the phrase "Good is knowing when to stop," which the story proceeds to explore as it delineates the necessary limits between self and other, past and present, the natural and supernatural. Indeed, a clear awareness of limits appears critical to the final "miracle of redemption or salvation in [Morrison's] novel, [which] is clearly a *communal* affair, instigated by diverse heroes."[12]

Looking at the shape the myth of redemption takes in *Beloved*, as both communal and mundane, one realizes how far we have come from its traditional representation as relying on "a *single* hero,"[13] and taking us to a beatific afterlife. In Morrison's fiction, the Bible is a profound source of wisdom when interpreted in the context of actual African-American circumstances. In this perspective, the writer's stance towards the Book might be regarded as less "oppositional" than revisionary,[14] which her handling of the metaphorical biblical cosmos will also show.

II "A View of Heaven as Life; Not Heaven as Post-Life": Morrison's Postsecular Religious Space

Paradise Lost: The Fortunate Fall of the Plantation Myth

In *Beloved*, the implicit intertext to which the novel responds is the southern plantation myth. Projecting the classic biblical imagery and its hierarchical picture of the cosmos onto the southern slave society, the plantation myth posited the plantation as an Eden of harmonious relationships between master and slaves, ruled over by the benevolent figure of the patriarchal slave owner. In *Beloved*, such an idealized place of perfection is given shape through the symbolically named Sweet Home, the Garners' plantation where Sethe and Paul D were slaves. There, both husband and wife behave as protective parents to their slaves, as illustrated by Mrs Garner's benevolence at the time of Sethe and Halle's "marriage" or her husband's proud, fatherly insistence on "raising [his slaves] into men" (220).

Envisioned through the black protagonists' memories, however, the Garners' Eden soon appears flawed, precisely because of its lack of realism. As Baby Suggs perceives, the Garners' "special kind of slavery" both respected and denied the slaves' human nature: "The Garners [...] ran a special kind of slavery, treating them like paid labor, listening to what they said, teaching what they wanted known. And he didn't stud his boys. [...] It surprised and pleased her, but worried her too. Would he pick women for them or what did he think was going to happen when those boys ran smack into their nature?" (140). Banishing both sex and death ("Nobody counted on Garner dying. Nobody thought he could," 220), Sweet Home thus masquerades as a prelapsarian world of innocence, until Garner does actually die. Like the serpent in Genesis, the new overseer schoolteacher will then grant the slaves the knowledge of evil they had so far recoiled from. Symbolically imprinting it on Sethe's back in the shape of the tree formed by the scars produced by his violent beating, schoolteacher makes the fall from this false Eden both necessary and fortunate. As Paul D later realizes, in Sweet Home, "they had been isolated in a wonderful lie, dismissing Halle's and Baby Suggs' life before Sweet Home as bad luck": "Ignorant of or amused by Sixo's dark stories. Protected and convinced they were special. Never suspecting the problem of Alfred, Georgia; being so in love with the look of the world, putting up with anything and everything, just to stay alive in a place where a moon he had no right to was nevertheless there" (221). Leaving that "cradle" (219) will enable the slaves to develop a self-awareness they had been totally deprived of. As Sethe enthuses, recounting her escape to Paul D: "'I did it. I got us all out. [...] Up till then it was the only thing I ever did on my own. [...] I had help, of course, lots of that, but still it was me doing it; [...] It was a kind of selfishness I never knew nothing about before. It felt good. Good and right'" (162). Although she did not have to escape, Baby Suggs experienced the selfsame exhilarating effects of freedom as she was taken into free territory: "She didn't know what she looked like and was not curious. But suddenly she saw her hands and thought with a clarity as simple as it was dazzling, 'These hands belong to me. These *my* hands.' Next she felt a knocking in her chest and discovered something else new: her own heartbeat. [...] She felt like a fool and began to laugh out loud" (141). Both Sethe's sense of "selfishness" and Baby Suggs's sudden physical realization of her own, individual existence will, however, lead the women to develop a hubristic sense of self resulting in their own downfall.

From Heaven to Hell, or When Pride Goes before a Fall

Just as Sweet Home could masquerade as a prelapsarian Eden based on the suppression of evil, so 124 comes close to a kind of terrestrial paradise after Sethe's arrival with her newborn baby girl Denver in her arms: "Sethe had had twenty-eight days [...] of unslaved life. [...] Days of company: knowing the names of forty, fifty other Negroes, their views, habits. [...] One taught her the alphabet; another a stitch. All taught her how it felt to wake up at dawn and *decide* what to do with the day. [...] Bit by bit, at 124 and in the Clearing, along with the others, she had claimed herself" (95).

"A cheerful, buzzing house where Baby Suggs, holy, loved, cautioned, fed, chastised and soothed" (86–7), 124 becomes a heaven of shared company, sustained by Baby Suggs's "Word" (178) until the "Misery," as Stamp Paid names Sethe's infanticide (177). Subsequently, the fall of 124, like that of Sweet Home, will be due to its inhabitants' enchanted ignorance of evil. Only this time, when evil comes in the shape of the four apocalyptic horsemen, "schoolteacher, one nephew, one slave catcher and a sheriff" (148) and disrupts the joyful harmony, hubris has replaced innocence. Years later, defending her infanticide to Paul D, Sethe still claims the "selfishness" that allowed her to stop schoolteacher, causing Paul D to reflect that she "didn't know where the world stopped and she began" (164). While exposing the demonic nature of Sethe's claim, Paul D's thought also reflects back on the kind of place 124 has become: a nether world deprived of safety.

If "hell is the world we live in when we are compelled to do so by [...] the folly and cruelty of others" (*WP*, 231), then 124 does seem to qualify. Left "desolate and exposed at the very hour when everybody stopped dropping by" (163), it is haunted for years by Beloved's ghost and becomes the space of alienation that Frye sees as the defining feature of the lower world (*WP*, 179). Shunned by the rest of the community, 124 becomes a place of retreat where its inhabitants deliberately shut themselves in.

Baby Suggs is the first to do this. As she later realizes, her fault was excessive generosity. The feast she organized, "a celebration of blackberries that put Christmas to shame" (147) was the last straw: faced with such bounty, the black community started to question her inordinate claim to love: "124, rocking with laughter, goodwill and food for ninety, made them angry. Too much they thought. Where does she get it all, Baby Suggs, holy? Why is she and hers always the center of things? How come she always knows exactly what to do and when? Giving advice; passing messages; healing the sick, hiding fugitives, loving, cooking [...] preaching, singing, dancing and loving everybody like it was her job and hers alone" (137). So they refrained from trying to prevent the "Misery." Defeated at last by such spite just as much as by Sethe's own murderous transgression, Baby Suggs takes to bed, "too ashamed of God to say so" (177). Likewise, Denver's timid attempt to venture outside 124 as a little girl is cut short by a classmate's question regarding her mother's infanticide. 124 and the field behind it then become "all the world she knew or wanted" (101). When her grandmother dies, Sethe and herself become its only and lonely inhabitants.

Alienated from others as well as from grace, haunted by the ghost of the dead baby, 124 turns into a recognizable form of hell because of the hubris of its female tenants. As Frye suggests, however, the original descent may be "complemented by a creative ascent, in the form of the revolutionary release of repressed elements, whether political or psychological": "The exploration of repressed worlds, and the study of techniques for releasing them, are, of course, what make Freud and Marx such portentous figures in the contemporary world. In the Old Testament the central image of this emancipating revolt is Exodus; in the New Testament it is the Resurrection, Christ's escape from death as well as hell" (*WP*, 238). Such a creative ascent appears as the impetus behind the narrative.

Creative vs Demonic Ascents

At the beginning of the novel, 124 and its inhabitants are prey to the repressed forces of the past, in the shape of the haunting presence of the dead baby's ghost or Sethe's own treacherous memory. Then, the release of this traumatic past starts with the arrival of Paul D, whose own escape from slavery is modelled on the resurrection pattern: the sunken quarters of the chain gang he is sent to after trying to kill his new master are likened to a grave and escape from it during a providential flood episode is a moment of collective resurrection: "One by one, from Hi Man back on down the line, they dove. Down through the mud under the bars, blind, groping. [...] The chain that held them would save all or none, and Hi Man was the Delivery. [...]. Like the unshriven dead, zombies on the loose, holding the chains in their hands, they trusted the rain and the dark, yes, but mostly Hi Man and each other" (110).

Instrumental as Paul D's presence will be to rid 124 of the dead baby's ghost, his own repressed memories are locked in his tobacco tin heart in just the same way as Sethe's hide behind her "iron eyes," and things would have remained so but for the other newcomer to the house: the supernatural, flesh-and-blood Beloved.

In this sense, Beloved's return from the dead first appears as a creative response to the characters' traumatic alienation, were it not for the destructive narcissistic circle into which she gradually entraps Sethe and Denver, then Sethe alone. Best expressed by the three women's monologues fusing into one to the same rapturous refrain of "you are mine," this enchanted, narcissistic coming together leads to a final erasure of self. As indicated by the recurring phrase "nobody saw them fall" in the skating episode preceding Sethe's realization of Beloved's identity, the return of the latter will cause yet another fall, deeper into alienation. The "no-time" Sethe anticipates as blissful liberation from the past thanks to her daughter's return (191) will, in fact, prove to submerge her in that past, an experience of time as "pure duration and power of annihilation" characteristic of the demonic world (*WP*, 179). This is the time of Beloved's world, the everlasting present of unredeemed death: "All of it is now it is always now there will never be a time when I am not crouching and watching others who are crouching too I am always crouching the man on my face is dead" (210).

To put it in Frye's terms again, the conversion of this ultimate demonic descent into a creative ascent that will finally liberate Sethe requires the external intervention of a loving being. For "only a 'Thou,' who is both another person and the identity of ourselves, releases the ability to love that gets us out of the world of shades and echoes [...] into the world of sunlight and freedom" (*WP*, 271). Denver, Paul D, and the community will play such a role for Sethe.

For Denver, such a rescue will require a personal act of resurrection. Not only must she disengage herself from the fateful trio, she will then have to leave 124, that is, "step off the edge of the world and die" (239) in order to "save" both Sethe and herself: "Somebody had to be saved, but unless Denver got work, there would be no one to save, no one to come home to, and no Denver either. It was a new thought, having a self to look out for and preserve" (252).

As for Paul D and the community, Sethe's salvation will require a physical, psychological, and spiritual regression. When they walk back to 124 for the first time in years, the first thing the thirty black women see is their past selves: "Younger, stronger, even as little girls lying in the grass asleep. [...] The fence they had leaned on and climbed over was gone. The stump of the butternut had split like a fan. But there they were, young and happy, playing in Baby Suggs' yard, not feeling the envy that surfaced the next day" (258). In similar fashion, Paul D's return to 124 "is the reverse route of his going" (263), the product of introspection and examination of "how he left and why" (267). In both cases – the women's communion with past days of communal felicity or Paul D's memory of his first feel of free life – the regression is no osmotic fusion with an irrepressible past like the "brainless urge to stay alive" that coupling with Beloved felt like to Paul D (264). Transmuting this demonic experience of a descent to "some ocean-deep place [he] once belonged to" (264) – the metaphorical hell of those who did not survive the Middle Passage – the women take a redemptive step "back to the beginning": "They stopped praying and took a step back to the beginning. In the beginning there were no words. In the beginning was the sound, and they all knew what that sound sounded like" (259). Connecting back with a prelapsarian and preverbal life force, the women free Sethe from Beloved, "the devil-child" (261). Their work of faith is then completed by Paul D's work of grace, as his "blessedness" (272) resurrects Sethe's endangered sense of self:

> "You your best thing, Sethe. You are." His holding fingers are holding hers.
> "Me? Me?" (273)

Resurrecting the personal and collective self from beneath layers of oppression and repressed memories seems to be the purpose of the mythical and metaphorical pattern underpinning the book: a pattern of fall from innocence, tragic hubris, and fall into death before the redemptive ascent to a redeemed sense of self. The novel thus offers no spiritual guidance for entering the other world but rather one for inhabiting our secular world as religious space: not in the usual sense of the word implying a separation between the sacred and profane but in its etymological sense of reconnection. Indeed, the novel suggests, our world could become paradise, "heaven as life; not heaven as post-life,"[15] were it cleansed of the demons of the past, while keeping them alive through storytelling so as not to permit relapse into fateful innocence. Then this world could become a place of caring interaction between people, based on clear limits between self and other. The model for it is, of course, the world of the novel. Indeed, Morrison's phrase in her Nobel lecture cited above seems to suggest that such a redemptive effect is the very function of literature. Frye would have assented, if one is to judge from his own words: "In proportion as we try to approach literature with a sense of personal involvement or commitment, one pole of it begins to look like the revelation of a paradisal state [...]. It is a world of individuals but not of egos, and a world where nature is no longer alien but seems to be, in the medieval phrase, our 'natural place'" (*WP*, 88). For fiction to acquire such a redeeming power, what are the implications regarding the relationship to language?

III Words with Power

Metaphorical Literalism and the Dangers of Ecstatic Identification

> The question has often been raised about the moral benefits of studying literature. [...] Almost any serious writer, if asked what kind of contact he wanted to make with his public, would say that his aim had something to do with making his reader a different person from what he was before. (*WP*, 77)

Exploring what might be called the "mechanics" of literature's transformative potential leads Frye to focus on metaphor. Starting from the premise that "literature always assumes, in its metaphors, a relation between human consciousness and its natural environment that passes beyond [...] the ordinary common sense based on a permanent separation of subject and object" (*WP*, 71), Frye then proceeds to delineate the specificity of what he calls "existential" metaphor. According to him, this particular kind of metaphor "not merely identifies one thing with another in words, but something of ourselves with both" (*WP*, 75–6). In "this conception of personally involving metaphor," the form of identity involved is no "identity *as*, which is a basis of ordinary knowledge," but "an identity *with* that is not found in ordinary experience" and implies "in every such form of identification [...] a renunciation of egocentric or subjective identity" (*WP*, 77–81). Quoting Montaigne – who declared his own book "consubstantial with his author" – as an illustration of this type of identity, Frye proceeds to suggest the similarity between the relation of the writer to his creation and "the elements of the Eucharist to the body of Christ" (*WP*, 81–2). This participative stance, which makes a creation true for us "whether we have been in on the making of it or on the responding to it" (*WP*, 82) recalls Nancy Berkowitz Bate's analysis of *Beloved* as Eucharistic:

> Morrison's book is Eucharistic in its comparisons of eating to reading, in its frequent juxtapositions of episodes of storytelling and images of eating or food preparation, and finally, in its inclusion of three symbolic Eucharists in the novel. [...] Novels, then, are similar to communion, in which the Christian remembers the life and crucifixion of Jesus, the "beloved Son." The communicant internalizes – eats – that memory, thus integrating Jesus with the self. In kind, Morrison desires that readers consume or internalize

> her ideas and her *Beloved*/Beloved. [...] *Beloved* dusts off the cliché of the Eucharist and revitalizes it.[16]

In a previous article, I suggested that Morrison's metaphorical writing, particularly as evidenced in *Beloved*, was a fundamental technique enabling the reader to partake in the characters' inner experiences.[17] My tentative labelling of this technique "magic realist" was an attempt to make sense of a strongly evocative narrative strategy, based on concrete imagery. Actually, in *Beloved*, the metaphorical quality of the narrative strives to make manifest what Denver terms "the downright pleasure of enchantment, of not suspecting but *knowing* the things behind things" (37). In her own case, her secret inner life – a mystery to all those surrounding her – is disclosed and made alive, shareable, through metaphors. One instance is the time when her anxiety about losing Beloved is rendered as an experience of actual dislocation: "She feels like an ice cake torn away from the solid surface of the stream, floating on darkness, thick and crashing against the edges of things around it. Breakable, meltable and cold" (123).

This illustrates Frye's remark that "of all images in literature, the most important are the characters, the personalities that do most to mediate between the author and its public" (*WP*, 71). In Morrison's novel, the main metaphorical kernel is, of course, Beloved herself, who actualizes the invisible presence of the haunting memory of slavery. Through her, Morrison seems to have given full literary expression to Frye's often-repeated contention that "real literal meaning is an imaginative and poetic one" (*WP*, xv). As the embodiment of cherished though suppressed collective and individual memory, Beloved is a manifestation of the meaning of her name, seven letters carved on a tombstone through forced procreation, becoming a living person through an act of imaginative creation. Throwing open "the doors of perception in the psyche, the doors of dream and fantasy as well as of waking consciousness" (*WP*, 83), Morrison's narration illustrates the liberating power of the imaginative mode with its capacity to disclose people's hidden, sometimes unconscious inner drama for all to share. Besides, as it resurrects Sethe's dead child, her narration also produces "some kind of union between the imaginative and the actual" (*WP*, 90) where we enter "the mysterious borderlands between the poetic and the kerygmatic" (*WP*, 111). Similarly, the plot appears to rest on what remained a carefully marginalized possibility in *The Scarlet Letter*: the romantic conception of letters (Beloved's name) becoming alive.[18]

As Frye warns, "every image of revelation, whether in the Bible or not, has its demonic parody or contrast" (*WP*, 87). Accordingly, the apparently redemptive power of the existential metaphor *Beloved* may be read as turned into its opposite: destructive osmosis. As Bate suggests, the Eucharistic Salvation described in the St John Gospel as "mutual indwelling" has risks when "experienced by Denver, Sethe, and the resurrected Beloved as a merging of identities."[19] For both Denver and Sethe, it spells death, as "Denver feels that she does not live when Beloved leaves her alone,"[20] while Sethe is ready to surrender her own life to Beloved's bottomless hunger for love. In both cases, Sethe and Denver experience selflessness not as the liberating renunciation of egocentrism but as a threat of annihilation. When enchantment becomes possession and the promises of redemption turn into the certainty of alienation, some kind of ultimate divisive power is needed to sever the ecstatic bond turned destructive.

Redeeming the Word

Frye's basic definition of metaphor signals the possible transgression of the redemptive process potentially coterminous with metaphorical identity. As he puts it, "literature always assumes, in its metaphors, a relation between human consciousness and its natural environment that *passes beyond –in fact, outrages and violates* – the ordinary common sense based on a permanent separation of subject and object" (*WP*, 71; emphasis added). In Morrison's novel, the threat of subjective disintegration caused by Sethe's ecstatic identity with Beloved is fully revealed: "Dressed in Sethe's dresses, [Beloved] stroked her skin with the palm of her hand. She imitated Sethe, talked the way she did, laughed her laugh and used her body the same way down to the walk, the way Sethe moved her hands, sighed through her nose, held her head. Sometimes coming upon them [...], it was difficult for Denver to tell who was who" (241).

While the aim of all spiritual quests is such self-absorbing identity in a higher force (the Holy Spirit for Christians), which leads to redemption through the limited ego's fusion in the non-limited nature of that higher force, the danger of such ecstatic identity is obvious when the "object" identified with is the individual and collective living force of the past and of the unconscious embodied by Beloved. Then the spirit becomes that of demonic possession, whose hold on the subject must be broken if she or he is to survive. In *Beloved*, this is achieved through a collective return to "the sound" that there was "in the beginning [when] there were no words" (259), that is, the Word: "The voices of women searched for the right combination, the key, the code, the sound that broke the back of words. Building voice upon voice until they found it, and when they did it was a wave of sound wide enough to sound deep water and knock the pods off chestnut trees. It broke over Sethe and she trembled like the baptized in its wash" (261). Interestingly, as Frye remarks, "the 'Word,' in the New Testament, has associations of division and discrimination" (*WP*, 89). So, the women's Wordlike chant will sever the fusional and destructive bond between mother and demonic child, driving Beloved away and making it possible for Sethe to come to some eventual, tentative sense of self. While this echoes McClure's reading of *Beloved* as a secular Epistle on the art of discernment warning against "the perils of enchanted enclosure,"[21] the efficiency of the collective Word does call for a further examination of Morrison's prose, particularly in the novel's epilogue.

Viewed from a metaliterary perspective, the novel's last two pages appear as the story of the genesis, birth, and death of Beloved as existential metaphor, leaving in its place a felt symbolic presence expressed through the last seven letters.

The embodiment of an initial feeling of "loneliness," equipped with "arms crossed" and "knees drawn up," "she" first appears in the position of a foetus, before the issue of her name suggests the aborted birth of an individual identity: for "everybody knew what she was called, but nobody anywhere knew her name" (274). Swallowed by the "chewing laughter" and forgotten "like a bad dream," Beloved's anonymous physical presence gradually dissolves as people's memory absorbs it, so they "began to believe that, other than what they themselves were thinking, she hadn't said anything at all" (274). Remaining as "weather" and the bare suggestion of a "clamor for a kiss," her conversion from haunting presence into peaceful epitaph ("Beloved") is complete. In the end, the letters of her name are like Sethe's house: "unloaded" and "quiet" (264).

In a way, the epilogue would thus seem to consecrate the death of metaphorical language as haunted language. In place of the threatened annihilation of the subject through identity with a demonic object, the epilogue suggests a way towards a dispossessed language: no longer haunted, though not empty, it becomes suggestive of a subtle Presence. In the final inscription of Beloved's name, this paradoxical sense of presence evoked through her absence points in the direction of a "verbal communication coming from a Word made flesh, a presence in whom the distinction between the end and the means of communication has disappeared" (*WP*, 110). Such verbal communication, which is the definition of the New Testament as Gospel according to Frye, produces "truthful fiction." Such fiction, as Jean Wilson notes, depends on a re-creation of language: "In her 'recreating of language,' as Frye would put it, Morrison [...] revives 'that original, metaphorical sense of immediacy' that Frye associates with the first phase of language. [...] Morrison [...] offers what Frye would describe as 'a vision of reality that is something other than history or logic'; hers is an imaginative vision whose transformative power begins 'to remake the world.'"[22]

In other words, Morrison's imaginative mode manages to become redemptive thanks to its "literary literalism," which reinstates language's original "metaphorical immediacy," for "the true literal sense ... is metaphorical."[23] While Jean Wilson also notes Morrison's "astonishingly concrete vocabulary" as a sign of that "metaphorical immediacy" at work in the novel, my preceding analysis would purport to suggest that such immediacy revives metaphorical language as the medium of spiritual unity rather than subjective alienation. As Wilson points out, not only is Morrison working against the contemporary grain and the tendency to use a falsely literal language, "the narrative's work of reclaiming 'what language was made for' involves a re-imagining and reconfiguring of conventional relationships and conceptions of love."[24] The model for such a reconfiguration in the novel is suggested by Beloved's departure and Paul D's return, a conversion of fusional into spiritual love: "For the New Testament, the Word clarifies, the Spirit unifies, and the two together create what is the only genuine form of human society, the spiritual kingdom of Jesus, founded on the *caritas* or love which for Paul is not one virtue among others but the only virtue there is" (*WP*, 89).

To illustrate the "renunciation of egocentric or subjective identity" conveyed in the ecstatic or existential metaphor, Frye takes the example of the lover, the poetic one-flesh metaphor being a good representation of the "identification with" process at stake in existential metaphor. As *Beloved* shows, however, carried to its ultimate conclusion, the actual merging of two bodies leads to the death of the subject. The difference between Paul D's final offer of care and Beloved's self-consuming demand for love is one between redemptive love and its demonic parody. As Frye states: "The capacity to merge with another person's being without violating it seems to be at the center of love, just as the will to dominate one conscious soul-will externally by another is the center of all tyranny and hatred" (*WP*, 126).

Such respectful inner merging seems precisely what Morrison's poetic prose aims at, attesting to the fact that the essential function of literature is, at heart, profoundly redemptive.

Conclusion: Kerygma and the Promises of Postsecular Imagination in Postmodern Times

There is a tradition of viewing American cultural history, particularly as expressed by its literature, as a kind of fall from innocence. Famously introduced by R.W.B. Lewis, the myth of the American as Adam has been, in its author's own terms, "frowned quite out of existence" and what began "as a valuable corrective to the claims of innocence in America [...] has declined into a cult of original sin," generating a culture of scepticism, the "chilling skepticism of the mid-twentieth century" which, in Lewis's own terms, "represents one of the modes of death."[1] Likewise, Leslie Fiedler notes, "the American writer [...] lives on the last horizon of an endlessly retreating vision of innocence,"[2] while Tony Tanner contends that the naïve wonderer, a characteristic of American literature, "has become more and more alienated."[3]

Still, those same critics also agree that "there is, undoubtedly, an occasional vitality in American fiction. And wherever we find it, we encounter again traces of the hopeful or Adamic tradition."[4] In Tanner's words, "it is hard to think of many major American novels which do not in some way incorporate in them the notion of a search, a quest, a more than physical journey."[5] Is this, then, to say that all we are left with to achieve some kind of coherent vision of American fiction is Emerson's classic division into the parties of Memory and Hope,[6] which might be rephrased as that of Scepticism and Faith?[7]

What the preceding study hopes to have shown would be more in keeping with Mark C. Taylor's analysis of the "paradoxical faith" that seems to have emerged as a result of the immanence of transcendence that Taylor thinks was conceptualized in the nineteenth century and actualized in the twentieth.[8] In fact, as this work hopes to suggest, the history of American fiction and that of modern theology and religion as delineated by Taylor seem to run curiously parallel courses. As my analysis of the relationship to transcendence in *The Scarlet Letter* and *The Europeans* has meant to explore, Hawthorne's and James's novels read like two steps in an overall process leading to "the death of the moral God, [which] creates the possibility of the birth of the divine artist whose creative activity is beyond good and evil."[9] In turn, this initiates a gradual immanentizing of transcendence oscillating between the opposed poles of an anguished call for transcendence (*The Great Gatsby, On the Road*) and developing awareness of secular sacrality (*The Grapes of Wrath, Beloved*), strangely echoing Taylor's history of modern theology as "grow[ing] out of the repeated 'altarnation' between the monism of immanence and the dualism of transcendence."[10] Defining "altarity" as "a dimension of sacrality, which is neither simply transcendent nor immanent but is an immanent transcendence that disrupts and dislocates systems, structures, and schemata that seem to be secure,"[11] Taylor offers an interesting way of considering the complex interrelation between immanence and transcendence in American fiction, making them anything but polar opposites while suggesting that this notion of immanent transcendence might be a way of developing "an account of the divine as the infinite life of creative emergence."[12] In Taylor's words: "The immanent transcendence of altarity transforms human agents into vehicles of a creative process that is more encompassing than their individual activity. The artist, as Nietzche observes, is the *medium* through which 'the true Subject celebrates His redemption in illusion.'"[13]

While I would not follow Taylor in his view of virtual reality as "something like an immanent transcendence,"[14] his notion of creative emergence does offer an interesting way of assessing the religious valence of secular fiction in a non-dichotomic way, while curiously rephrasing the romantic belief that "God and the imagination become one in the bacchanalian revel of a world that is a work of art."[15]

This brings me back to Frye's avowedly romantic theory of literature. When considered from a Frygian perspective, the previous chapters suggest a tentative vision of the literature of the United States as that of a dialogue between human imagination and the divine. In this dialogue, there is the suggestion of an evolution best described as a spiralling process, away from a state of bondage to a frightful transcendent divinity, to an immanent experience of Charity, "the only genuine element that has survived the 'appalling historical record of Christianity' with its long list of heresy hunt, militancy, intolerance, and demonic perversions,"[16] through periodic lapses into disoriented alienation.[17] A first step in this evolution, Hawthorne and James appear as hopeful literary advocates of secularization and its promises of worldly felicity. While for Hawthorne, still very much a hostage to the Puritan mindset, such a perspective remains utopian, James's *The Europeans* happily claims its advent, despite forebodings of an increasingly complex relationship to meaning and reality. Conversely, with Fitzgerald, the time for rejoicing is long gone. In his modernist world of alienating materialism, meaningful relationships and true love are fading memories, and the quest for transcendence has turned into a doomed effort to rise above the wasteland of worldly parties. Erring in a spiritless world devoid of meaning, human beings have exchanged enchantment for excitement to hide the vacuity eating at their hearts. Wholly echoing this tragic vision, Kerouac only intensifies the pace of the purposeless quest, in the deluded hope that trance might bring felicity. However, although also extolling a pseudoheroic character who embodies the narrator's own search for transcendence, Kerouac's quest somewhat differs from Fitzgerald's: far from bemoaning the loss of a Platonic kind of transcendence, his own journey is firmly rooted in secular experience, and the ecstasy sought is just as much sexual as mystical. Still, even if girls are part and parcel of the envisioned treasure at the end of the road, the beat goal much transcends human love in its wild yearning for "everything" (*On the Road*, 10).

A perceptible shift thus seems to have occurred between the "lost" twenties and the beat fifties as regards the literary outlook on transcendence. This change might probably best be described as entry into a postsecular world, where transcendence again becomes a possibility. Its shape, however, dramatically differs from the omniscient and omnipotent God happily deposed by modernity. In the postsecular universe, the heavy moral weight attached to the divine has gone, leaving in its wake a potent human longing for spiritual experience. Such a turn to immanence as the site of revelation is visible in Steinbeck's *Grapes of Wrath*, which might be considered as a transitional work, both permeated with a still recognizable Christian type of faith and discarding its traditional teleological outlook. With Kerouac's beat novel, a further feature of postsecularity is introduced: the hybridization of religious referents. Both Christian and Buddhist, his search for beatitude is a good introduction to the "religious innovation constitutive of postsecular fiction."[18] While thus fully endorsing McClure's analysis regarding this characteristic articulation of "hybridized forms of belief" as defining literary postsecularism,[19] I am only in partial agreement with his statement that this postsecular treatment of scripture corresponds to a "weakened" form of belief. True, "postsecular narratives affirm the urgent need for a turn toward the religious even as they reject [...] the most familiar dream of full return to an authoritative faith."[20] Still, if based on the rejection of religious discourse as voicing "absolute conviction and doctrinal conformity,"[21] postsecular expressions of faith are anything but weak. In the literary works reviewed, postsecular spirituality claims resurrecting and redemptive power. As already evidenced with the dramatization of kerygma in *The Scarlet Letter*, the literature of the United States seems driven by an imaginative quest for the full power of the Word, the actual heaven of its pilgrims' journey. Nonetheless, in its progression between the dialectic poles of immanence and transcendence, it sometimes falls prey to the deceptive inflation of the ego: "'Without a contrary,' Michael Dolzani has written in a seminal essay, the Blakean identification of the human and divine 'will result in what Jung called inflation, when the ego puffs itself up into a transcendental ego ... The only thing that can follow, in a manic-depressive cycle, is deflation.'"[22] Such is the case with Kerouac's beat progress and already before that, Fitzgerald's nostalgic romanticism. Yet, each fall into the demonic pit of despair is answered by a fulfilled kerygmatic form in another work: prophecy in *The Grapes of Wrath* and interpenetration in *Beloved* are two of them.

Defining insight as "kerygma with a subjective focus, [which] prophetic writers have" (*LN*, 1: 418), Northrop Frye suggests the potentially varied expressions of the kerygmatic. This interpenetration of the human and the divine may, indeed, take various narrative forms, itself being "all content and so without form."[23] With its focus on "the human medium transmitting the kerygmatic to the idiom of ordinary language" (*WP*, 118), the prophetic seems to be the shape it assumes in *The Grapes of Wrath* with its Christlike characters and polysemous realism aiming at symbolic vision. Frye's definition of love as interpenetration, on the other hand, sums up the very point made by Morrison's narrative of transgression in *Beloved*: "'Love is interpenetration, but it has to extend beyond the sexual interpenetrating of intercourse. Every act of hostility is penetration with a threat, with a desire to dominate or acquire for oneself. Love means entering into and identifying with other people and things without threats or domination, in fact without retaining an ego-self' (*LN*, 1: 209–10)."[24]

Still, notwithstanding their differing narrative strategies, these two instances of kerygmatic fiction produce the same kind of reading experience: one of unity as identity without uniformity, a spiritual experience of the literary that Frye seems to have striven to theorize through his focus on metaphor and the concept of interpenetration. Such a reading experience manifests the "evidence of things not seen," the "reality of what is created in the production and response to literature"[25] that Frye grappled with in his attempt to define the kerygmatic mode.[26] Such intangible yet transformative reality, in turn, answers "Frye's aspiration in *Words with Power* [...] to show the possibility of a 'more inclusive mode of verbal communication' usually called imaginative, one that 'takes us into a more open-ended world, breaking apart the solidified dogmas that ideologies seem to hanker for' [...] [and that] releases the creative energy needed to transform the alienated 'It-world' into a home."[27] In the current postmodern context, this redemptive potential of the literary experience seems in urgent need of being addressed.

In *Intimations of Postmodernity*, Zygmunt Bauman defined postmodernity as a "state of mind marked above all by its all-deriding, all-eroding, all-dissolving *destructiveness*, [...] a critique caught at the moment of its ultimate triumph, [when] it has destroyed everything it used to be critical about."[28] This is true, though, we would hopefully argue, only of one phase in the postmodern process. Just as modernity's self-confident trust in its capacity to do away with transcendence was to founder on the rocks of materialistic sterility and modernist despair, so postmodernity's claim to nihilistic subversion encounters its own limitation in the human search for fullness. In this sense, if "the postmodern state of mind is the radical [...] victory of modern (that is, inherently critical, restless, unsatisfied, insatiable) culture over the modern society it aimed to improve through throwing it wide open to its potential,"[29] its victory has its positive expression in the very "potential" it makes manifest. "A new Copernican revolution [...] not in cosmology but in consciousness [...], postmodernity affects not simply how we think about the world, but how we actually *experience* it."[30] Indeed, when all ideological constructs have been deconstructed, sole experience is what remains. Interestingly, Derrida himself wrote that "what remains irreducible to any deconstruction, what remains as undeconstructible as the possibility itself of deconstruction is, perhaps, a certain *experience* of the emancipatory promise."[31] Also defined as "a messianism without religion,"[32] such an experience is the basis of

Derrida's idea of justice as well as, we would contend, the foundation of postsecular imagination.

In the end, Jean-Luc Nancy's call for a deconstruction, or rather dis-enclosure, of Christianity should have the last word, as it most beautifully phrases the very spirit of this project: "Is is such a knowledge – if it is a knowledge at all – that we approach here: a knowledge of a very simple, even elementary, disposition toward the 'outside the world' ['hors du monde'] in the very midst of the world, a disposition toward a transcendence *of* immanence."[33]

Notes

Introduction

1 Despite the controversy surrounding the exact terms of this prediction, which Malraux himself disowned, we have retained it precisely because the heated debate it has engendered is indicative of its cultural perceptiveness.
2 Charles Taylor, *A Secular Age* (Cambridge MA: Belknap Press, 2007), 15.
3 Ibid., 539.
4 Ibid., 21.
5 Ibid., 19.
6 Ibid., 19.
7 Ibid., 589.
8 Ibid., 545.
9 Peter L. Berger, *The Desecularization of the World: Resurgent Religion and World Politics* (Grand Rapids, MI: William B. Eerdmans, 1999), 6; original emphasis.
10 Ibid., 9–10.
11 Ibid., 10; original emphasis.
12 Ibid.
13 Christopher Partridge, *The Re-Enchantment of the West* (London: T&T Clark International, 2004), 39.
14 Ibid., 38.
15 Ibid., 1.
16 Ibid., 4.
17 This phrase is used by Partridge to refer to "the new subculture of dissent and opposition" that he sees as replacing the "deteriorating/secularized Christian culture" (ibid., 40). See also Jeffrey Kaplan and Heléne Lööw's *The Cultic Milieu* (Walnut Creek, CA: AltaMira Press, 2002).

18 George Levine, *Darwin Loves You: Natural Selection and the Re-enchantment of the World* (Princeton, NJ: Princeton University Press, 2006), xiii.
19 Ibid., xv.
20 Ibid., xvi.
21 Ibid., xv.
22 Mark C. Taylor's introduction to *Critical Terms for Religious Studies* (Chicago: University of Chicago Press, 1998), 2.
23 Ibid., 4.
24 William E. Connolly, "Refashioning the Secular," in Judith Butler, John Guillory, and Kendall Thomas, eds., *What's Left of Theory? New Work on the Politics of Literary Theory* (New York: Routledge, 2000), 157. See also William E. Connolly, *Why I Am Not a Secularist* (Minneapolis, MN: University of Minnesota Press, 1999).
25 Graham Ward, "Introduction: Where We Stand," in Graham Ward, ed., *The Blackwell Companion to Postmodern Theology* (Oxford: Blackwell, 2001), xv.
26 John A. McClure, *Partial Faiths: Postsecular Fiction in the Age of Pynchon and Morrison* (Athens, GA: University of Georgia Press, 2007), 7.
27 Graham Ward, ed., *The Postmodern God: A Theological Reader* (Oxford: Blackwell, 1997), xxii, xlii.
28 Regina Schwartz, ed., *Transcendence: Philosophy, Literature, and Theology Approach the Beyond* (New York: Routledge, 2004), ix.
29 Kevin J. Vanhoozer, ed., *The Cambridge Companion to Postmodern Theology* (Cambridge: Cambridge University Press, 2003), 4.
30 Ibid., 14.
31 Graham Ward, "Introduction: Where We Stand," xv.
32 Brian D. Ingraffia, "Is the Postmodern Post-Secular?" in Merold Westphal, ed., *Postmodern Philosophy and Christian Thought* (Bloomington, IN: Indiana University Press, 1999), 44–68.
33 Vanhoozer, *The Cambridge Companion*, 21–2.
34 See Brian D. Ingraffia, *Postmodern Theory and Biblical Theology* (Cambridge: Cambridge University Press, 1995).
35 Vanhoozer, *The Cambridge Companion*, 23.
36 Ibid., 23–4; original emphasis.
37 Ward, *The Postmodern God*, xliii.
38 Vanhoozer, *The Cambridge Companion*, 24.
39 Ibid., 23; original emphasis.
40 Paul S. Fiddes, ed., *The Novel, Spirituality and Modern Culture: Eight Novelists Write about Their Craft and Their Context* (Cardiff: University of Wales Press, 2000), 11.

41 Philip Sheldrake, *A Brief History of Spirituality* (Oxford: Blackwell, 2007), xi.

42 Andrew Tate, in *Contemporary Fiction and Christianity* (London: Continuum, 2008), speaks of a "non-creedal spirituality" (128). In *Postmodern Belief: American Literature and Religion since 1960* (Princeton, NJ: Princeton University Press, 2010), Amy Hungerford even defines postmodern belief as "belief without content" or "belief in meaninglessness" (xiii–xiv), suggesting a creative side to Vanhoozer's view of postmodernity as an ailing spiritual condition.

43 Sheldrake, *A Brief History*, xi.

44 Arthur Holder, ed., *The Blackwell Companion to Christian Spirituality* (Oxford: Blackwell, 2011), 1.

45 Though lying outside the scope of the present work, Kevin Hart and Barbara Wall, in *The Experience of God: A Postmodern Response* (New York: Fordham University Press, 2005), provide illuminating insight into the conceptual complexity of the word "experience" when "placed near that wild word 'God'" (xi).

46 Vanhoozer's view of postmodernity's interest in language and his previous analysis of "the postmodern condition of knowledge," interestingly, tie up with our own concept of "experience" as central to the postmodern condition, though adding a Christian colouring to it: "The mark of the postmodern condition of knowledge, then, is a move away from the authority of universal science toward narratives of local knowledge. Eating from the postmodern tree of knowledge occasions a new 'fall' and loss of innocence. No longer can we aspire to the knowledge of angels, much less a God's eye point of view" (*The Cambridge Companion*, 10). This also lends support to Charles Taylor's observation regarding the loss of religious naïveté as a feature of our secular age, which accounts for the plural character of postsecular spirituality.

47 Vanhoozer, *The Cambridge Companion*, 13.

48 Likewise, it could be argued that the cinema's direct appeal to sensual experience may account for the cultural power it has acquired as well as for the fact that it has arguably come to displace literature in much the same way that literary theory has done for philosophy.

49 Mark Knight and Thomas Woodman, eds., *Biblical Religion and the Novel, 1700–2000* (Aldershot: Ashgate, 2006), 5. Likewise, Fiddes writes: "There seems [...] to be [...] a potential for convergence between the spiritual journey and the effects of a novel, and this might be strengthened by the more general idea of a story" (*The Novel, Spirituality and Modern Culture*, 1).

50 Martin Corner, "Opening the Literal: Spirituality in Updike and Ford," in Knight and Woodman, *Biblical Religion and the Novel*, 150.

51 Knight and Woodman, *Biblical Religion*, 5. While I am here focusing on the theological dialogue with postmodern theory – as in Graham Ward, *Theology and Contemporary Critical Theory* (London: Macmillan, 1996) – the postmodern philosophical engagement with theology will be dealt with in the latter part of this introduction.
52 Vanhoozer, *The Cambridge Companion*, 25; emphasis added.
53 In *Partial Faiths*, 4.
54 Tate, *Contemporary Fiction and Christianity*, 1.
55 McClure, *Partial Faiths*, ix.
56 Tate, *Contemporary Fiction*, 126–8.
57 Hungerford, *Postmodern Belief*, xiii.
58 Being concerned with tracking signs of "ontological opening" (McClure, *Partial Faiths*, 3) in our Western (post)modern culture, as expressed by some of its literature, the present study will not address the issue of contemporary fundamentalism.
59 Dennis Taylor, "The Need for a Religious Literary Criticism," *Religion and the Arts* 1/1, 1997, no page number. As Dennis Taylor also notes: "To say there is a great vacuum in discussions of spirituality in literature is, of course, unfair to those who have long been working in this field, and whose work might be associated with journals like *Religion and Literature, Christianity and Literature, Literature and Theology, Renascence*, and others. But even the editors and writers of these journals would probably agree that their discourse is not yet one of the major discourses in the academy" (n.p.). In *Towards A Christian Literary Theory* (New York: Palgrave Macmillan, 2003), notably, Luke Ferretter examines some of the most important work done in the field of religion and literature, which has become an established discipline in the United States since the 1950s.
60 Even though America does not equate the United States, in this work, American fiction is understood to refer exclusively to literary works from the United States.
61 Beyond the French context, Mark C. Taylor, in *After God* (Chicago: University of Chicago Press, 2007), notes that "there are […] forces beyond as well as within the university that make responsible reflection on [the influence of religion] difficult if not impossible. […] Political correctness on the left becomes religious correctness on the right. The deepening entrenchment of opposing views creates a growing resistance to every form of criticism and makes constructive dialogue virtually impossible. It is precisely this resistance that underscores the urgent need for renewed critical analysis" (4).

62 In *Palimpsests* (1984), Gérard Genette examines the various types of relationships a text may have with prior texts, the latter being referred to as "hypotexts." Gerald Prince notes: "Any text is a hypertext, grafting itself onto a hypotext, an earlier text that it imitates or transforms; any writing is rewriting; and literature is always in the second degree" (foreword to Gérard Genette, *Palimpsests: Literature in the Second Degree,* trans. Channa Newman and Claude Doubinsky (Lincoln, NB: University of Nebraska Press, 1997), ix).
63 Knight and Woodman, *Biblical Religion*, 4.
64 David Bevan, ed., *Literature and the Bible* (Amsterdam: Rodopi, 1993), 3; original emphasis.
65 Ibid., 4.
66 The following quote is from Northrop Frye, *Words with Power: Being a Second Study of* The Bible and Literature (Harcourt Brace Jovanovich, 1990), xxi–xxii. Hereafter *WP*.
67 Robert D. Denham, ed., *Northrop Frye: Religious Visionary and Architect of the Spiritual World* (Charlottesville: University of Virginia Press, 2004). Hereafter *RV*.
68 Ibid., 1.
69 Ibid., xi.
70 Ibid., 2.
71 Ibid., 5–7.
72 "One of the United Church's organizational aims was to move personal relationships out of dogmatic straitjackets. Denominationalism in particular was thought by many religious leaders in Canada and abroad to be a highly discreditable straitjacket. Religiously speaking, Frye was a child of his times in Canada" (Ian Sloan, "The Reverend H. Northrop Frye," in David Rampton, ed., *Northrop Frye: New Directions from Old* (Ottawa: University of Ottawa Press, 2009), 106.
73 Ibid., 112.
74 Ibid.
75 This conception of language appears in *The Great Code*, stated as follows: "To use a convenient French distinction: there is in addition to the *langue* that separates English and French and German, also a *langage* that makes it possible to express similar things in all three languages. [...] Human creative expression all over the world has some degree of mutual intelligibility and communicating power. [...] What we call *langage,* then, is a very positive linguistic force. One wonders whether it is substantial enough for there to be such a thing as a history of *langage,* a sequence

of modes of more or less translatable structures in words, cutting across the variety of *langues* employed, affected and conditioned but not wholly determined by them" (Northrop Frye, *The Great Code* (New York: Harcourt Brace Jovanovich, 1982), 5; hereafter *GC*).

76 One could even go as far as to view some theories such as Baudrillard's regarding the ultimately virtual character of reality as the perverse result of an alienated subjectivity's fundamentally unexamined assumptions concerning its own positioning to the reality it theorizes. As Zygmunt Bauman puts it, in *Intimations of Postmodernity* (London: Routledge, 1992), 154–5: "The world [Jean Baudrillard] paints seems to be one likely to be seen by a person glued to the television screen; a person who replaced with TV screens the windows in the apartment he inhabits and in the car in which he travels to his university lectures. [...] One suspects, *pace* Baudrillard, that there is life after and beyond the television." In the same vein, Sára Tóth, in her essay "Recovery of the Spiritual Other: Martin Buber's 'Thou' in Northrop Frye's Late Work" (in Rampton, *Northrop Frye*), examines the way Frye "transforms [...] Lacan's narrative of alienation into a redemptive vision" (124).

77 Denham, *RV*, ix.

78 Abbreviated to *AC*.

79 Denham, *RV*, 14.

80 Ibid., 13.

81 Rampton, introduction to his *Northrop Frye*, xx.

82 "Literature in Education," in Jean O'Grady, ed., *Interviews with Northrop Frye*, vol. 24 of the Collected Works of Northrop Frye (Toronto: University of Toronto Press, 2008), 461–2.

83 Robert D. Denham, ed., *Northrop Frye's Late Notebooks, 1982–1990: Architecture of the Spiritual World*, vol. 5 of the Collected Works of Northrop Frye (Toronto: University of Toronto Press, 2000), hereafter *LN*, quoted in Denham, *RV*, 260.

84 Denham, *RV*, 260.

85 Sloan ("The Reverend H. Northrop Frye," 111) is quoting Frye's Notebook 44, quote 496, from *LN*, 209.

86 Nelson Hilton, *Literal Imagination: Blake's Vision of Words* (Berkeley: University of California Press, 1983), 4–8; original emphasis.

87 Alvin A. Lee, "Sacred and Secular Scripture(s) in the Thought of Northrop Frye," in Jeffery Donaldson and Alan Mendelson, eds., *Frye and the Word: Religious Contexts in the Writings of Northrop Frye* (Toronto: University of Toronto Press, 2004), 29.

88 Tóth, "Recovery of the Spiritual Other," 123.
89 One also finds Frye's central concern for the Word within the word expressed as the quest for the "word within the Word," as in Garry Sherbert's essay "Frye's 'Pure Speech': Literature and the Sacred without the Sacred," in Rampton, *Northrop Frye*. I take this possible inversion in the succession of capital and lower case as the sign of the interpenetrating process between the secular and sacred poles in literature, the order of precedence depending on the pole being stressed. Sherbert's aim was to study "Frye's way of interrogating the 'secularised sacred' in literature, a sacredness that goes beyond the determined faiths, our inherited religious traditions, toward a 'sacred without the sacred'" (142). My own approach would rather tend to emphasize the spiritual potential of secular literature, thus the Word within the word rather than the other way round.
90 This magnum opus is made up of *The Great Code* (*GC*, 1982) and its sequel *Words with Power* (*WP*, 1990).
91 Denham's introduction to *Northrop Frye's Late Notebooks*, xxv.
92 Denham, *RV*, 255.
93 Quoted in Imre Salusinszky, "'In the Climates of the Mind': Frye's Career as a Spiritual Curriculum," in Donaldson and Mendelson, *Frye and the Word*, 51.
94 Frye himself referred to the "spiral alchemical shape" his projected Third Book was to have (quoted in Salusinszky, ibid., 55).
95 Ibid.
96 Denham, *RV*, 252.
97 Salusinszky, "'In the Climates of the Mind,'" 54.
98 For a study of Frye's vision of imagination as well as of his key concepts of *Aufhebung* and interpenetration, see Denham's magisterial study *Northrop Frye: Religious Visionary and Architect of the Spiritual World*.
99 Salusinszky, "'In the Climates of the Mind,'" 52.
100 Jeffery Donaldson's introduction to Donaldson and Mendelson, *Frye and the Word*, 11.
101 Northrop Frye, "The Koine of Myth: Myth as a Universally Intelligible Language," in Robert D. Denham, ed., *Myth and Metaphor: Selected Essays, 1974–1988* (Charlottesville: University Press of Virginia, 1990), 7.
102 See n75.
103 Robert D. Denham, introduction to Robert D. Denham, ed., *Northrop Frye's Notebooks and Lectures on the Bible and Other Religious Texts*, vol. 13 of the Collected Works of Northrop Frye (Toronto: University of Toronto

Press, 2003), xl–xliii; hereafter *RT*, to take up Denham's own abbreviation in *RV*.

104 Denham, *RV*, 95.

105 Ibid., 77.

106 Ibid., 78.

107 Ibid., 79.

108 Denham, *RT*, xlvi.

109 Denham, *RV*, 55.

110 Ibid.

111 Frye (*GC*, 30) acknowledged his debt to Bultmann, despite openly disagreeing with him regarding the latter's view of myth: "The word *kerygma* is associated mainly with the theology of Bultmann, and in Bultmann's view *kerygma* is to be opposed to myth, which he regards as an obstacle to it. In the next chapter I shall give my reasons for saying that myth is the linguistic vehicle of *kerygma*, and that to 'demythologize' any part of the Bible would be the same thing as to obliterate it."

112 Indeed, Frye made "frequent assertions that the myths and metaphors of secular literature are always hypothetical, whereas those of the Bible are existential, having designs on the reader's consciousness and aiming to change his life. [...] In fact it is mostly in the more uninhibited context of his notebooks that the word 'kerygma' is used in connection with secular writers" (Jean O'Grady, "Re-valuing Value," in Rampton, *Northrop Frye*, 234–5).

113 Ibid., 234.

114 Frye (*LN*, 1:61) himself defines the raising of consciousness as revelation (quoted in Denham, *RV*, 82).

115 Denham, *RV*, 260.

116 Sherbert, "Frye's 'Pure Speech,'" 151.

117 Frye's major concern with Christian Revelation is hardly perceptible in his famous *Anatomy of Criticism* (1957), while it very much shapes his line of argument in *Words with Power* (1990). Likewise, *Of Grammatology* (1967) seems very far from Derrida's later concerns with messianism, the gift or faith, though, as Caputo reminds us, very early on, deconstruction was – wrongly, he argues – likened to negative theology. See John D. Caputo, "The Apophatic," in *The Prayers and Tears of Jacques Derrida: Religion without Religion* (Bloomington, IN: Indiana University Press, 1997), 1–68.

118 Northrop Frye, *The Critical Path*, in Jean O'Grady and Eva Kushner, eds., The Critical Path *and Other Writings on Critical Theory 1963–1975*, vol. 27

of the Collected Works of Northrop Frye (Toronto: University of Toronto Press, 2009), 17.

119 Sherbert, "Frye's 'Pure Speech,'" 149–50.

120 Caputo, *Prayers and Tears*, xxi.

121 A distinction is to be made, however, between Frye and Derrida regarding their approach to theory as a structure of religious experience: for Frye, the impulse to theorize very much resulted from a number of personal epiphanies (see his previously quoted remark: "I've spent nearly eighty years trying to articulate intuitions that occupied about five minutes of my entire life," *LN*, 2: 636). Derrida, for his part, is a self-proclaimed atheist, as Caputo stresses, "with respect to the God of the orthodox faiths." Yet, his is a "broken alliance and ring that manages still to bind him to Judaism," a paradoxical stance that Caputo calls "the religion without religion of Jacques Derrida, in a new *alliance*" (*Prayers and Tears*, xviii–xix; original emphasis). Derrida's route to theory, as the attempt to translate theological concepts (such as messianism in *Specters of Marx*) or biblical episodes (like Abraham's sacrifice of Isaac in *The Gift of Death*) into theoretical insights into those concepts or episodes as structures of experience would thus appear a reverse one as compared with Frye's theorizing of experience.

122 Paul De Man, "The Return to Philology," in *The Resistance to Theory* (Manchester: Manchester University Press, 1986), 29.

123 Caputo, *Prayers and Tears*, xix.

124 Ibid., xix, xxiii.

125 In Caputo's words, "deconstruction arises from 'a certain experience of the promise' *sans* the dogmatics of any particular faith [...], where 'experience' is taken [...] in messianic terms as the expectation of something unrepresentable, [...] a certain absolute experience. [...] This promise is the passion of deconstruction, [...] the religious aspiration of deconstruction. Deconstruction [...] is driven mad by the promise, by an impossible deal, by a covenant cut with the *tout autre*" (ibid., xxi; original emphasis).

126 Lars Sandbeck, "God as Immanent Transcendence in Mark C. Taylor and John D. Caputo," *Studia Theologica* 65 (2011), 20.

127 Mark C. Taylor, *Erring: A Postmodern A/theology* (Chicago: University of Chicago Press, 1984), 103.

128 "Taylor develops his notion of God as immanent transcendence by referring to Hegel's interpretation of God's incarnation in Jesus Christ. This irruptive movement marks the end of God's transcendence. The God who comes after the incarnation and death of God is, according to Taylor,

not Hegelian spirit but the imagination [...]. Taylor's work thereby suggests an abiding faith in a certain unfathomable creativity (God) that is definitely more aesthetical than ethical, a God beyond good and evil" (Sandbeck, "God as Immanent Transcendence," 33).

129 I feel that the increasingly complex relationship to reality in James's fiction, generally interpreted as signalling the advent of modernism, does betray a kind of existentialist anguish pertaining to the disappearance of the God of transcendence as warrant of reality's stable and decipherable meaning. In this sense, *The Europeans* has been chosen as the most unambiguous illustration in James's fiction of a wholehearted celebration of artistic creativity premised upon the death of the transcendent God of ethics.

130 Taylor, *Erring*, 142.

131 Walter Lowe, "A Deconstructionist Manifesto: Mark C. Taylor's *Erring*," *Journal of Religion* 66/3 (1986), 327.

132 Taylor, *Erring*, 103, original emphasis.

133 Sandbeck, "God as Immanent Transcendence," 23.

134 The term is borrowed from Linda Hutcheon, *A Poetics of Postmodernism: History, Theory, Fiction* (Milton Park, Oxon: Routledge, 1988).

135 Contrary to the implications of an ideological pre-construct attached to the concept of the metanarrative, the present work results from a close reading of the texts selected in terms of their relationship to transcendence. That it should reach a conclusion in terms of a general direction that seems to be taken away from the God of transcendence to the emergence of an immanent transcendence should not be misconstrued as a pre-critical assumption. As Mark C. Taylor quips, in *After God*: "What poststructuralists cannot imagine is a nontotalizing structure that nonetheless acts as a whole" (310).

136 Sára Tóth, "What Does Literature Say? The Problem of Dogmatic Closure – from Romanticism to Northrop Frye," *ESC* (*English Studies in Canada*) 37/2 (2011), 198.

137 See my section on "The Spiral and the Cross: Northrop Frye's Theoretical Imagination."

138 Sandbeck, "God as Immanent Transcendence," 32–3.

139 Ibid., 35.

140 Ibid.

141 Indeed, for Mark C. Taylor (in *Erring*): "By enacting the death of the transcendent(al) Father/signified, the word becomes the wayward, rebellious, errant 'son.' [...] The death of the father opens the reign of the word that is embodied in scripture. Since this word enacts absolute

passage, it is forever liminal and eternally playful. [...] This play is a play of differences that forms and reforms the word itself" (106–7). As my study of the kerygmatic potential of literature purports to show, there might be another way of looking at writing than as a playfully differential network of signs, which does not mean regressing to a naïve, pre-deconstructionist understanding of transcendence.

142 In *Love and Death in the American Novel* (New York: Stein and Day, 1966), Leslie A. Fiedler also regards American fiction as marked by its "inheritance from Puritanism," which he defines as a "'typical' (even allegorical) way of regarding the sensible world" (29). A recurring concern of the following analyses is the allegorical basis of the works under study.

143 Fiedler makes a similar observation in his introduction to *Love and Death in the American Novel*, when he comments on Hawthorne's phrase saying that among "certain obsessive concerns of our national life," there is "not least of all, the uneasiness of the writer who cannot help believing that the very act of composing a book is Satanic revolt" (27).

144 Edition used: Nathaniel Hawthorne, *The Scarlet Letter* (London: Dent, 1967), 16; hereafter *SL*.

145 To be opposed to the "literal" reading of the Bible that Frye seeks to theorize, which is closer to Blake's romantic conception of the power of the letter. See our preceding remarks regarding Blake's influence on Frye in the section entitled "Religious vs Spiritual Criticism: Further Methodological Remarks."

146 For a review of the extent of Frye's practical literary criticism, see Imre Salusinszky, ed., *Northrop Frye's Writings on the Eighteenth and Nineteenth Centuries*, vol. 17 of the Collected Works of Northrop Frye (Toronto: University of Toronto Press, 2005), and Glen Robert Gill, ed., *Northrop Frye on Twentieth Century Literature*, vol. 29 of the Collected Works of Northrop Frye, (Toronto: University of Toronto Press, 2010).

147 Denham, *RV*, 45–6.

148 Ibid., 46.

149 Gill, *Northrop Frye*, xxxvii.

150 Ibid., xlv.

151 O'Grady, "Re-valuing Value," 238.

152 Donaldson, introduction to Donaldson and Mendelson, *Frye and the Word*, 14.

153 This is extracted from Frye's *The Stubborn Structure* and quoted by David Rampton at the end of his introduction to *Northrop Frye: New Directions from Old*, xxix.

1 *The Scarlet Letter*

1 This theme of redemption remains surprisingly little addressed by the substantial body of criticism dedicated to the novel. Preston M. Browning, Jr's opening remark in his essay "Hester Prynne as Secular Saint," in Harold Bloom, ed., *Hester Prynne* (Philadelphia, PA: Chelsea House, 2004), might account for this critical blind spot. As he states: "While the centrality of *The Scarlet Letter* as a literary fact of our national history is a matter beyond dispute, its significance for our *religious* history has not received, I feel, the attention which it deserves" (95; original emphasis). As Browning proceeds to add, if there is no dearth of critical material pertaining to Puritanism in Hawthorne's fiction and *The Scarlet Letter*, in particular, a relatively overlooked matter is the contemporary relevance of the "alternative to Puritanism [...] which the novel adumbrates" (95). This relevance, Browning suggests, has everything to do with "the modernity of [Hester's] vision of redemption" (96). Relating this vision of redemption to a development in contemporary Christian thought referred to as "religionless Christianity" and deriving from Dietrich Bonhoeffer's work, Browning contends that Hester enacts Bonhoeffer's secular view of Christianity as "voluntary participation in the suffering of the world [...] – for which Jesus Christ is the ultimate paradigm" (101). This analysis thus supports my own Christic reading of Hester. More importantly, though, the opposition Browning draws between Hester's modern vision of the secular character of redemption as opposed to Arthur's more traditional one, which is linked to his conception of God as transcendent, ties up with my central thesis of Hawthorne's novel as a transitional work in the global evolution towards immanentized forms of transcendence that I see as characterizing the history of American fiction. See "The Impetus behind This Project and Its Corpus" in the introduction.

2 The obvious similarity of Hester's and the minister's experiences is a fact often overlooked, as critics rather tend to focus on the two characters' contrasted religious attitudes. See, for instance, the opposition between Hester's antinomianism and Dimmesdale's Puritanism in Michael J. Colacurcio's "Footsteps of Ann Hutchinson: The Context of *The Scarlet Letter*," in Bloom, *Hester Prynne*.

3 "Thou hast escaped me!" he repeated more than once. "Thou hast escaped me!" (Hawthorne, "The Revelation of the Scarlet Letter," *SL*, 308).

4 Jacques Cabau, *La prairie perdue* (Paris: Seuil, 1966), 114 (my translation). For a detailed discussion of Hester's political subversive potential, see Nina Baym, "Who? The Characters," in Bloom, *Hester Prynne*.

5 For a most insightful analysis of Pearl as standing outside the symbolic and thus legal and moral order, manifesting and mediating an ontological rather than semiological experience, see Christophe Chambost, "Signification et intensité de la lettre écarlate," in Marc Amfreville and Antoine Cazé, eds., *The Scarlet Letter* (Paris: Ellipses, 2005), 87–97. Chambost also refers to Jean-Jacques Mayoux's analysis of Pearl in *Vivants piliers, le roman anglo-saxon et les symboles* (Paris: Maurice Nadeau, 1985) as being situated in a state before the separation of law and nature, recalling Charles H. Feidelson's statement that "[Pearl's] beauty and grace [...] suggest a prelapsarian child of Adam, a throwback to Eden before the fall" ("*The Scarlet Letter*," in Bloom, *Hester Prynne*, 58; originally published in R.H. Pearce, ed., *Hawthorne Centenary Letters* (Columbus, OH: Ohio State University Press, 1964)). While all these views support my own reading of the ontological character of the subversion embodied by Pearl in *The Scarlet Letter*, Chambost makes an additional important point: no matter how attractive Pearl's evasion of the symbolic order may be to contemporary postmodern and poststructuralist sensitivities, as the very energy of life, "she is closer to a reading experience emphasizing the feeling of presence. In this respect, she is at odds with interpretive attempts taking place in the absence of what is being referred to. Thanks to the child, immediacy replaces mediation and sensation wins over the intellect" (93; my translation).

6 The point I am making may at first feel conspicuously close to new historicist approaches of the novel, stressing the fictionalization of history in *The Scarlet Letter*. For a review of these approaches, see Ross C. Murfin, "The New Historicism and *The Scarlet Letter*," in Ross C. Murfin, ed., *The Scarlet Letter* (Boston: St Martin's, 1991), 330–44. Most of these analyses, however, are interested in the ideological purport of the novel, as reflecting the "concerns and biases [...] of the author's nineteenth-century American culture" for which "the Puritan past in which the novel is set is thus a kind of disguise" (338). In contrast, my concern is with the spiritual import of the novel, which Frye's delineation of poetic myth's two directions of development enables me to address.

7 Feidelson, "*The Scarlet Letter*," 38–9.

8 This interpretation of Hawthorne's novel as profoundly subversive would seem to contradict Sacvan Bercovitch's analysis of the conservative thrust of the narrative, which he sees illustrated by its eventual construction of Hester as "an agent of social cohesion and continuity" ("Hawthorne's A-Morality of Compromise," in Murfin, *The Scarlet Letter*, 345). Feidelson, for his part, mediates between a conservative vs subversive interpretation

of the novel by reading Hester's decision to stay on and endure not as a "devastating critique of Hester's radicalism" (344) but as a "dialectical conversion" of the Puritans' "negative" vision of "modern liberty as fearful freedom" into Hester's version of freedom: "an affirmative individualism, humanism, and naturalism" (Feidelson, "*The Scarlet Letter*," 43), thus reflecting Hawthorne's own narrative strategy to "construct an image of positive human enterprise" "out of the negative world that he inherits" (32). While voicing a comparable claim in his study of *The Scarlet Letter* as romance, Michael Davitt Bell is much more straightforward in his focus on the subversive and even "anarchic" quality of Hawthorne's narrative. For Bell, "behind th[e] mask of 'acquired wisdom,' Hester has been nurturing a thoroughly subversive sense of her individuality" and "paradoxically enough, it is by *forsaking* open rebellion, by reassuming her part in society, that Hester is at last able to realize her individuality and freedom" ("Arts of Deception: Hawthorne, 'Romance,' and *The Scarlet Letter*," in Michael J. Colacurcio, ed., *New Essays on The Scarlet Letter* (Cambridge: Cambridge University Press, 1985), 51–4; original emphasis). As Bell contends, this indirect rebellion is duplicated in Hawthorne's narrative strategy of "ironic subversion," as, beneath a genteel façade, Hawthorne is actually masking a claim for the imaginative freedom granted by romance, formerly "less a neutral generic label than a revolutionary, or at least antisocial, slogan" (37). While I agree that subversion in *The Scarlet Letter* has everything to do with the "authority of romance" (44), I also wish to contend that the imaginative freedom thus claimed is not just that of private fantasy and impulse versus normative reason but the specific authority granted Hester through her individual experience of transcendence as secular saint endowed with "sympathetic 'imagining'" (43) and characteristic of Hawthorne's romantic imagination (see the part on romantic kerygma).

9 "In an allegory what is primarily signified – that is to say the literal meaning – is contingent, and what is signified secondarily, the symbolic meaning itself, is external enough to be directly accessible. Hence, there is a relation of translation between the two meanings; once the translation is made, the henceforth useless allegory can be dropped" (Paul Ricoeur, *The Symbolism of Evil*, translated by Emerson Buchanan (Boston: Beacon Press, 1969), 16).

10 "In the symbol, I cannot objectify the analogical relation that connects the second meaning with the first. It is by living in the first meaning that I am led by it beyond itself; the symbolic meaning is constituted in and by the literal meaning which effects the analogy in giving the analogue. Maurice Blondel said: 'Analogies are based less on notional resemblances

(*similitudines*) than on an interior stimulation, on an assimilative solicitation (*intentio ad assimilationem*).' In fact, unlike a comparison that we *consider* from outside, the symbol is the movement of the primary meaning which makes us participate in the latent meaning and thus assimilates us to that which is symbolized without our being able to master the similitude intellectually. It is in this sense that the symbol is donative; it is donative because it is a primary intentionality that gives the second meaning analogically" (Ricoeur, *The Symbolism of Evil*, 15–16; original emphasis).

11 Regarding characterization in *The Scarlet Letter*, critics often like to focus on its psychological realism when divested of its allegorical and symbolic trappings. See, e.g., F.O. Matthiessen's classic "Allegory and Symbolism," in John C. Gerber, ed., *Twentieth-Century Interpretations of The Scarlet Letter* (Englewood Cliffs, NJ: Prentice-Hall, 1968); Baym, "Who? The Characters"; David Van Leer, "Hester's Labyrinth: Transcendental Rhetoric in Puritan Boston," in Colacurcio, *New Essays on The Scarlet Letter*, 99; Armand Hage, "*The Scarlet Letter* Characters: Allegories, Symbols and Individuals," in Amfreville and Cazé, *The Scarlet Letter*, 77–97. A notable exception is A.N. Kaul, "*The Scarlet Letter* and Puritan Ethics," in Harold Bloom, ed., *Nathaniel Hawthorne's* The Scarlet Letter (New York: Chelsea House, 1986, 9–20), which observes the same opposition as I do between the conservative, ostracizing rigidity of Puritan allegorical semiology and the subversive function of romantic symbolism, resulting in a portrayal of New England society as "a society which claimed to have based itself on the highest principles of moral idealism but which turns out at the first test to be utterly lacking in the elementary Christian virtues of love and compassion" (14). Generally paying scarce attention to the implications of a distinction between allegory and symbol, critics' historical consciousness seems future-oriented, mainly concerned with tracking the way Hawthorne might "prefigure a concern of Henry James that afterward became central to much modern fiction" (Hage, "*The Scarlet Letter*," 85) or in delineating the way he operated as a psychologist heralding Freud's work half a century later (Baym, "Who? The Characters," 143). What such approaches seem to miss, however, is the specificity of the "reality" Hawthorne's romantic imagination struggles to mediate. Indeed, the realistic bias of such critical perspectives tends to psychologize the "inner truth" Hawthorne was famously so intent on, even when admitting its romantic root (142). The unfortunate consequence of such a reductive view can be perceived in Van Leer's analysis of what he calls the "pragmatic semantics in *The Scarlet Letter*" ("Hester's Labyrinth," 99), resulting in his assertion that "although characters frequently think differently, there is

really no such thing as 'revelation' in the book" (86). Van Leer then proceeds to argue for this on the basis of the semantic indeterminacy the community is confronted with in the scene of Dimmesdale's final exposure of his chest. Ignoring the consistency of this interpretive instability with the book's overall subversive symbolic versatility, Van Leer's interpretation also conflates immateriality and non-existence, thereby missing the unsubstantiality characterizing the energy of rebellion in *The Scarlet Letter*. According to Hélène Guillaume: "In the wake of the Transcendentalist focus on the physical dimension of life, and of the stoic corporeal theory, the book is unified around the symbol of energy and the images of its manifestation. [...] As the abusive patriarchal power exerts its power by impressing shapes upon matter – the letter A – non-substantial events happening within matter *escape it*, as Pearl escapes through the open window and as the meaning of the scarlet letter 'evad[es the narrator's] analysis' until he retrieves it by resurrecting the characters' experience through art. This value of energy translates into manifestations and changes of state perceived through matter" ("Energy and Truth: 'The Custom House,' 'The Scarlet Letter,' and *The Scarlet Letter*," in Amfreville and Cazé, *The Scarlet Letter*, 52–3; original emphasis, parentheses added). Of course, such an analysis suggests a conception of truth and meaning as corporeal though unsubstantial experiences rather than as concepts, in accordance with Hawthorne's narrator's romantic perception of reality and Frye's conception of the kerygmatic.

12 Interestingly, as Austin Warren reminds us, Boston critic E.P. Whipple once remarked that "Hawthorne's 'great books appear not so much created by him as through him. They have the character of revelations, – he, the instrument'" ("The Scarlet Letter," in Bloom, *Hester Prynne*, 63).

2 Henry James's *The Europeans*

1 See F.O. Matthiessen's chapter on "Allegory and Symbolism" in his *American Renaissance: Art and Expression in the Age of Emerson and Whitman* (New York: Oxford University Press, 1941) or Robert Emmet Long's book *The Great Succession: Henry James and the Legacy of Hawthorne* (Pittsburgh, PA: University of Pittsburgh Press, 1979). In his full-length study of the Hawthorne/James literary relationship, Long also quotes Marius Bewley's *The Complex Fate: Hawthorne, Henry James, and Some Other Americans* (London: Chatto and Windus, 1952) as one relatively rare instance of an extended study on this issue.

2 Long, *The Great Succession*, 7.

3 Ibid., 4.
4 Ibid., 6.
5 John Carlos Rowe, *Henry Adams and Henry James: The Emergence of a Modern Consciousness* (Ithaca, NY: Cornell University Press, 1976), 10–11.
6 In *The Form of Victorian Fiction* (Notre Dame, IN: Notre Dame University Press, 1968), quoted in Rowe, *Henry Adams and Henry James*, 39.
7 This part is dedicated to the close analysis of the often remarked problematic centrality of allegory in the novel (see Ward, Tuttleton, Tanner, Nazare, Lustig), following a double movement of construction and subversion of the allegorical mode that I will study sequentially and that illustrates Richard Poirier's contention regarding the tension between dramatic and allegorical impulses in James's early fiction (*The Comic Sense of Henry James: A Study of the Early Novels* (New York: Oxford University Press, 1960), 9). Such analyses, however, are often interested in drawing conclusions regarding James's vision of cultural identity (Ward, Tuttleton, and Tanner) or concerning issues of genre (*The Europeans'* link with Shakespearean comedy – Nazare – or Hawthorne's romance – Lustig – for instance). By contrast, my analysis focuses on the construction/subversion of the sin vs virtue pattern (supposedly represented by the European/American encounter) traditionally at the basis of the Puritan view of life, which I hold to be an invitation to read the novel as the illustration of a significant shift in American religious imagination towards the moral indeterminacy of modernity. See J.A. Ward, *The Search for Form: Studies in the Structure of James's Fiction* (Chapel Hill, NC: the University of Carolina Press, 1967); J.W. Tuttleton, "Propriety and Fine Perception: James's *The Europeans*," *Modern Language Review* 73/3 (1978); Tony Tanner, introduction to *The Europeans*, by Henry James (New York: Penguin, 1984); Joseph Nazare, "Enter Touchstone: Manners of Comedy in James's *The Europeans*," *Henry James Review* 18/2 (1997), 149–60; T.J. Lustig, "Sunspots and Blindspots in *The Europeans*," *E-rea revue d'études Anglophones* 3/2 (2005), 6–18.
8 Edward A. Geary makes a similar claim when he notes the Europeans' role as tempters bearing the fruit of knowledge to arguably ambiguous innocents, both inhabited by a sense of evil and utterly lacking in worldliness ("*The Europeans*: A Centennial Essay," *Henry James Review* 4/1 (1982), 31–49). This approach to the novel as biblical allegory has also been noted by Deborah Austin, "Innocents at Home: A Study of *The Europeans* of Henry James," *Journal of General Education* 14 (1962), 103–29. Austin argues that Felix and Eugenia may be read as postlapsarian Adam and Eve coming back to Eden. However, as, Eric Haralson and Kendall Johnson suggest, "the fallen Eden of New England is not without redemption"

(*Critical Companion to Henry James: A Literary Reference to His Life and Work* (New York: Facts on File, 2009), 78), since "it also provides an atmosphere in which young lovers can achieve bliss and in which innocence can never be sullied" (Ward, *The Search for Form*, 97).

9 Tanner, introduction to *The Europeans*, 9.

10 James's *Hawthorne* (1879), quoted by Tanner, ibid., 14.

11 For a detailed analysis of the "complicated symbolism of youth and age" as one of the devices used to complexify the Manichean character of the basic opposition between the Europeans and the Americans, see Ward, *The Search for Form*, 108–9.

12 For an analysis of duplicity as not being confined to Eugenia but as also characterizing the New Englanders, see, notably, Poirier, *The Comic Sense of Henry James*; and Judith Caesar, "James's *The Europeans*," *Explicator* 62/3 (2004), 151–3.

13 See Ward's analysis (in *The Search for Form*) of this contrast as the basis of the novel's structure.

14 This actualization of human potential is what Poirier (*The Comic Sense of Henry James*) seems to define as the spirit of comedy in James's fiction.

15 This well-known fact is stated by Henry James himself in his famous letter to William Dean Howells published in the *Atlantic* in 1878, where he calls his future novel "a joyous little romance" (quoted by Tanner in his introduction to *The Europeans*, 7).

16 Marta Banta, *Henry James and the Occult: The Great Extension* (Bloomington, IN: Indiana University Press, 1972), 3.

17 Ibid., 3–4.

18 Ibid., 4.

19 In a way, Gertrude could be seen as the embodiment of rebellion against the "old evangelical and utilitarian hostility to the novel [that] surfaced again and again in various forms throughout the nineteenth century" (Roslyn Jolly, *Henry James: History, Narrative, Fiction* (New York: Oxford University Press, 1993), 10) but was at its height in the first quarter of the nineteenth century (6), the time frame for *The Europeans*. This is one more sign of the novel's overall strategy to destabilize the traditionally ethical function of art.

20 Ward, *The Search for Form*, 111.

21 This is also Poirier's view (in *The Comic Sense of Henry James*), which has generated a whole critical debate about whose viewpoint is privileged in the novel (Eugenia's or Felix's), leading to various conclusions as to the unalloyed comic quality of the novel. As the title suggests, however, both European characters are central novelistic focuses, seemingly preventing

a reading of the novel as either comic (should emphasis be laid on Felix's perspective and the final happy marriages) or tragic (when one considers Eugenia's fate). Besides, my contention is that, notwithstanding the indisputable comic tone prevailing in the novel, as James explicitly intended, this comic tone is qualified from the start, within the text itself, by the "tragi-comical power" of Felix's sketch in the introductory scene (*The Europeans*, 38), suggesting a metafictional comment on the following tale as being endowed with the same quality.

22 This is also what Ward points out: "The New Englanders can regard forms of artfulness only in terms of ethics because they can express themselves only by a moralistic rhetoric. But the Europeans convert moral questions to aesthetic ones" (*The Search for Form*, 110). In this sense, I would side with Geary ("*The Europeans*," 38) in his analysis of Eugenia and Felix as tempters who "have no sense of sin" and "have made worldliness into an art" illustrating James's outcry over "the Protestant idea that art 'is supposed [...] to have some vaguely injurious effect upon those who make it an important consideration'" (Leon Edel and Mark Wilson, eds., *Henry James: Literary Criticism*, quoted in Jolly, *Henry James*, 74), rather than with Gail Fincham's view that Felix reconciles the aesthetic and the moral ("'The Alchemy of Art': Henry James's *The Europeans*," *English Studies in Africa* 23/2 (1980), 83–92). As I have tried to show, that Felix should sometimes express himself using a vocabulary belonging to the realm of ethics (as in his expressed concern to do the Wentworths *good*) does not necessarily mean that the nature of his concern is ethical.

23 For Tuttleton, Felix is also "gaily idealized and constitutes an allegorical type" ("Propriety and Fine Perception: James's *The Europeans*," 495).

24 Phillip Blond, "Introduction: Theology before Philosophy," in Phillip Blond, ed., *Post-Secular Philosophy: Between Philosophy and Theology* (New York: Routledge, 1998), 9.

25 Michel Haar, "Nietzsche and the metamorphosis of the divine," in Blond, *Post-Secular Philosophy*, 158.

26 Ibid., 159.

27 Quoted in ibid., 161; original emphasis.

28 In the *Merriam-Webster's Collegiate Dictionary*, redemption is defined as "the act, process or an instance of redeeming," i.e., "buy[ing] back," "get[ting] or winning back." This is exactly what Eugenia is trying to do, going to America in the hope of finding the husband and financial means she had in Europe.

29 This fairy tale quality has been abundantly remarked upon. See, notably, Peter Buitenhuis, "Comic Pastoral: Henry James's *The Europeans*,"

University of Toronto Quarterly 31 (1962), 152–63; Geary, "*The Europeans*"; Fincham, "'The Alchemy of Art'"; and Long, *The Great Succession*.

30 Merle A. Williams, *Henry James and the Philosophical Novel* (Cambridge: Cambridge University Press, 1993), 2.

31 For a detailed study of theatricality in *The Europeans*, see Tanner's introduction to the novel.

32 In *Philosophie de la volonté*, vol. 2, *Finitude et culpabilité* (Paris: Aubier, 1988 [1960]), 179; previously quoted in the part dealing with the kerygmatic mode in *The Scarlet Letter*.

33 Thomas J.J. Altizer, *The Gospel of Christian Atheism* (London: Collins, 1967), 74–5.

34 Ibid., 22.

35 Ibid.

36 See Charles Thomas Samuels, *The Ambiguity of Henry James* (Urbana, IL: University of Illinois Press, 1971), where this distinction operates as a structuring principle.

3 Fitzgerald's *The Great Gatsby*

1 Altizer, *The Gospel of Christian Atheism*, 22.

2 The phrase is used by John A. McClure, in *Partial Faiths*, to characterize postsecularism. According to him, "a feature of literary thinking since the romantics," postsecularism manifests as a "turn to the religious" and "process of ontological opening" (3).

3 Maxwell Geismar, *Writers in Crisis: The American Novel, 1925–1940* (Boston: Houghton Mifflin, 1942), 28.

4 Ibid., 29.

5 John F. Callahan, *The Illusions of a Nation: Myth and History in the Novels of F. Scott Fitzgerald* (Urbana, IL: University of Illinois Press, 1972), 8.

6 Ibid., 7.

7 Ibid., 8.

8 Ibid., 14.

9 Ibid.

10 Ibid., 16.

11 T.S. Eliot's words in a letter he wrote Fitzgerald after reading *The Great Gatsby*. Quoted in Letha Audhuy, "The *Waste Land* Myth and Symbols in *The Great Gatsby*," in Harold Bloom, ed., *F. Scott Fitzgerald, The Great Gatsby* (New York: Chelsea House, 1986), 110. This has led critics to connect James and Fitzgerald in various ways, ranging from thematic concerns (see next endnote) to the spatial dichotomy both authors rely on, opposing Europe

and New England in the one case, East and West in the other (Ornstein), or stressing their differing use of the spectatorial stance to tell a story (Samuels), while some focus on the stylistic novelty Eliot's remark is perceived to adumbrate (George Garrett, "Fire and Freshness: A Matter of Style in *The Great Gatsby*," in Matthew J. Bruccoli, ed., *New Essays on* The Great Gatsby (Cambridge: Cambridge University Press, 1985)). My own concern is to compare the two writers' narrative strategies with the allegorical and dramatic structure of traditional moralities so as to assess James's and Fitzgerald's respective stances to the God of morality and transcendence. Robert Ornstein, "Scott Fitzgerald's Fable of East and West," in Ernest Lockridge, ed., *Twentieth-Century Interpretations of* The Great Gatsby (Englewood Cliffs, NJ: Prentice-Hall, 1968); Charles Thomas Samuels, "The Greatness of 'Gatsby,'" in Henry Dan Piper, ed., *Fitzgerald's* The Great Gatsby*: The Novel, the Critics, the Background* (New York: Charles Scribner's Sons, 1970).

12 See, e.g., Kermit Vanderbilt, "James, Fitzgerald and the American Self-Image," *Massachussetts Review* 6/2 (1965), 289–304; R.J. Wilson, "Henry James and F. Scott Fitzgerald: Americans Abroad," *Research Studies Pullman* 45/2 (1977), 82–91; or more recently, Bryan R. Washington, "The Daisy Chain: The Great Gatsby and Daisy Miller or the Politics of Privacy," in *The Politics of Exile: Ideology in Henry James, F.S. Fitzgerald, and James Baldwin* (Evanston, IL: Northeastern University Press, 1995), 35–54.

13 Brian Way, "The Great Gatsby," in Bloom, *F. Scott Fitzgerald*, 87.

14 While critics have traditionally noted this dualistic structure and/or the allegorical dimension of characters in the novel (see, e.g., Lockridge, Raleigh, Berman), they usually draw conclusions in terms of symbolic significance rather than generic filiations. Once again, my interest in connecting *The Great Gatsby* with the allegorical strategy of moralities is to pursue the same type of enquiry as in my study of James's *The Europeans* so as to assess the evolution of the relationship of American literary imagination to the Puritan moral and religious mindset. Brian Way conducts a curiously similar analysis in his *F. Scott Fitzgerald and the Art of Social Fiction* (Boston: St Martin's Press, 1980) when he discusses Fitzgerald's "place in the American literary tradition" in terms of "a moral sense" that Gatsby's author would notably share with Henry James, "which is [...] a secularized version of American Puritanism" (25). Interestingly, Way then proceeds to make his point via a compared analysis of James's *The Europeans* and Fitzgerald's *The Great Gatsby*. Lockridge, *Twentieth-Century Interpretations of* The Great Gatsby; John Henry Raleigh, "F. Scott Fitzgerald's *The Great Gatsby*: Legendary Bases and Allegorical Significances," in Piper,

Fitzgerald's The Great Gatsby; Ronald Berman, "*The Great Gatsby* and the Twenties," in Ruth Prigozy, ed., *The Cambridge Companion to F. Scott Fitzgerald* (Cambridge: Cambridge University Press, 2002).

A last point to be made is that, contrary to what might have been expected, my approach is closer to this type of reading and to formalist close readings of the text than to the comparatively few analyses dedicated to Fitzgerald's religious imagination in *The Great Gatsby*, which often focus on the author's Catholic sensitivity. For a survey of the latter type of discussion, see Tracy Fessenden, "F. Scott Fitzgerald's Catholic Closet," in *Culture and Redemption: Religion, the Secular, and American Literature* (Princeton, NJ: Princeton University Press, 2007).

15 Way, "The Great Gatsby," 89.

16 Ibid., 88.

17 For an analysis of the realistic handling of Nick as first person narrator, see James E. Miller Jr, "Boats against the Current," in his *F. Scott Fitzgerald: His Art and His Technique* (New York: New York University Press, 1964). For an early defence of Nick's moral role as first person narrator, see Thomas A. Hanzo, "The Theme and Narrator of The Great Gatsby," in Lockridge, *Twentieth-Century Interpretations*, 61–9, originally published in 1957. In his later essay, "The Untrimmed Christmas Tree: The Religious Background of The Great Gatsby," in Piper, *Fitzgerald's* The Great Gatsby, Henry Dan Piper complexifies the moral issue by examining the evolution of Fitzgerald's religious imagination from his short story "Absolution," which was to have been about Gatsby's early years, prior to *The Great Gatsby*. By suggesting that, with Nick, Fitzgerald kept "the residual tradition of moral values represented by the advice given Nick by his father without the sectarian [Catholic] dogma" still to be found in "Absolution" (99), the critic also illuminates the way Fitzgerald's novel at once unites and takes Hawthorne's and James's stances to transcendence one step further. With Nick as the embodiment of morality without the ornament of Catholic dogma, Fitzgerald completes Hawthorne's break away from religion. With Gastby as representative of a romantic quest for transcendence without the trappings of morality, Fitzgerald dramatizes James's rebellion against stifling ethics. The result of such a secularization of ethics, however, hardly seems fulfilling as it appears premised on a schizophrenic pattern (severing morals from transcendence) and ultimate modernist sense of loss.

18 Marius Bewley also records the opposition between Tom and Gatsby as one between body and spirit, in his essay "Scott Fitzgerald's Criticism of America," in Lockridge, *Twentieth-Century Interpretations*, 37–53.

Raleigh, however, stresses a dichotomy between materialism and idealism ("F. Scott Fitzgerald's *The Great Gatsby*, 141–4).

19 Lockridge characterizes Myrtle Wilson as "body without spirit" (*Twentieth-Century Interpretations*, 8). Ronald Berman speaks of "carnal intelligence," in "*The Great Gatsby* and the Twenties," 89.

20 Charles Thomas Samuels makes the same point in "The Greatness of 'Gatsby,'" when he analyses this passage of the kiss: "[Gatsby] renounces the innocent, pre-sexual, other-worldliness which alone brings one in contact with ideality to marry the temporal, perishable, sexual world. Like God, he renounces unlimited promise for love of humanity" (155–6); this supports my reading of the novel as (partly at least) a literary expression of the death of God theology introduced by Altizer's quote at the start of this chapter. As the next section will proceed to demonstrate, however, the death of the transcendent ideality Gatsby stands for will not resolve itself into a kenotic expression of immanent divinity, as, through Gatsby's failed love and eventual death, the novel seems intent on mourning the very possibility of ideality.

21 Richard D. Lehan, *The Great Gatsby: The Limits of Wonder* (New York: Twayne, 1989), 41. For an analysis of Gatsby's Christic value, see also Thomas Dilworth, "The Passion of Gatsby: Evocation of Jesus in Fitzgerald's *The Great Gatsby*," *Explicator* 68/2 (2010), 119–21.

22 See the chapter on "Commerce as the New Religion" in *The Great Gatsby*, in Michael Grawe, *Expatriate American Authors in Paris: Disillusionment with the American Lifestyle as Reflected in Selected Works of Ernest Hemingway and F. Scott Fitzgerald* (Munich: Grin Verlag, 2001).

23 Way, "The Great Gatsby," 101.

24 Ibid., 101–2.

25 Audhuy, "The *Waste Land* Myth and Symbols in *The Great Gatsby*," 114.

26 Ibid., 109, 116. See also Robert Emmitt, "Love, Death and Resurrection in *The Great Gatsby*," in Donna G. Fricke and Douglas C. Fricke, eds., *Aeolian Harps: Essays in Literature in Honor of Maurice Browning Cramer* (Bowling Green, OH: Bowling University Press, 1976).

27 This is the explicit theme in William A. Fahey, *F. Scott Fitzgerald and the American Dream* (New York: Thomas Y. Crowell, 1973), but is also famously focused on in Bewley, "Scott Fitzgerald's Criticism of America," originally published in 1954, and in Richard D. Lehan's analysis of the novel in his *F. Scott Fitzgerald and the Craft of Fiction* (Carbondale, IL: Southern Illinois University Press, 1966).

28 The interlocking of the personal, historical, and metaphysical is notably studied by Lehan in *F. Scott Fitzgerald*.

29 See Lehan's study of Fitzgerald's religious rhetoric and the "godlike proportions" taken by Dan Cody, Gatsby's "Father," whose "business" he attends to (*The Limits of Wonder*, 35). As Lehan shows, the perversion of the Dream entails a linguistic shift away from spiritual concerns to financial ones.

30 This remark is made by Richard Lehan in the context of his analysis of Fitzgerald's short story "Absolution," one of "*The Great Gatsby* satellite stories" "originally written as a part of the novel that explored Gatsby's boyhood" (*The Limits of Wonder*, 35–6).

31 The aim of this part, dedicated to Nick's narration, is not one more assessment of the failure or success of Fitzgerald's handling of the first person narrator. See, e.g., Gary J. Scrimgeour, "Against *The Great Gatsby*," in Lockridge, *Twentieth-Century Interpretations*, 70–81 vs Samuels's "The Greatness of 'Gatsby'" or Miller's "Boats against the Current." Rather, my point is to analyse whether Nick's spiritual growth through his gradual identification with Gatsby (Samuels, 157) is reflected in his narration in such a way as to fulfil the redemptive promise whose failure the plot dramatizes.

32 Neuhaus, 53.

33 Michael Leff's rhetorical criticism remains largely unknown in France, which Ruth Amossy tries to account for in her essay included in the special issue of the online review *Argumentation et Analyse du Discours* paying tribute to Leff's work: "L'analyse rhétorique aux Etats-Unis: Hommage à Michael Leff.'" See Ruth Amossy, "Introduction: Pour une analyse rhétorique des textes politiques," *Argumentation et Analyse du Discours* 6 (Apr. 2011), http://aad.revues.org/1081.

34 In her introduction to Michael Leff's rhetorical criticism (see n33), Amossy points out that Leff himself, whose close reading technique had up until then been reserved to literary texts, fought against literary/non-literary distinctions.

35 See Leff's essay "Rhetoric and Dialectic in Martin Luther King Jr's 'Letter from Birmingham Jail,'" in Frans H. van Eemeren et al., eds., *Anyone Who Has a View: Theoretical Contributions to the Study of Argumentation* (Dordrecht: Kluwer, 2003), 255–68.

36 Leff, 263.

37 The instrumental function of rhetoric refers to all the devices that make rhetoric an instrument of persuasion, while its constitutive or generative function corresponds to the operations of rhetoric whereby self is constituted, often via the persona of the rhetor. This is developed in a later version of Leff's essay on King's "Letter From Birmingham Jail" (see Michael

Leff and Ebony A. Utley, "Instrumental and Constitutive Rhetoric in Martin Luther King Jr's 'Letter From Birmingham Jail,'" *Rhetoric and Public Affairs* 7/1 (2004), 37–51), arguing for the interrelatedness of these two functions, which will also be my point in my study of Nick Carraway as narrative persona.

38 For related remarks, see Dilworth, "The Passion of Gatsby."

39 Audhuy, "The *Waste Land* Myth and Symbols," 111.

40 Ibid., 122. This is an idea already introduced by various critics such as Bewley ("Scott Fitzgerald's Criticism of America"), who calls Gatsby "mythic," i.e., "impersonal" (44). See also Raleigh, "F. Scott Fitzgerald's *The Great Gatsby*."

41 Arguing against a wholesale dismissal of Fitzgerald's hyperbolic imagery as bad art, tribute has been paid to its very effective realistic use, as in the suggestion of Meyer Wolfshiem's rapacious character through his way of eating with "ferocious delicacy" (77), or in the caricature of upper-class false gentility through the description of Tom Buchanan and Myrtle Wilson's New York flat: "The living-room was crowded to the doors with a set of tapestried furniture entirely too large for it, so that to move about was to stumble continually over scenes of ladies swinging in the gardens of Versailles" (35). In this second case, the general narrative tendency to hyperbolic imagery seems entirely justified by the excessively theatrical character of social life as displayed in this scene. In both the examples taken, the adequacy and humorous suggestiveness of the description construct a narrative persona who seems far more at ease with immediate, observable reality than with Gatsby's reconstructed flights of fancy, quite in keeping with Nick's down-to-earth genealogy.

42 "They were careless people, Tom and Daisy – they smashed up things and creatures and then retreated back into their money or their vast carelessness […] and let other people clean up the mess they had made" (186).

43 Leff, "Rhetoric and Dialectic," 266.

44 Ibid.

4 Immanent Christianity in *The Grapes of Wrath*

1 Warren French, "John Steinbeck and Modernism (A Speculation on His Contribution to the Development of the Twentieth-Century American Sensibility)," in John Ditsky, ed., *Critical Essays on Steinbeck's Grapes of Wrath* (Boston: G.K. Hall, 1989), 156, original emphasis.

2 Ibid., 155.

3 Ibid.

4 Ibid.
5 Ibid.
6 Ibid., 160.
7 Ibid.
8 Ibid., 161.
9 Frederic I. Carpenter, "The Philosophical Joads," in Peter Lisca and Kevin Hearle, eds., *The Grapes of Wrath: Text and Criticism* (New York: Penguin, 1997), 571 (originally published in *College English II* (Jan. 1941), 315–25).
10 Stephen Railton, "Pilgrim's Politics: Steinbeck's Art of Conversion," in David Wyatt, ed., *New Essays on* The Grapes of Wrath (Cambridge: Cambridge University Press, 1990), 43.
11 Ibid., 42.
12 Ibid., 45.
13 Ibid., 42.
14 Ibid., 38–9.
15 For Jesus' command affects both the external building and the inner temple of the body. As the biblical episode proceeds to explain, "Jesus answered and said unto them, Destroy this temple, and in three days I will raise it up. [...] But he spake of the temple of his body" (John 2:19–21).
16 John 2:16.
17 "And another angel came out from the altar [...] and cried a loud cry to him that had the sharp sickle, saying, Thrust in thy sharp sickle, and gather the clusters of the vine of the earth; for her grapes are fully ripe.
"And the angel thrust in his sickle into the earth, and gathered the vine of the earth, and cast it into the great winepress of the wrath of God" (Revelation 14:18–19).
18 The difference between empathy and sympathy rests in their prefixes. Whereas empathy indicates the capacity to commune with somebody else's feelings as if one were "within" the other person, sympathy suggests that one is not just privy to the other's feelings but actively shares them. Hence a distinction between empathy and sympathy as the passive vs active sides of compassion, which are discussed as two potential tools leading to the experience of Charity (the Christian virtue).
19 Luke 17:20–1.
20 This is demonstrated by Railton's study ("Pilgrim's Politics") regarding the centrality of the characters' conversion to a "redemptive discovery of their interrelatedness, their membership in a vastly extended family – the 'we'" (33).
21 Ibid., 29.
22 Ibid., 29–30.

23 Ibid., 28–9; emphasis added.

24 Chris Kocela, "A Postmodern Steinbeck, or Rose of Sharon Meets Oedipa Maas," in Barbara A. Heavilin, ed., *The Critical Response to John Steinbeck's* Grapes of Wrath (Westport, CT: Greenwood, 2000), 253.

25 Ibid.

26 See Ken Eckert, "Exodus Inverted: A New Look at *The Grapes of Wrath*," *Religion and the Arts* 13/3 (2009), 340–57, quoting J. Paul Hunter, "Steinbeck's Wine of Affirmation in *The Grapes of Wrath*," in Robert Con Davis, ed., *Twentieth-Century Interpretations: The Grapes of Wrath* (Englewood Cliffs, NJ: Prentice-Hall, 1982).

27 Eckert, "Exodus Inverted," 348.

28 John 2:17.

29 John 2:15.

30 John 2:18–21.

31 As Eckert notes, "The evolution of man from 'I' to 'we' is positive but must be painful and involve missteps and setbacks, and involves a humbling of self. Part of Christ's education of His disciples is to tell them one must 'deny himself and take up his cross and follow me' (Matt. 16:24), and Christ warns that wherever your possessions are your heart will be (Matt. 6:21). Similarly, in *The Grapes of Wrath* it is the growing material squalour of the Joads which finally teaches them to look beyond their narrow family interests to the shared 'we' of humanity" (Eckert, "Exodus Inverted," 349).

32 The phrase is taken from George Levine, *Darwin Loves You*, the first chapter of which is entitled "Secular Re-enchantment."

33 Regarding the critical response to Peter Lisca's analysis of the exodus pattern in "*The Grapes of Wrath* as Fiction" (in Lisca and Hearle, *The Grapes of Wrath*, 572–88; originally published in *PMLA* LXXII, Mar. 1957, 269–309), see J.R.C. Perkin, "Exodus Imagery in *The Grapes of Wrath*," in David Bevan, ed., *Literature and the Bible*, (Amsterdam: Rodopi, 1993), 79–93, quoted in Eckert's '"Exodus Inverted." See also Tamara Rombold, "Biblical Inversion in *The Grapes of Wrath*," *College Literature* 14/2 (1987), 146–66.

34 John Steinbeck, *Sea of Cortez*, 264–5, quoted in Lester Jay Marks, *Thematic Design in the Novels of John Steinbeck* (The Hague: Mouton, 1971), 20.

35 Elizabeth Napier, "*The Grapes of Wrath*: Steinbeck's *Pilgrim's Progress*," *Steinbeck Review* 7/1 (2010), 52.

36 Ibid., 55.

37 "I ain't gonna baptize. I'm gonna work in the fiel's, in the green fiel's, an' I'm gonna be near to folks. I ain't gonna try to teach 'em nothin'. I'm gonna try to learn" (96).

38 Robert J. Richards, "Darwinian Enchantment," in George Levine, ed., *The Joy of Secularism: 11 Essays for How We Live Now* (Princeton, NJ: Princeton University Press, 2011), 191.
39 Ibid., 185–6.
40 Ibid., 192.
41 Ibid., 194.
42 This reading of Tom Joad does not invalidate previous analyses "variously interpreting him as Moses" (Eckert, "Exodus Inverted," 341) or Saint Paul. See Gerard Cannon, "The Pauline Apostleship of Tom Joad," *College English* 24/3 (1962), 222–4; reprinted in Agnes McNeill Donohue, ed., *A Casebook on The Grapes of Wrath* (New York: Thomas Y. Crowell, 1968, 118–22). All of these are arguable symbolic dimensions of the character. My reading rather wishes to emphasize the Christlike dimension of his final prophecy regarding his future spiritual omnipresence.
43 Richards, "Darwinian Enchantment," 193.
44 Ibid., 199.
45 Woodburn O. Ross, "John Steinbeck: Naturalism's Priest," in Heavilin, *The Critical Response to John Steinbeck's* Grapes of Wrath, 65 (originally published in *College English*, May 1949, 432–8).
46 Railton, "Pilgrim's Politics," 28.
47 Steinbeck, *Sea of Cortez*, quoted in Marks, *Thematic Design*, 23.
48 Marks, *Thematic Design*, 25.
49 Mark's full quotation is: "I do not believe, however, that Steinbeck's conclusions are any more 'mystical' than [...] those reached by Darwin, Einstein, or Emerson, all of whom went to the physical world, the world of matter, and found that man in nature was a microcosm of a greater design" (ibid.).
50 "[Darwin's] natural world breaks down the absolute borders that separate species from each other, puts the world in motion, opens sublime vistas of past and future, ennobles a humanity that constantly threatens to denigrate the body [...] and submit itself to some noncorporeal Other beyond the reach of time and change. Darwin's world – which is our world – is an enchanted one, if we would allow ourselves to look with his eye for detail and aberration, movement and connection, and his reverence for living things; [...] and if we acquired the strength to confront without metaphysical equipment the astonishing richness of the material world" (Levine, "Secular Re-enchantment," in *Darwin Loves You*, 12).
51 See, e.g., McClure, *Partial Faiths*; Tate, *Contemporary Fiction and Christianity*; and Hungerford, *American Literature and Religion since 1960*.
52 Kocela, "A Postmodern Steinbeck," 248.

53 Robert Con Davis in Kocela, 248.
54 Gloria Gaither, "John Steinbeck: The Postmodern Mind in the Modern Age," *Steinbeck Review* 3/1 (2006), 57.
55 Kocela, "A Postmodern Steinbeck," 250.
56 Ibid.; original emphasis.
57 Ibid., 251.
58 Ibid., 253.
59 Ibid.
60 Ibid., 251.
61 Ibid., 252.
62 Gaither, "John Steinbeck," 64.
63 Steinbeck, *The Winter of Our Discontent*, 75, in ibid., 54.
64 The context of Frye's expression is his analysis of the metaliterary and its capacity to "extend one's vision," provoking identification with the narrative, "as in Eliot's famous phrase about listening to music so deeply that we become the music while it lasts. [...] The existential movement of the nineteen-forties, also, revolved around a number of figures [...] who were primarily literary figures, the word existential referring to tendencies in them that were metaliterary, *trying to get past the limitations of literature into a different kind of identity with their readers*" (*WP*, 114–16; emphasis added).
65 "Modernist faith in rationality, science, and freedom had by year 2000 precipitated deep-rooted skepticism, and the formulas for everything and the structures to house them began to be deconstructed and disassembled. Fluidity, unfixed boundaries, and the absence of definable distinctions began to emerge as earmarks of the postmodern mindset" (Gaither, "John Steinbeck," 56).
66 See, e.g., Robert Griffin and William Freedman, "Machines and Animals: Pervasive Motifs in *The Grapes of Wrath*," *Journal of English and Germanic Philology* 62/3 (1963), 569–80; reprinted in Lisca and Hearle, *The Grapes of Wrath*, 589–602.
67 Tate, *Contemporary Fiction and Christianity*, 10.
68 Knight and Woodman, *Biblical Religion and the Novel, 1700–2000*, quoted in Tate, *Contemporary Fiction and Christianity*, 12.
69 Jean-François Côté, "*The Grapes of Wrath*: Un réalisme moderniste," in Claude Le Fustec, ed., *Lectures de Steinbeck: Les raisins de la colère* (Rennes: Presses Universitaires de Rennes, 2007), 125–39.
70 Barry G. Maine, "Steinbeck's Debt to Dos Passos," in Heavilin, *The Critical Response to John Steinbeck's* Grapes of Wrath, 158.
71 Ibid., 160.
72 Ibid., 158.

73 Ibid., 159.
74 Ibid.
75 Ibid., 160.
76 Côté, "*The Grapes of Wrath*," 132.
77 Ibid., 136; my translation.
78 Steinbeck quoted in Warren French, "The Education of the Heart," in *John Steinbeck's Fiction Revisited* (New York: Twayne, 1994), 82.
79 French, "The Education of the Heart," 83.
80 Ibid.
81 See Clara Mallier, "Le quatrième sens de l'écriture dans *The Grapes of Wrath*," paper presented at the conference "Imaginaires Américains: Steinbeck et Ford," Toulouse Le Mirail University, 25 Jan. 2008; available at http://w3.cas.univ-tlse2.fr/spip. http://w3.cas.univ-tlse2.fr/spip.php?article126 php?article126 . I will translate all further references to this essay.
82 "Guess who I been thinkin' about ? Casy! He talked a lot. Used ta bother me. But now I been thinkin' what he said, an' I can remember – all of it. Says one time he went out in the wilderness to find his own soul, an' he foun' he didn' have no soul that was his'n. Says he foun' he jus' got a little piece of a great big soul. Says a wilderness ain't no good, 'cause his little piece of a soul wasn't no good 'less it was with the rest, an' was whole. Funny how I remember. Didn' think I was even listenin'. But now I know a fella ain't no good alone" (418).
83 Mallier, "Le quatrième sens."
84 Ibid.
85 Ibid.
86 French, "The Education of the Heart," 83.
87 "There does seem to be a movement in time, which is the *mythos* properly speaking, up to and followed by an act of understanding where the *mythos* is 'seen,' or apprehended as a unit. It is this final act of understanding the whole [...] that has made the word *structure* so pervasive a metaphor in literary criticism, although the traditional term *anagnorisis* seems to me less misleading" (Frye, "The Koine of Myth," 6).
88 John Ditsky, "The Ending of *The Grapes of Wrath*: A Further Commentary," in Ditsky, *Critical Essays*, 117.
89 Ibid.
90 In this sense, my understanding of Steinbeck's postmodernity is at odds with Kocela's reading of the final scene as "emphasizing the constructedness of meaning in self-conscious role-play" ("A Postmodern Steinbeck," 262). If this final scene "explodes the allegorical frameworks of [the]

novel" (ibid.), I would rather see it as the effect of the attempted suppression of any distance between the literal/realistic quality of the scene and its symbolic dimension rather than the result of increased awareness on the part of the character (and reader) regarding the presumed heterogeneity of those two levels. Just as Rose of Sharon *becomes* a Madonna, so we are made to *experience* her silent and intimate revelation by watching it. Such, in any case, seems to be the aim of Steinbeck's kerygmatic realism.

91 As Joseph Fontenrose notes regarding the whole novel: "The wine of this new gospel is poured into the old bottle of Christian scripture" ("*The Grapes of Wrath*," in Heavilin, *The Critical Response*, 83).

92 Graham Ward, *Theology and Contemporary Critical Theory*, 2nd ed. (London: Macmillan, 2000), 170.

5 "In the Name of the Lost Father"

1 Jason Spangler, "We're on a Road to Nowhere: Steinbeck, Kerouac, and the Legacy of the Great Depression," *Studies in the Novel* 40/3 (2008), 316.

2 Ibid., 322.

3 Ibid., 309.

4 McClure, *Partial Faiths*, 7.

5 Ben Giamo, *Kerouac, the Word and the Way: Prose Artist as Spiritual Quester* (Carbondale, IL: Southern Illinois University Press, 2000), 198.

6 Ibid., 20.

7 Ibid.

8 See, e.g., André LaCocque's analysis of the psalm in André LaCocque, and Paul Ricoeur, *Penser la Bible* (Paris: Le Seuil, 1998), 254–86.

9 See Ann Charters' introduction to the 1991 Penguin edition of the novel (xxiii).

10 Giamo, *Kerouac*, 21.

11 Spangler, "We're on a Road to Nowhere," 309.

12 One explicit instance of Dean's manic-depressive behaviour occurs in part 4:

> "'Hup! Hup!' Dean was saying, tugging at his shirt, rubbing his belly, jumping up and down. [...] Then Dean suddenly grew quiet and sat in a kitchen chair between Stan and me and stared straight ahead with rocky doglike wonder and paid no attention to anybody. He simply disappeared for a moment to gather up more energy. If you touched him he would sway like a boulder suspended on a pebble on the precipice of a cliff. [...] Then the boulder exploded into a flower and his face lit up with a lovely smile and he looked around like

a man waking up [...]. And he stood swaying in the middle of the room, eating his cake and looking at everyone with awe" (239).

13 Giamo, *Kerouac*, 21.

14 Mario L. D'Avanzo, "Melville's *Bartleby* and Carlyle," in Howard P. Vincent, ed., *A Symposium: Bartleby the Scrivener* (Melville Annual, 1965) (Kent, OH: Kent State University Press, 1966), 124.

15 Ibid., 116.

16 Ibid., 115.

17 Ibid., 120–1.

18 Ibid., 121.

19 Ibid., 133–4.

20 Carlyle, in ibid., 115–16.

21 Carlyle, Book 2, chapter 4.

22 Giamo, *Kerouac*, 29.

23 Ibid., 43.

24 See Ricoeur's essay entitled "La plainte comme prière" in LaCocque and Ricoeur, *Penser la Bible*, 287–313.

25 "Libérée du souci de justifier Dieu et renonçant à toute théodicée où l'homme prétendrait prouver l'innocence de Dieu, la prière questionnante de la plainte n'attend rien d'autre que la compassion d'un Dieu dont l'orant ne sait pas comment il peut être à la fois juste et compatissant. C'est pourquoi il ne lui reste qu'à crier: Pourquoi ?" (ibid., 311–12).

26 Carole Gottlieb Vopat, "Jack Kerouac's *On the Road*: A Re-evaluation," in Harold Bloom, ed., *Jack Kerouac's* On the Road (Philadelphia, PA: Chelsea House, 2004), 7.

27 "Si la plainte comme prière est encore susceptible d'actualisation, c'est dans la mesure où l'exemplarité qu'elle doit à la forme poétique est une source permanente de transposition et d'historisation nouvelle dans des conditions culturelles inédites. [...] A quoi il faut ajouter que la reprise de la plainte biblique dans le 'grand cri' du Christ en croix ne peut devenir un modèle pour la prière que si elle suscite à son tour une continuelle innovation de la prière de plainte dans des expressions verbales qui peuvent être très éloignées de la forme littéraire du psaume original. [...]

Une dernière condition à satisfaire par le suppliant d'aujourd'hui serait peut-être qu'il découvre une secrète parenté entre ce qu'on pourrait se risquer à appeler souffrance de Dieu [...] et l'appel à une pratique personnelle et communautaire de la compassion à l'égard de frères humains souvent plus souffrants que coupables" (Ricoeur, "La plainte comme prière," 312–13).

28 Giamo, *Kerouac*, 209.

29 Ibid., 209–10.
30 Ann Charters' introduction to the 1991 Penguin edition of Kerouac's *On the Road*, xiv.
31 D'Avanzo, "Melville's *Bartleby* and Carlyle," 122–3.
32 Commenting on this surprisingly early inclusion of Buddhist imagery, Giamo turns to the narrator's own admission about this moment of illumination: "I was too young to know what had happened" (31). Stressing how this remark "highlights the aesthetic distance between Kerouac and the character of Sal Paradise, while also taking the reader beyond the limits of this *Road*," Giamo notes: "it seems as if the visionary passage is less a foreshadowing of Kerouac's keen interest in Buddhism and more of a retrofit once his self-study was underway in 1954, almost three years since he completed the *Road* manuscript, which was not published until 1957, thus allowing much time to play with various insertions and perform related editorial tasks" (*Kerouac*, 31–2).
33 Sheldrake, *A Brief History of Spirituality*, 20.
34 Ibid., 18–19.
35 Robert Holton, "Kerouac among the Fellahin: *On the Road* to the Postmodern," in Bloom, *Jack Kerouac's* On the Road, 83.
36 Alex Albright, "Ammons, Kerouac, and Their New Romantic Scrolls," in Bloom, *Jack Kerouac's* On the Road, 117.
37 Douglas Malcom, "'Jazz America': Jazz and African American Culture in Jack Kerouac's *On the Road*," in Bloom, *Jack Kerouac's* On the Road, 112.
38 Hungerford, *Postmodern Belief*, 38.
39 Ibid., 37–8.
40 Giamo, *Kerouac*, 31.
41 As critics have noted, this spontaneous quality was seriously impaired by the editing process the narrative went through.
42 Malcom, "'Jazz America,'" 111.
43 Hungerford, *Postmodern Belief*, 50.
44 Ibid., 41. In Kerouac's case, I would argue that this quest for a language beyond intelligibility is part of his general – admittedly regressive – craving for osmosis. As Sal enthuses about Dean's logorrhoea: "There was nothing clear about the things he said, but what he meant to say was somehow made pure and clear. [...] These were the first days of his mysticism, which would lead to the strange, ragged W.C. Fields saintliness of his later days" (109). Sal's remark reads as a metaliterary comment on Kerouac's own effort to arrive at the same type of immediate understanding, beyond surface nonsense, which Sal always presents as a kind of mystical connection, though it results from his fusional relationship

with Dean. This again raises the issue of the necessary distinction between mystical discipleship and regressive osmosis, whose conflation the novel appears to rest on.

45 Ibid., xiii.

6 "I Will Call Them My People"

1 Giamo, *Kerouac, the Word and the Way*, 199–201.

2 Giamo, quoting James, ibid., 200.

3 McClure, *Partial Faiths*, 118–19.

4 Beat stands both for defeat and beatitude.

5 McClure, *Partial Faiths*, 119.

6 Ibid., 119.

7 "In a grumpy letter written to Nanda Pivano (13 Apr. 1964), an Italian translator of American literature who wanted to publish a beat anthology of poetry, Kerouac griped about being associated with other beat writers. […]:
"There is no relation between my purely literary motives and their really political motives […]. You'll find that 'Visions of Gerard' is truly honest because it minds its own business and doesnt try to sell insurrection and discontent in our streets, but only reverts to what I finally believe in, peaceful sorrow at home" (Giamo, *Kerouac*, 206).

8 McClure, *Partial Faiths*, 119.

9 Ibid., 122.

10 Ibid., 121.

11 Ibid., 122.

12 Nancy Berkowitz Bate, "Toni Morrison's *Beloved*: Psalm and Sacrament," in Shirley A. Stave, ed., *Toni Morrison and the Bible: Contested Intertextualities* (New York: Peter Lang, 2006), 61; original emphasis.

13 Ibid.

14 In her introduction to *Toni Morrison and the Bible*, Shirley Stave divides the intertextual study of Morrison's fiction and the Bible into essays that either "remain very close to the Bible in their analyses of Morrison's work" or "argue that Morrison's stance toward the Bible is oppositional, that she employs biblical or theological concepts in such a way as to reveal their limitations" (1–2). The present study would hope to strike a middle ground, in keeping with my own essay: "'Never break them in two. Never put one over the other. Eve is Mary's mother. Mary is the daughter of Eve': Toni Morrison's Womanist Gospel of Self," *E-rea* 8/2 (2011). There, my line of argument consisted in showing that, after exposing the racist and sexist uses made of the doctrinal reading of the Fall in her first four novels, as

from *Beloved*, Morrison's aim seems not so much to subvert biblical theology as to explore its potential actualization.

15 Morrison's words in her Nobel lecture.

16 Bate, 53.

17 See Claude Le Fustec, "Le réalisme magique dans Beloved, ou l'écriture de l'unité," in G. Fabre and C. Raynaud, eds., *"Beloved She's Mine": Essais sur* Beloved *de Toni Morrison* (Paris: Cetanla, 1993), 101–8.

18 Just as Beloved is the living actualization of her name, so Pearl is the embodiment of the scarlet letter. As has been demonstrated, however, the kerygmatic power of the letter to actually become alive is consistently safely put at a distance in Hawthorne's text, both in the plot, through the ostracism both Pearl and her mother, as the wearer of the scarlet letter, are subjected to, and through the theatrical form given to its expression in Dimmesdale's public addresses. Morrison, for her part, being free from the Puritan distrust for human creation still plaguing Hawthorne's conscience, bases her novel on the full expression of the kerygmatic power of her imagination.

19 Bate, "Toni Morrison's *Beloved*," 55.

20 Ibid.

21 McClure, *Partial Faiths*, 119, 122–7.

22 Jean Wilson, "Toni Morrison: Re-Visionary Words with Power," in Donaldson and Mendelson, *Frye and the Word*, 237–8.

23 Jean Wilson, quoting Frye, ibid., 238.

24 Ibid., 242.

Conclusion

1 R.W.B. Lewis, *The American Adam: Innocence Tragedy and Tradition in the Nineteenth Century* (Chicago: University of Chicago Press, 1955), 197.

2 Fiedler, *Love and Death in the American Novel*, 27.

3 Tanner, *The Reign of Wonder*, 356.

4 Lewis, *The American Adam*, 198.

5 Tanner, *The Reign of Wonder*, 352.

6 Lewis, *The American Adam*, 6.

7 I am here indebted to Rédouane Abouddahab's suggestion, though made in a different context, that American literature might be regarded as revolving around the two opposed but not mutually exclusive poles of faith and suspicion. "Introduction: De l'Amérique à ses textes," in *Textes d'Amérique: Ecrivains et artistes américains entre américanité et originalité* (Lyon: Presses Universitaires de Lyon, 2008), 12.

8 Taylor, *After God*, xvi–xvii.
9 Ibid., 123.
10 "The foundational principle of immanence entails a monistic schema in which God, self, and world are different manifestations or expressions of the same underlying reality. Transcendence shatters monism by introducing a radical Other, which forms the foundation of the principle of oppositional difference constitutive of every dualism. The monistic and dualistic schemata illuminate the close relationship between religion and secularity by showing the contrasting ways in which God or the divine seems to disappear. In monism, God and the gods disappear by becoming indistinguishable from the world [...]. In dualism, God and the gods vanish by becoming so distant that they are inconsequential" (ibid., 133).
11 Ibid., 127.
12 Ibid., 391.
13 Ibid., 127.
14 Ibid., 311.
15 Ibid.
16 Denham quoting Frye, *RV*, 265.
17 This is an obviously simplified outline, more interested in the general direction taken by American literature than in the complex particulars regarding the admittedly diverse religious and spiritual impulses at play in the history of its fiction.
18 McClure, *Partial Faiths*, xi.
19 Ibid., 4.
20 Ibid., 6.
21 Ibid., 5.
22 Tóth, "Recovery of the Spiritual Other," 124–5.
23 Denham, *RV*, 68.
24 Ibid., 49.
25 Ibid., 66.
26 As Denham notes, in his effort to elucidate the nature of spiritual reality or presence, which kerygma makes manifest, Frye always returns to "Hebrews 11:1, ('the substance of things hoped-for, the evidence of things not seen'), which he translates into 'the reality of hope and illusion'" (Denham, *RV*, 66). The link with literature (and the arts generally) is illuminated in *Words with Power* in the passage about "the two kinds of illusion": "the negative illusion that merely fails to be an objective reality, and the positive illusion which is a potential, a something hoped for that can be actualized by a creative effort. To realize an illusion is to abolish its future and turn it into a presence" (*WP*, 131). This could be read as

a definition of the kerygmatic potential of literature and, interestingly, intersects with Mark C. Taylor's notion of "creative emergence."

27 Tóth, "Recovery of the Spiritual Other," 138.

28 Bauman, *Intimations of Postmodernity*, vii–viii.

29 Ibid., viii.

30 Vanhoozer, *The Cambridge Companion to Postmodern Theology*, 14.

31 Jacques Derrida, *Specters of Marx: The State of the Debt, the Work of Mourning and the New International*, trans. Peggy Kamuf (New York: Routledge, 1994), 74.

32 Ibid.

33 Jean-Luc Nancy, *Dis-enclosure: The Deconstruction of Christianity*, trans. Bettina Bergo, Gabriel Malenfant, and Michael B. Smith (New York: Fordham University Press, 2008), 177; original emphasis.

Bibliography

Frye Corpus

Frye, Northrop. *The Great Code: The Bible and Literature*. New York: Harcourt Brace Jovanovich, 1982.

Frye, Northrop. *Words with Power: Being a Second Study of the Bible and Literature*. New York: Harcourt Brace Jovanovich, 1990.

Frye, Northrop. *The Double Vision: Language and Meaning in Religion*. Toronto: University of Toronto Press, 1991.

Literary Corpus

Fitzgerald, F. Scott. *The Great Gatsby* (1926). Harmondsworth: Penguin Modern Classics, 1968.

Hawthorne, Nathaniel. *The Scarlet Letter* (1850). London: Dent, 1967.

James, Henry. *The Europeans* (1878). London: Penguin Classics, 1985.

Kerouac, Jack. *On The Road* (1957). New York: Penguin Classics, 2000.

Morrison, Toni. *Beloved* (1987). London: Chatto and Windus (Picador), 1988.

Steinbeck, John. *The Grapes of Wrath* (1939). New York: Penguin, 1997.

SECONDARY SOURCES

Introduction

Bauman, Zygmunt. *Intimations of Postmodernity*. London: Routledge, 1992.

Bevan, David, ed. *Literature and the Bible*. Amsterdam: Rodopi, 1993.

Berger, Peter L. *The Desecularization of the World: Resurgent Religion and World Politics*. Grand Rapids, MI: William B. Eerdmans, 1999.

Caputo, John D. *The Prayers and Tears of Jacques Derrida: Religion without Religion*. Bloomington, IN: Indiana University Press, 1997.

Connolly, William E. "Refashioning the Secular." In *What's Left of Theory? New Work on the Politics of Literary Theory*, edited by Judith Butler, John Guillory, and Kendall Thomas, 157–91. New York: Routledge, 2000.

De Man, Paul. "The Return to Philology." In *The Resistance to Theory*, 21–6. Manchester: Manchester University Press, 1986.

Denham, Robert D., ed. *Northrop Frye's Late Notebooks, 1982–1990: Architecture of the Spiritual World*. Vols. 5 and 6 of the Collected Works of Northrop Frye. Toronto: University of Toronto Press, 2000.

Denham, Robert D., ed. *Northrop Frye's Notebooks and Lectures on the Bible and Other Religious Texts*. Vol. 13 of the Collected Works of Northrop Frye. Toronto: University of Toronto Press, 2003.

Denham, Robert D., ed. *Northrop Frye: Religious Visionary and Architect of the Spiritual World*. Charlottesville, VA: University of Virginia Press, 2004.

Donaldson, Jeffery, and Alan Mendelson, eds. *Frye and the Word, Religious Contexts in the Writings of Northrop Frye*. Toronto: University of Toronto Press, 2004.

Ferretter, Luke. *Towards A Christian Literary Theory*. New York: Palgrave Macmillan, 2003.

Fiddes, Paul S., ed. *The Novel, Spirituality and Modern Culture: Eight Novelists Write about Their Craft and Their Context*. Cardiff: University of Wales Press, 2000.

Fiedler, Leslie A. *Love and Death in the American Novel* New York: Stein and Day, 1966.

Frye, Northrop. *The Anatomy of Criticism* (1957). London: Penguin, 1990.

Frye, Northrop. *The Critical Path: An Essay on the Social Context of Literary Criticism*. In The Critical Path *and Other Writings on Critical Theory 1963–1975*. Vol. 27 of the Collected Works of Northrop Frye, edited by Jean O'Grady and Eva Kushner, 3–117. Toronto: University of Toronto Press, 2009.

Frye, Northrop. *The Great Code: The Bible and Literature*. New York: Harcourt Brace Jovanovich, 1982.

Frye, Northrop. *Words with Power: Being a Second Study of the Bible and Literature*. New York: Harcourt Brace Jovanovich, 1990.

Frye, Northrop. "The Koine of Myth: Myth as a Universally Intelligible Language." In Robert D. Denham, ed., *Myth and Metaphor: Selected Essays, 1974–1988*, 3–17. Charlottesville: University Press of Virginia, 1990.

Frye, Northrop. *The Double Vision: Language and Meaning in Religion*. Toronto: University of Toronto Press, 1991.

Gill, Glen Robert, ed. *Northrop Frye on Twentieth Century Literature*. Vol. 28 of the Collected Works of Northrop Frye. Toronto: University of Toronto Press, 2010.

Hilton, Nelson. *Literal Imagination: Blake's Vision of Words*. Berkeley: University of California Press, 1983.

Holder, Arthur, ed. *The Blackwell Companion to Christian Spirituality* (2005). Oxford: Blackwell, 2011.

Hungerford, Amy. *Postmodern Belief: American Literature and Religion since 1960*. Princeton, NJ: Princeton University Press, 2010.

Ingraffia, Brian D. *Postmodern Theory and Biblical Theology*. Cambridge: Cambridge University Press, 1995.

Ingraffia, Brian D. "Is the Postmodern Post-Secular? The Parody of Religious Quests in Thomas Pynchon's *The Crying of Lot 49* and Don DeLillo's *White Noise*." In *Postmodern Philosophy and Christian Thought*, edited by Merold Westphal, 44–68. Bloomington: Indiana University Press, 1999.

Knight, Mark, and Thomas Woodman, eds. *Biblical Religion and the Novel, 1700–2000*. Aldershot: Ashgate, 2006.

Levine, George. *Darwin Loves You: Natural Selection and the Re-enchantment of the World*. Princeton, NJ: Princeton University Press, 2006.

Lowe, Walter. "A Deconstructionist Manifesto: Mark C. Taylor's *Erring*." *Journal of Religion* 66/3 (July 1986): 324–31.

McClure, John A. *Partial Faiths: Postsecular Fiction in the Age of Pynchon and Morrison*. Athens, GA: University of Georgia Press, 2007.

McHale, Brian. *Postmodernist Fiction*. London: Routledge, 1987.

O'Grady, Jean, ed. *Interviews with Northrop Frye*. Vol. 24 of the Collected Works of Northrop Frye. Toronto: University of Toronto Press, 2008.

O'Grady, Jean. "Re-valuing Value." In *Northrop Frye: New Directions from Old*, edited by David Rampton, 223–43. Ottawa: University of Ottawa Press, 2009.

Partridge, Christopher. *The Re-Enchantment of the West: Alternative Spiritualities, Sacralization, Popular Culture and Occulture*. Vol. 1. London: T&T Clark International, 2004.

Rampton, David, Introduction to *Northrop Frye: New Directions from Old*, edited by David Rampton, viii–xxix. Ottawa: University of Ottawa Press, 2009.

Salusinszky, Imre. "'In the Climates of the Mind': Frye's Career as a Spiritual Curriculum." In *Frye and the Word: Religious Contexts in the Writings of Northrop Frye*, edited by Jeffery Donaldson and Alan Mendelson, 43–56. Toronto: University of Toronto Press, 2004.

Sandbeck, Lars. "God as Immanent Transcendence in Mark C. Taylor and John D. Caputo." *Studia Theologica* 65 (2011): 18–38.

Schwartz, Regina, ed. *Transcendence: Philosophy, Literature, and Theology Approach the Beyond*. New York: Routledge, 2004.

Sheldrake, Philip. *A Brief History of Spirituality*. Oxford: Blackwell, 2007.

Sherbert, Garry. "Frye's 'Pure Speech': Literature and the Sacred without the Sacred." In *Northrop Frye: New Directions from Old*, edited by David Rampton, 141–63. Ottawa: University of Ottawa Press, 2009.

Sloan, Ian. "The Reverend H. Northrop Frye." In *Northrop Frye: New Directions from Old*, edited by David Rampton, 105–22. Ottawa: University of Ottawa Press, 2009.

Tate, Andrew. *Contemporary Fiction and Christianity*. London: Continuum, 2008.

Taylor, Charles. *A Secular Age*. Cambridge MA: Belknap Press, 2007.

Taylor, Dennis. "The Need for a Religious Literary Criticism." *Religion and the Arts* 1/1 (1997). http://www.bc.edu/publications/relarts/supplements/excerpts/v1-1taylor2.html

Taylor, Mark C. *Erring: A Postmodern A/theology*. Chicago: University of Chicago Press, 1984.

Taylor, Mark C., ed. *Critical Terms for Religious Studies*. Chicago: University of Chicago Press, 1998.

Taylor, Mark C. *After God*. Chicago: University of Chicago Press, 2007.

Tóth, Sára. "Recovery of the Spiritual Other: Martin Buber's 'Thou' in Northrop Frye's Late Work." In *Northrop Frye: New Directions from Old*, edited by David Rampton, 123–40. Ottawa: University of Ottawa Press, 2009.

Tóth, Sára. "What Does Literature Say? The Problem of Dogmatic Closure – from Romanticism to Northrop Frye." *ESC* (*English Studies in Canada*) 37/2 (June 2011): 185–200.

Vanhoozer, Kevin J., ed. *The Cambridge Companion to Postmodern Theology*. Cambridge: Cambridge University Press, 2003.

Ward, Graham, ed. *The Postmodern God: A Theological Reader*. Oxford: Blackwell, 1997.

Ward, Graham, ed. *The Blackwell Companion to Postmodern Theology*. Oxford: Blackwell, 2001.

1 *The Scarlet Letter*

Baym, Nina. "Who? The Characters." In *Hester Prynne*, edited by Harold Bloom, 137–49. Philadelphia, PA: Chelsea House, 2004.

Bell, Michael Davitt. "Arts of Deception: Hawthorne, 'Romance,' and *The Scarlet Letter*.' In *New Essays on The Scarlet Letter*, edited by Michael J. Colacurcio, 29–56. Cambridge: Cambridge University Press, 1985.

Bercovitch, Sacvan. "Hawthorne's A-Morality of Compromise." In *The Scarlet Letter*, edited by Ross C. Murfin, 344–58. Boston: St Martin's, 1991.

Browning, Preston M. Jr. "Hester Prynne as Secular Saint." In *Hester Prynne*, edited by Harold Bloom, 95–101. Philadelphia, PA: Chelsea House, 2004.

Chambost, Christophe. "Signification et intensité de la lettre écarlate." In *The Scarlet Letter*, edited by Marc Amfreville and Antoine Cazé, 87–97. Paris: Ellipses, 2005.

Colacurcio, Michael J. "Footsteps of Ann Hutchinson: The Context of *The Scarlet Letter*." In *Hester Prynne*, edited by Harold Bloom, 105–36. Philadelphia, PA: Chelsea House, 2004.

Cabau, Jacques. *La prairie perdue*. Paris: Seuil, 1966.

Feidelson, Charles, Jr. "*The Scarlet Letter*." In *Hester Prynne*, edited by Harold Bloom, 29–60. Philadelphia, PA: Chelsea House, 2004. Originally published in *Hawthorne Centenary Letters*, edited by R.H. Pearce, 31–77 (Columbus, OH: Ohio State University Press, 1964).

Guillaume, Hélène. "Energy and Truth: 'The Custom House,' 'The Scarlet Letter,' and *The Scarlet Letter*.' In *The Scarlet Letter*, edited by Marc Amfreville and Antoine Cazé, 47–56. Paris: Ellipses, 2005.

Hage, Armand. "*The Scarlet Letter* Characters: Allegories, Symbols and Individuals." In *The Scarlet Letter*, edited by Marc Amfreville and Antoine Cazé, 77–97. Paris: Ellipses, 2005.

Kaul, A.N. "*The Scarlet Letter* and Puritan Ethics." In *Nathaniel Hawthorne's The Scarlet Letter*, edited by Harold Bloom, 9–20. New York: Chelsea House, 1986.

Matthiessen, F.O. "Allegory and Symbolism." In *Twentieth-Century Interpretations of The Scarlet Letter*, edited by John C. Gerber, 57–64. Englewood Cliffs, NJ: Prentice-Hall, 1968.

Murfin, Ross C. "The New Historicism and *The Scarlet Letter*." In *The Scarlet Letter*, edited by Ross C. Murfin, 330–44. Boston: St Martin's, 1991.

Ricoeur, Paul. *The Symbolism of Evil* (1967). Translated by Emerson Buchanan. Boston: Beacon Press, 1969.

Van Leer, David. "Hester's Labyrinth: Transcendental Rhetoric in Puritan Boston." In *New Essays on The Scarlet Letter*, edited by Michael J. Colacurcio, 57–100. Cambridge: Cambridge University Press, 1985.

Warren, Austin. "The Scarlet Letter." In *Hester Prynne*, edited by Harold Bloom, 61–80. Philadelphia, PA: Chelsea House, 2004.

2 Henry James's *The Europeans*

Austin, Deborah. "Innocents at Home: A Study of *The Europeans* of Henry James." *Journal of General Education* 14 (1962): 103–29.

Banta, Marta. *Henry James and the Occult: The Great Extension*. Bloomington, IN: Indiana University Press, 1972.

Blond, Phillip. "Introduction: Theology before Philosophy." In *Post-Secular Philosophy: Between Philosophy and Theology*, edited by Phillip Blond, 1–66. New York: Routledge, 1998.

Buitenhuis, Peter. "Comic Pastoral: Henry James's *The Europeans*." *University of Toronto Quarterly* 31 (1962): 152–63.

Caesar, Judith. "James's *The Europeans*." *Explicator* 62/3 (2004): 151–3.

Fincham, Gail. "'The Alchemy of Art': Henry James's *The Europeans*." *English Studies in Africa* 23/2 (Sept. 1980): 83–92.

Fogel, Daniel Mark. *A Companion to Henry James Studies*. Westport, CT: Greenwood, 1993.

Frye, Northrop. "Henry James and the Comedy of the Occult." In *Genre, Trope, Gender: Critical Essays by Northrop Frye, Linda Hutcheon, and Shirley Neuman*, edited by Barry Ruthland, 13–31. Ottawa: Carleton University Press, 1992.

Geary, Edward A. "*The Europeans*: A Centennial Essay." *Henry James Review* 4/1 (1982): 31–49.

Haar, Michel. "Nietzsche and the metamorphosis of the divine." In *Post-Secular Philosophy: Between Philosophy and Theology*, edited by Phillip Blond, 157–76. New York: Routledge, 1998.

Haralson Eric and Kendall Johnson, eds. *Critical Companion to Henry James: A Literary Reference to His Life and Work*. New York: Facts on File, 2009.

Jolly, Roslyn. *Henry James: History, Narrative, Fiction*. New York: Oxford University Press, 1993.

Long, Robert Emmet. *The Great Succession: Henry James and the Legacy of Hawthorne*. Pittsburgh, PA: University of Pittsburgh Press, 1979.

Long, Robert Emmet. *Henry James: The Early Novels*. Boston: Twayne, 1983.

Lustig, T.J. "Sunspots and Blindspots in *The Europeans*." *E-rea revue d'études Anglophones* 3/2 (2005): 6–18.

Matthiessen, F.O. *American Renaissance: Art and Expression in the Age of Emerson and Whitman*. New York: Oxford University Press, 1941.

Nazare, Joseph. "Enter Touchstone: Manners of Comedy in James's *The Europeans*." *Henry James Review* 18/2 (1997): 149–60.

Poirier, Richard. *The Comic Sense of Henry James: A Study of the Early Novels*. New York: Oxford University Press, 1960.

Rowe, John Carlos. *Henry Adams and Henry James: The Emergence of a Modern Consciousness*. Ithaca, NY: Cornell University Press, 1976.

Samuels, Charles Thomas. *The Ambiguity of Henry James*. Urbana, IL: University of Illinois Press, 1971.

Tanner, Tony. Introduction to *The Europeans*, by Henry James, 7–29. New York: Penguin, 1984.

Tanner, Tony. *Henry James: The Writer and His Work*. Amherst, MA: University of Massachussets Press, 1985.

Tuttleton, J.W. "Propriety and Fine Perception: James's *The Europeans*." *Modern Language Review* 73/3 (1978): 481–95.

Wallace, Ronald. *Henry James and the Comic Form*. Ann Arbor, MI: University of Michigan Press, 1975.

Ward, J.A. *The Search for Form: Studies in the Structure of James's Fiction*. Chapel Hill, NC: University of Carolina Press, 1967.

Williams, Merle A. "Traces of James's Later Manner in 'New England's Silvery Prime': A Reading of *The Europeans*." *English Studies in Africa* 36/2 (1993): 21–9.

Williams, Merle A. *Henry James and the Philosophical Novel*. Cambridge: Cambridge University Press, 1993.

3 Fitzgerald's *The Great Gatsby*

Altizer, Thomas J.J. *The Gospel of Christian Atheism*. London: Collins, 1967.

Amossy, Ruth. "Introduction: Pour une analyse rhétorique des textes politiques." *Argumentation et Analyse du Discours* 6 (Apr. 2011). http://aad.revues.org/1081.

Audhuy, Letha. "The *Waste Land* Myth and Symbols in *The Great Gatsby*." In *F. Scott Fitzgerald, The Great Gatsby*, edited by Harold Bloom, 109–22. New York: Chelsea House, 1986.

Bewley, Marius. "Scott Fitzgerald's Criticism of America." in *Twentieth-Century Interpretations of* The Great Gatsby, edited by Ernest Lockridge, 37–53. Englewood Cliffs, NJ: Prentice-Hall, 1968.

Berman, Ronald. "*The Great Gatsby* and the Twenties." In *The Cambridge Companion to F. Scott Fitzgerald*, edited by Ruth Prigozy, 79–94. Cambridge: Cambridge University Press, 2002.

Bruccoli, Matthew J., ed. *New Essays on* The Great Gatsby. Cambridge: Cambridge University Press, 1985.

Callahan, John F. *The Illusions of a Nation: Myth and History in the Novels of F. Scott Fitzgerald*. Urbana, IL: University of Illinois Press, 1972.

Curnutt, Kirk. *The Cambridge Introduction to F. Scott Fitzgerald*. Cambridge: Cambridge University Press, 2007.

Dilworth, Thomas. "The Passion of Gatsby: Evocation of Jesus in Fitzgerald's *The Great Gatsby*." *Explicator* 68/2 (2010): 119–21.

Fessenden, Tracy. "F. Scott Fitzgerald's Catholic Closet." In *Culture and Redemption: Religion, the Secular, and American Literature*, 181–212. Princeton, NJ: Princeton University Press, 2007.

Geismar, Maxwell. *Writers in Crisis: The American Novel, 1925–1940*. Boston: Houghton Mifflin, 1942.

Grawe, Michael. *Expatriate American Authors in Paris: Disillusionment with the American Lifestyle as Reflected in Selected Works of Ernest Hemingway and F. Scott Fitzgerald*. Munich: Grin Verlag, 2001.

Hanzo, Thomas A. "The Theme and Narrator of *The Great Gatsby*." In *Twentieth-Century Interpretations of* The Great Gatsby, edited by Ernest Lockridge, 61–9. Englewood Cliffs, NJ: Prentice-Hall, 1968.

Lehan, Richard D. *F. Scott Fitzgerald and the Craft of Fiction*. Carbondale, IL: Southern Illinois University Press, 1966.

Lehan, Richard D. *The Great Gatsby: The Limits of Wonder*. New York: Twayne, 1989.

Leff, Michael. "Rhetoric and Dialectic in Martin Luther King's 'Letter from Birmingham Jail.'" In *Anyone Who Has a View: Theoretical Contributions to the Study of Argumentation*, edited by Frans H. van Eemeren, J. Anthony Blair, Charles A. Willard, and A. Francisca Snoeck Henkemans, 255–68. Dordrecht: Kluwer, 2003.

Lockridge, Ernest, ed. *Twentieth-Century Interpretations of* The Great Gatsby. Englewood Cliffs, NJ: Prentice-Hall, 1968.

McClure, John A. *Partial Faiths: Postsecular Fiction in the Age of Pynchon and Morrison*. Athens, GA, Georgia: University of Georgia Press, 2007.

Miller, James E., Jr. *F. Scott Fitzgerald: His Art and His Technique*. New York: New York University Press, 1964.

Neuhaus, Ron. "Gatsby and the Failure of the Omniscient 'I.'" In *F. Scott Fitzgerald, The Great Gatsby*, edited by Harold Bloom, 45–55. New York: Chelsea House, 1986.

Ornstein, Robert. "Scott Fitzgerald's Fable of East and West." In *Twentieth-Century Interpretations of* The Great Gatsby, edited by Ernest Lockridge, 54–60. Englewood Cliffs, NJ: Prentice-Hall, 1968.

Piper, Henry Dan. "The Untrimmed Christmas Tree: The Religious Background of *The Great Gatsby*." In *Fitzgerald's* The Great Gatsby: *The Novel, the Critics, the Background*, edited by Henry Dan Piper, 93–100. New York: Charles Scribner's Sons, 1970.

Prigozy, Ruth, ed. *The Cambridge Companion to F. Scott Fitzgerald*. Cambridge: Cambridge University Press, 2002.

Raleigh, John Henry. "F. Scott Fitzgerald's *The Great Gatsby*: Legendary Bases and Allegorical Significances." In *Fitzgerald's* The Great Gatsby: *The Novel, the Critics, the Background*, edited by Henry Dan Piper, 141–4. New York: Charles Scribner's Sons, 1970.

Samuels, Charles Thomas. "The Greatness of 'Gatsby.'" In *Fitzgerald's* The Great Gatsby: *The Novel, the Critics, the Background*, edited by Henry Dan Piper, 151–9. New York: Charles Scribner's Sons, 1970.

Way, Brian. *F. Scott Fitzgerald and the Art of Social Fiction*. London: Edward Arnold, 1980.

Way, Brian. "The Great Gatsby." In *F. Scott Fitzgerald, The Great Gatsby*, edited by Harold Bloom, 87–108. New York: Chelsea House, 1986.

4 Immanent Christianity in *The Grapes of Wrath*

Carpenter, Frederic I. "The Philosophical Joads." In *The Grapes of Wrath, Text and Criticism*, edited by Peter Lisca and Kevin Hearle, 562–71. New York: Penguin, 1997. Originally published in *College English II* (Jan. 1941): 315–25.

Côté, Jean-François. "*The Grapes of Wrath*: Un réalisme moderniste." In *Lectures de Steinbeck: Les raisins de la colère*, edited by Claude Le Fustec, 125–39. Rennes: Presses Universitaires de Rennes, 2007.

Ditsky, John. "The Ending of *The Grapes of Wrath*: A Further Commentary." In *Critical Essays on Steinbeck's* The Grapes of Wrath, edited by John Ditsky, 116–24. Boston: G.K. Hall, 1989.

Eckert, Ken. "Exodus Inverted: A New Look at *The Grapes of Wrath*." *Religion and the Arts* 13/3 (Summer 2009): 340–57.

Fontenrose, Joseph. "*The Grapes of Wrath*." In *The Critical Response to John Steinbeck's* Grapes of Wrath, edited by Barbara A. Heavilin, 71–86. Westport, CT: Greenwood, 2000. Originally published in Joseph Fontenrose, *John Steinbeck: An Introduction and Interpretation* (New York: Barnes and Noble, 1963, 67–83).

French, Warren. "John Steinbeck and Modernism (A Speculation on His Contribution to the Development of the Twentieth-Century American Sensibility)." In *Critical Essays on Steinbeck's Grapes of Wrath*, edited by John Ditsky, 152–62. Boston: G.K. Hall, 1989.

French, Warren. "The Education of the Heart." In *John Steinbeck's Fiction Revisited*, 75–84. New York: Twayne, 1994.

Gaither, Gloria. "John Steinbeck: The Postmodern Mind in the Modern Age." *Steinbeck Review* 3/1 (Spring 2006): 53–68.

Kocela, Chris. "A Postmodern Steinbeck, or Rose of Sharon Meets Oedipa Maas." In *The Critical Response to John Steinbeck's* Grapes of Wrath, edited by Barbara A. Heavilin, 247–66. Westport, CT: Greenwood, 2000.

Levine, George. *Darwin Loves You: Natural Selection and the Re-enchantment of the World*. Princeton, NJ: Princeton University Press, 2006.

Lisca, Peter. "*The Grapes of Wrath* as Fiction." In *The Grapes of Wrath: Text and Criticism*, edited by Peter Lisca and Kevin Hearle, 572–88. New York: Penguin, 1997. Originally published in *PMLA* LXXII (Mar. 1957: 269–309).

Maine, Barry G. "Steinbeck's Debt to Dos Passos." In *The Critical Response to John Steinbeck's* Grapes of Wrath, edited by Barbara A. Heavilin, 151–61. Westport, CT: Greenwood, 2000. Originally published in the *Steinbeck Quarterly* 23/1–2 (Winter/Spring 1990: 17–27).

Mallier, Clara. "Le quatrième sens de l'écriture dans *The Grapes of Wrath*." Paper presented at the conference "Imaginaires Américains: Steinbeck et Ford," Toulouse Le Mirail University, France, 25 Jan. 2008. http://w3.cas.univ-tlse2.fr/spip.php?article126.

Marks, Lester Jay. *Thematic Design in the Novels of John Steinbeck* (1969). The Hague: Mouton, 1971.

Napier, Elizabeth. "*The Grapes of Wrath*: Steinbeck's *Pilgrim's Progress*." *Steinbeck Review* 7/1 (Spring 2010): 51–6.

Railton, Stephen. "Pilgrim's Politics: Steinbeck's Art of Conversion." In *New Essays on* The Grapes of Wrath, edited by David Wyatt, 27–46. Cambridge: Cambridge University Press, 1990.

Richards, Robert J. "Darwinian Enchantment." In *The Joy of Secularism: 11 Essays for How We Live Now*, edited by George Levine, 185–204. Princeton, NJ: Princeton University Press, 2011.

Ross, Woodburn O. "John Steinbeck: Naturalism's Priest." In *The Critical Response to John Steinbeck's* Grapes of Wrath, edited by Barbara A. Heavilin, 57–66. Westport, CT: Greenwood, 2000. Originally published in *College English* (May 1949: 432–38).

Ward, Graham. *Theology and Contemporary Critical Theory* (2nd ed.). London: Macmillan, 2000.

5 "In the Name of the Lost Father"

Albright, Alex. "Ammons, Kerouac, and Their New Romantic Scrolls." In *Jack Kerouac's* On the Road, edited by Harold Bloom, 115–40. Philadelphia, PA: Chelsea House, 2004.

D'Avanzo, Mario L. "Melville's *Bartleby* and Carlyle." In *A Symposium: Bartleby the Scrivener* (Melville Annual, 1965), edited by Howard P. Vincent, 113–39. Kent, OH: Kent State University Press, 1966.

Giamo, Ben. *Kerouac, the Word and the Way: Prose Artist as Spiritual Quester*. Carbondale, IL: Southern Illinois University Press, 2000.

Holton, Robert. "Kerouac Among the Fellahin: *On the Road* to the Postmodern." In *Jack Kerouac's* On the Road, edited by Harold Bloom, 77–92. Philadelphia, PA: Chelsea House, 2004.

Hungerford, Amy. *Postmodern Belief: American Literature and Religion since 1960*. Princeton, NJ: Princeton University Press, 2010.
LaCocque, André, and Paul Ricoeur. *Penser la Bible*. Paris: Seuil, 1998.
Le Pellec, Yves. *Jack Kerouac*. Paris: Belin, 1999.
Malcom, Douglas. "'Jazz America': Jazz and African American Culture in Jack Kerouac's *On the Road*." In *Jack Kerouac's* On the Road, edited by Harold Bloom, 93–114. Philadelphia, PA: Chelsea House, 2004.
Sheldrake, Philip. *A Brief History of Spirituality*. Oxford: Blackwell, 2007.
Spangler, Jason. "We're on a Road to Nowhere: Steinbeck, Kerouac, and the Legacy of the Great Depression." *Studies in the Novel* 40/3 (Fall 2008): 308–27.
Vopat, Carole Gottlieb. "Jack Kerouac's *On the Road*: A Re-evaluation." In *Jack Kerouac's* On the Road, edited by Harold Bloom, 3–18. Philadelphia, PA: Chelsea House, 2004.

6 "I Will Call Them My People"

Bate, Nancy Berkowitz. "Toni Morrison's *Beloved*: Psalm and Sacrament." In *Toni Morrison and the Bible: Contested Intertextualities*, edited by Shirley A. Stave, 26–70. New York: Peter Lang, 2006.
Giamo, Ben. *Kerouac, the Word and the Way: Prose Artist as Spiritual Quester*. Carbondale, IL: Southern Illinois University Press, 2000.
Le Fustec, Claude. "'Never break them in two. Never put one over the other. Eve is Mary's mother. Mary is the daughter of Eve': Toni Morrison's Womanist Gospel of Self.' *E-rea* 8/2 (2011). http://erea.revues.org/1680.
McClure, John A. "Enclosures, Enchantments, and the Art of Discernment." In *Partial Faiths: Postsecular Fiction in the Age of Pyncheon and Morrison*, 100–30. Athens, GA: the University of Georgia Press, 2007.
Stave, Shirley A., ed. *Toni Morrison and the Bible: Contested Intertextualities*. New York: Peter Lang, 2006.
Wilson, Jean. "Toni Morrison: Re-Visionary Words with Power." In *Frye and the Word, Religious Contexts in the Writings of Northrop Frye*, edited by Jeffery Donaldson and Alan Mendelson, 235–50. Toronto: University of Toronto Press, 2004.

Conclusion

Abouddahab, Rédouane. *Textes d'Amérique: Ecrivains et artistes américains entre américanité et originalité*. Lyon: Presses Universitaires de Lyon, 2008.
Bauman, Zygmunt. *Intimations of Postmodernity*. London: Routledge, 1992.

Denham, Robert D., ed. *Northrop Frye's Late Notebooks, 1982–1990: Architecture of the Spiritual World.* Vols. 5 and 6 of the Collected Works of Northrop Frye. Toronto: University of Toronto Press, 2000.

Denham, Robert D., ed. *Northrop Frye: Religious Visionary and Architect of the Spiritual World.* Charlottesville, VA: University of Virginia Press, 2004.

Derrida, Jacques. *Specters of Marx: The State of the Debt, the Work of Mourning and the New International.* Translated by Peggy Kamuf. New York: Routledge, 1994.

Fiedler, Leslie A. *Love and Death in the American Novel.* New York: Stein and Day, 1966.

Lewis, R.W.B. *The American Adam: Innocence, Tragedy, and Tradition in the Nineteenth Century.* Chicago: University of Chicago Press, 1955.

McClure, John A. *Partial Faiths: Postsecular Fiction in the Age of Pynchon and Morrison.* Athens, GA: University of Georgia Press, 2007.

Nancy, Jean-Luc. *Dis-enclosure: The Deconstruction of Christianity.* Translated by Bettina Bergo, Gabriel Malenfant, and Michael B. Smith. New York: Fordham University Press, 2008.

Tanner, Tony. *The Reign of Wonder: Naivety and Reality in American Literature.* Cambridge: Cambridge University Press, 1965.

Taylor, Mark C. *After God.* Chicago: University of Chicago Press, 2007.

Tóth, Sára. "Recovery of the Spiritual Other: Martin Buber's 'Thou' in Northrop Frye's Late Work." In *Northrop Frye: New Directions from Old,* edited by David Rampton, 123–40. Ottawa: University of Ottawa Press, 2009.

Vanhoozer, Kevin J., ed. *The Cambridge Companion to Postmodern Theology.* Cambridge: Cambridge University Press, 2003.

Index

www.ingramcontent.com/pod-product-compliance
Lightning Source LLC
La Vergne TN
LVHW090156080826
844660LV00013B/838/J

* 9 7 8 1 4 4 2 6 4 7 6 9 5 *